A Time Beyond Fate

Ralf Carter

Copyright © 2024 by [Author or Pen Name]

All rights reserved.

No portion of this book may be reproduced in any form without written permission from the publisher or author, except as permitted by U.S. copyright law.

Contents

1. Prologue — 1
2. Chapter 1 — 17
3. Chapter 2 — 28
4. Chapter 3 — 38
5. Chapter 4 — 48
6. Chapter 5 — 63
7. Chapter 6 — 74
8. Chapter 7 — 84
9. Chapter 8 — 99
10. Chapter 9 — 108
11. Chapter 10 — 120
12. Chapter 11 — 138
13. Chapter 12 — 149
14. Chapter 13 — 158
15. Chapter 14 — 169
16. Chapter 15 — 185
17. Chapter 16 — 199

18.	Chapter 17	217
19.	Chapter 18	228
20.	Chapter 19	238
21.	Chapter 20	248
22.	Chapter 21	262
23.	Chapter 22	273
24.	Chapter 23	281
25.	Chapter 24	292
26.	Chapter 25	300
27.	Chapter 26	311
28.	Chapter 27	320
29.	Epilogue	330

Prologue

ARIA
2nd October, 2025

I stared at my computer screen, the presentation slides blurring into a monotonous haze. My eyes stung from hours of relentless screen time. Despite it being the 2nd of October, today was no exception. My schedule was crammed with back-to-back meetings, each one bleeding into the next.

A little after one, my co-worker leaned over my cubicle wall. "Aria, the boss wants an update on the Luca Everett story."

I sighed as I gathered my laptop and the necessary documents before making my way to Mateo's office. The thought of yet another meeting about this was almost too much to bear, but the Luca Everett story had been a thorn in our side for weeks.

Mateo's office was a spacious corner room, framed with floor-to-ceiling windows that let in a flood of natural light. The sleek glass walls created an open, airy feel, contrasting with the dark wooden desk at the center, which was cluttered with papers, files, and a couple of empty coffee cups. Mateo sat behind his desk, his usually immaculate hair disheveled, exhaustion etched into his features—a stark reminder of the all-nighter he'd pulled to manage a client's crisis. Across from him sat Olivia, my cousin, colleague, and best friend. Her shirt was wrinkled, and more empty coffee cups surrounded her, clear signs of shared fatigue.

I knocked lightly on the glass door before entering. "Hey, heard you wanted an update on the story."

Mateo looked up, eyes sharp despite the weariness. "Yeah. Did their PR department approve the latest storyboard?"

"After three weeks of constant nitpicking and annoying demands, they finally did. Now all we have to do is get the interview done. The headshots are scheduled for this afternoon. The team has everything set up, and it's on track to be published as scheduled."

"Great. So we're good to go. Finally!" Olivia chimed in, running a hand through her tangled hair. She looked as exhausted as I felt.

"You know, this doesn't change the fact that I hate working with them," I said, crossing my arms. "It's always on their terms and conditions. We're an independent media company."

Mateo leaned back in his chair, a satisfied smile creeping onto his face. "But because of our polite cooperation, all of their clients major advertising and endorsement contracts are being given to us. That means funds we can use to cover stories we really care about—corruption scandals, politics!"

I rolled my eyes but couldn't suppress a small smile. "And when am I going to be put on one of those? You both are really two-faced. First, you poach me from my well-paying content strategy job with the promise that I will get to work on real-world topics. But all I've had in the last five months is sports gossip nonsense."

"I promise you, cousin, soon! All we need is some more money. And the story you wish to chase is all yours. It's election season soon. I am sure we will find you the budget and resources for you to unearth the scandal you desire and ruin some poor politician's life," Olivia said jokingly.

"First of all, which politicians you know are poor? You make it sound like all I want to do is ruin people. But in reality all I want is to chase topics that matter."

Mateo chuckled. "And you shall!"

Mateo was Olivia's senior from university. With his rich business family background and Olivia's knack for real-world strategy, they decided to start this independent media agency three years ago. Their drive to make a difference in the media industry, in a world of short attention spans was inspiring enough for me to join them. Also compelled by lots of false promises regarding the bright future I could have and a bit of blackmail. After discussing a few more details about the upcoming photo shoot and going over some documents, Mateo said, "You can go home now."

"But it's just 2 o'clock," I stated blankly.

"It's the 2nd of October. I know you have to visit your parents. So go! This company can function without you for half a day," Olivia said. Once they decided on something, they didn't back down. That's what made them such an amazing team. So I agreed.

I was at my desk, packing my stuff when the lights went off. The whole floor went slightly dark—as one of my co-workers brought a cake towards me with a burning candle on top. Dim yellow lights from multiple desks were switched on. The whole floor looked magical and then in unison, fifteen of my colleagues sang the happy birthday song.

Why was this happening? I could feel my heart pounding faster and harder against my chest. My breathing became shallow, and a cold sweat broke out on my forehead and palms. A wave of dizziness almost swept over me, making it difficult to focus.

I did not celebrate my birthday. Not once since I turned fifteen. But how did they find out that my real birthday was today? I made sure to skip that question in all social media accounts and the HR forms.

Immediately, one of my co-workers gushed, "Blow the candle and make a wish!" My face had gone slightly pale but I did not want to cause a scene, so I complied, reluctantly. Olivia and Mateo realized what was happening, so they were about to yell at everyone when I exclaimed in fake excitement, "Thank you so much. This is such a lovely surprise! I love this office ritual."

I only said it because I didn't want to cause a scene. There was no way I was going to be excited to celebrate my birthday. The 2nd of October was a day I despised. A day that was the living reminder of the pain, emptiness, and loss.

After the cake cutting was over and everyone wished me, I thanked everyone and told them to get back to work, and left as soon as it was possible.

When I was waiting for the elevator to come, Olivia rushed towards me, "Are you okay? I had no idea they were planning to do this. Had I known, I would have stopped it immediately."

Even Mateo came running. "I am so sorry this happened. I will make sure it's not repeated."

I took a deep breath. "It's fine, guys. I am fine. It's officially been ten years now. They didn't know, and I would prefer to keep it that way."

Olivia held my hands firmly and whispered, "Don't pretend to be strong in front of me. Do you want me to come with you to visit aunt and uncle?"

"No. I would prefer to go alone," I said softly.

"Are you sure?" she asked, to which I nodded.

Mateo then asked, "Want to have a drink later tonight?"

I smiled. "That sounds perfect."

After driving for almost an hour, I finally reached my destination. The sky was a vivid shade of blue, with the sun hanging high at its center. But October in Portmaine city was no joke. As soon as I stepped out of the car, the warmth I had felt inside evaporated, replaced by the biting chill of the wind. It was a cold, windy day. The weather mirrored my emotions perfectly—bright and sunny on the outside, cold and turbulent on the inside. The grass lawns stretched endlessly before me, a patchwork of bright and dark spots glittering in the sunlight. A solitary yew tree swayed rhythmically with the wind, its leaves whispering secrets.

I hugged my jacket tighter, trying to reassure myself. Everything is going to be okay. The soft grass cushioned my steps as I walked until I stood before them: the gravestones of my parents. Their epitaphs were simple yet deep:

'In loving memory of Ethan Gibson. A dear son, husband, and father. History nerd to most, passionate professor to few, but missed by all. April 1967 - October 2015' and 'In loving memory of Emily Gibson. A dear daughter, wife, and mother. Beloved tech geek to most and a true dreamer at heart. Missed by all. November 1970 - October 2015.'

Moss had crept over their gravestones, mingling with tiny wildflowers. I stood there, feeling the echoes of their souls. When I was fifteen, people told me that time heals all wounds, but today it had been ten years, and it still hurt. It was as if someone had taken out a deep integral piece of me and never put it back.

In truth, I envied my parents. Their bond was so special that even death couldn't separate them. And yet, on the other hand, there was me on the receiving end of the worst present possible. I sat before their gravestones for a long time, sharing the recent happenings of my life. Each word I spoke felt like a fragile bridge to the past, connecting me to the warmth and love I once knew. I missed them so much that it physically ached—the kind of ache that no words can heal, the kind that settles into your bones and never leaves. And yet, I knew—how blur their memories had become.

I strolled across the graveyard, reading other epitaphs, each one a testament to a lost loved one. A few of them were as old as the early 1900s. Victims of the war—I guessed. Despite the common perception of graveyards as places for ghosts, this place felt like a gathering of many souls, a testament to love and loss. It reminded me of the past when I spent hours every day, clinging to my parents' gravestones.

After my parents passed away, I lived with my aunt and uncle. No matter how amazing they were, they could never replace my parents. I often felt like a guest in their home, a lingering presence that didn't quite belong. And without my parents, I truly felt lost and unprepared to face the real world.

Olivia often had to drag me back home, forcefully. She would find me there, curled up on the cold ground, lost in my grief. "Come on, Aria," she'd say gently, kneeling beside me. "You can't stay here forever." Her voice was always steady, calm, and patient.

When I resisted, she'd sit with me, sometimes for hours, holding my hand and sharing stories of our childhood that brought fleeting smiles to my face. She'd talk about how my dad would bore her with long stories of the freedom struggle, of heroes like Demion Marshall, and how our nation, Agnor, fought back in those difficult times against the British Empire. As Agnorians, we took immense pride in our culture and history.

Agnor, our beloved country, is part of the European Union and is situated near the North Sea. We have the United Kingdom to our west and Germany to our east. Our journey to where we stand today as a nation took time—lots of it—and a very tumultuous history.

Then she'd laugh about how she once fell asleep in the middle of a story while my dad, unaware, continued his narration for hours. She told me about instances where my grandparents were furious with my mom because she broke their perfectly new smart speaker—simply because she wanted to test out how it reacted after its new update. Yet, on the hardest days, Olivia stayed with me through the night, simply being there for me. Her presence was a constant reminder that while the pain of losing my parents would never truly disappear, I was not facing it alone. As the sun began to set, casting long shadows across the city, I realized just how much time I had once again spent at the graveyard.

As I was making my way back to the car, I heard a voice call out, "Excuse me, dear girl...." So I turned around, and my intuition was correct. An old woman stood at the corner of the road. She wasn't frail and pitiable but rather a strong, fit woman with pronounced wrinkles and folds. She was tall, with dense, curly grey hair that framed her face like a wild halo. Her sharp, discerning eyes seemed to look right through me. She gestured for me to come towards her stall, and despite my lack of interest, I walked over out of respect. Ignoring her would have felt impolite.

"Dear girl, would you like to have a look at these trinkets? Each one of them has played its own role in shaping history." Her voice was rich and velvety, filled with an inexplicable allure that drew me in despite my hesitant thoughts.

I smiled politely and glanced at the table in front of her. It was covered with dozens of beautiful ornaments and unusual objects of all shapes and sizes. Most of them looked ancient, possibly archaic. One item caught my eye—a small, antique silver box with intricate engravings. It was adorned with delicate floral patterns and scrolling vines, each line meticulously etched by hand. The silver had aged beautifully, developing a soft patina that gave it an air of timeless elegance. Tiny, almost invisible hinges connected the lid to the base, and a small, ornate clasp held it shut. I picked it up to have a closer look.

"A very interesting choice, dear girl," she remarked.

I gave her a questioning look but she continued, "That box was custom-made by a young man in the late nineteenth century for his beloved. It symbolized his eternal promise to defy time and space to be with her again. This box is said to hold the power to help its owners fulfill their destiny. However to date, no one has been able to open it since that young couple's tragic death."

I almost laughed. "No offense, granny, but I highly doubt the contents of this box can help someone fulfill their destiny."

Her eyes gave me a funny look. "Oh really? Why don't you try to open it and find out? Remember, it's the box that chooses its owner, not the other way around."

I tried to open the lid. It was surprisingly tight—extremely tight. I put a cloth over it and tried again, but all my attempts were in vain. The lid barely budged. "Okay, fine. It's not opening, but that doesn't prove it holds some magical object inside."

"To each her own belief, dear girl. Clearly, the box has rejected you. Why don't you buy something else?"

"No, I'm good with this box. How much is it?"

"You still want to buy it?" Her all-knowing smile made me uneasy, as if she was baiting me.

"Yes, I like challenges. I'll figure out a way to open it and prove to you that it holds no magical object."

"To each her own belief, dear girl. Now, that will be one hundred dollars."

I should have checked the price before proudly declaring I'd buy it—I thought to myself. "A hundred dollars for this tiny box?"

"Dear girl, had I been selling this in my store, it would have been much more expensive. It's pure silver and vintage. Is it too expensive? Would you prefer buying something else?"

"No, it's fine." I opened my wallet and gave her my card. "Here you go."

Pointing at a small board on the table, she said, "The sign clearly says, 'cash only.'"

"Who doesn't accept cards or payment wallets in the twenty-first century? Granny, I strongly suggest you upgrade your payment methods. It will boost your business." After scavenging my wallet for a few minutes, I managed to find only seventy-three dollars and eighty-one cents.

I sighed with frustration. "I guess this box is not meant for me."

She gave me that weird smile again. "How about this? I'll give it to you for the seventy-three dollars and eighty-one cents only if you can pay the rest tomorrow."

"Are you sure? I'm a stranger to you. What if I don't come back? You shouldn't trust people so easily."

"Dear girl I have lived in this world for a long, long time. I have a very good insight into a human's true nature."

"Well, thank you for trusting me, I guess. I will bring the remaining cash back to you tomorrow." I said as she handed me the box. "Go on... see you then."

Holding the box in my hand, I walked back to my car and then drove home, feeling a nagging sense of uncertainty. Did I get tricked? What if the silver box was fake and barely worth anything? No wonder she gave it to me so easily. But if it was real silver, then she was kind enough to trust me to pay the remaining amount in such an untrusting world. What kind of person would that make me if I doubted her? I decided to get the silver on the box verified as soon as possible. I had to confirm my doubts. Was I tricked, or had I become so hard-hearted that I couldn't trust anyone anymore?

Roughly an hour after I reached home, Olivia and Mateo arrived. I got the beers out and some wine. They brought the snacks. As we all crashed on the couch, I could sense their hesitance to broach the topic.

However, it was Olivia who finally broke the silence. "So, how was your day?"

"Fine. Not too bad," I replied, taking a sip of my pinot noir.

"Have you eaten?" Mateo asked, trying to keep things light.

I nodded, smiling. "Dumplings and black bean noodles. The perfect remedy for hunger and the cure for low spirits."

Olivia wrinkled her nose. "Ugh, you know I can't stand black bean noodles. Too greasy."

Mateo chuckled and fist-bumped me. "Love it. Solid choice."

Turning to Olivia, he asked, "So, how's it going with Zack?"

Her face lit up. "It's going well. He's a bit annoying at times, but I really like him. What about you?"

Mateo blushed slightly. "Cameron and I are celebrating our fourth anniversary soon. I'd say we're doing great."

They both turned to me with that familiar judgey look. Before they could say anything, I quickly proclaimed, "I'm good. Happy being single as always," flashing a grin.

Olivia narrowed her eyes playfully. "You've never really dated, so you don't know what you're missing."

"Hey! I've dated before," I protested, feeling a bit defensive.

"Three months after high school doesn't count," she retorted. "We all know that wasn't serious."

"We kissed so it counts," I insisted firmly.

"That was a peck on the lips, and you talked about it for weeks," she teased. "You need to get out there more."

Mateo laughed, shaking his head. "Well, we all know who's going to get married first and who's going to get married last here." He pointed at himself for the first and me for the last. I just rolled my eyes.

Just then, his phone started vibrating. He grimaced and answered it, his cheerful demeanor fading. We waited in silence as he listened, his expression growing more serious by the second. Finally, he spoke, his tone laced with frustration. "Wait, again? No, it's fine... yeah. Can it please not get pushed again?"

Once he hung up, I immediately asked, "Everything okay?"

"The Luca Everett interview is getting pushed to next week," he said, sighing.

"Wait, why? We just confirmed it this morning!" I exclaimed.

"Well, the PR team confirmed it without consulting Luca's assistant, Jane. She had specifically instructed them not to schedule anything because Luca has personal commitments all week."

I sighed, "Well, at least the headshots are done. I can work on those and prep more for this great exclusive you both keep pushing me into."

"Hey—you know Luca's personal assistant asked for you, right? I wasn't even planning on putting you on the project. But then she specifically requested that you interview him."

"Why me?"

"Who knows? Maybe they liked one of your old articles. Do rich football players ever need an excuse to get things their way?" Olivia commented.

Luca Everett was not just anyone. He was a high-profile figure, known for his athletic abilities and devilishly handsome good looks. His piercing blue eyes and charismatic smile had graced the covers of many magazines. But he was also known to be kind, charming and a history fan. He had many donations in his name for historical restoration purposes. It was funny of sorts. A football player who is also a history fan. Securing an interview with him was a significant achievement, but his busy schedule made it a logistical nightmare.

"I don't get why so many people admire him. He's good-looking and athletic, sure, but a bit strange. I met him a couple of times—once at university where he blanked at my simple question, and later at a party and a business conference. On TV, he seems confident, but in person, he's quite nervous. It makes him less idol-like and more human."

"Really? That's interesting. I've never really met him, but that doesn't sound like his character at all. Whenever I see him on TV, posters, or ads, he looks so perfect," Mateo said.

"Bet his girlfriend might know," I joked, and both Mateo and Olivia started to laugh. Clearly I had said something funny.

"Luca Everett's girlfriend! If you find out who that is, please do tell me. That would be such a great scoop. I'm sure you'd get a huge promotion just for finding out her name, because that's how big of news it would be. No one knows why he is so single. Did you know he hasn't even dated once? The entertainment division would be at your feet."

"Wow," was all I could say.

Eventually, our conversation shifted, and we ended up watching Deadpool, a one-of-a-kind, science-fiction comedy. Actually, we didn't really watch much. By the time we got halfway through the movie, Olivia had already passed out on my couch. Mateo had fallen asleep in the guest bedroom. They were both clearly exhausted, yet they had made time to come see me today, simply because they didn't want me left alone.

I switched off the television and decided to head to bed. As I stepped into my dark bedroom, I fumbled for the light switch, bumping into a small table in the process. Objects clattered to the floor with chaotic clinks and thuds. I continued to blindly press random switches until, finally, the room was flooded with light.

Looking down, I saw the contents of my purse scattered across the floor. As I quickly began picking things up, my eyes were drawn to the silver box. It had split into two, miraculously opened. Whoa, the box with magical items opened! I had twisted my arm trying to pry this thing open before, but it hadn't budged a millimeter. Who knew all it needed was an accidental collision with the floor? Doesn't this count as the box choosing me as its owner? I smiled at the thought.

I picked up the box to have a closer look. Inside, the faded velvet cushioning had once been a rich burgundy but now showed signs of time with its muted, worn appearance. The velvet, though slightly discolored, still held a touch of its former luxury, providing a soft bed for the treasures it once contained. At the center of the box, nestled securely in the velvet, was space for two platinum bands. But only one ring lay inside. I wondered where the other one was. It was clearly part of a set.

According to that granny, this box held the power to help its owners fulfill their destiny, but no one had managed to open it since the young couple's tragic death. Is this the universe's twisted way of saying that I need to get married? But if this was indeed a real engagement ring made of platinum and diamonds, there was no way it would cost just $100. If I were to believe what she said was true, and this ring was in fact made in the nineteenth century, then it would be a priceless antique. Heavens, I had to return this! There was no way I could keep something as invaluable as this, especially when it doesn't belong to me.

After spiraling in my thoughts for a few minutes, I gave the ring a closer look. The band was enchanting, almost magical, a perfect blend of elegance. It was a thin band of platinum with a diamond embedded in its center, with an engraving of "Fine &" etched inside. Out of curiosity, I decided to try it on. The moment I wore it, the sky lit up, followed by a deafening sound of thunder.

What the hell! That scared the hell out of me.

It had been a clear night sky with no hint of rain or dark clouds, and rain in October was almost impossible in this city. I looked outside my window, but the sky was clear. Did I hallucinate the thunder? I looked at my finger once again. The ring was a perfect fit, as if it were made just for my left ring finger.

I was tipsy, and the ring felt so at home on my finger that I decided to wear it for a few more minutes. I crawled into my bed, under my cozy blanket, and switched off the lights. The soft blanket against my skin was warm, making me feel so comfortable. I put my head down on the pillow, which was miraculously in a perfect position. Within seconds, I drifted into a very deep sleep.

I should have heeded the words of that peculiar old woman.

The ring might indeed have possessed a strange magic—for what happened next was beyond my wildest dreams. One second, I was there—sleeping in my bed—and the next, I was there—in that strange place, at an unusual time—surrounded by strangers.

Chapter 1

ARIADNE

2nd October, 1899

It usually takes me a long time to fall asleep, but last night was different. The pinot noir surely helped, but there was something more to it. The day's mental exhaustion had finally kicked in, and when I slept, I slept deeply.

To be honest, I wasn't sure how long I slept. But it felt long—uncomfortably long. When I finally opened my eyes, everything was a blur. Instead of a peaceful start to my new day, my head was pounding as if someone was punching it from the inside. My chest burned. But I didn't drink enough to get a hangover... so why did this feel so different? The discomfort gnawed at me, a relentless ache that turned my body heavy and my mind foggy.

The ceiling above me wasn't the familiar off-white of my bedroom. Instead, dark, coffered brown beams crisscrossed in a grid pattern above me. The wood looked old, its surface rough and aged. Shadows gathered in the recessed panels, adding to the antique feel of the room. I tried to look around, but my vision remained a blur. Faint whispers drifted from one side of the room. It seemed like a group of four or five.

Why would anyone be in my room so early? Who were they talking about? I wondered. The sense of confusion deepened, a thick, murky fog clouding my thoughts. It was as if I was seeing the world through someone else's eyes. I felt almost drugged—intoxicated and uncomfortable. The fatigue was overwhelming, dragging me back under its heavy weight as the world slipped away once more into darkness.

When I finally woke up, those unfamiliar whispers were long gone, the burning sensation in my chest had dulled, and my vision was no longer a blur. I looked around, but no one was here except me. This wasn't my room. Where in the world was I?

I sat up on the bed. A faint scent of lavender filled the air, mingling with a peculiar earthy aroma, as if the room had been recently aired out. The open arch-shaped window to the right was the source of almost all those scents and the diffused light that lit the room in a faint honey color. The room was unnecessarily spacious with little furniture. Just a plain wooden chair, a small table with a tarnished brass lamp, and a simple wardrobe. The walls were bare, save for a single, faded painting of a serene countryside scene. Everything looked positively archaic.

Just as I was about to stand up, I noticed my outfit. What in the world was I wearing? The high-collared shirt was choking my neck, with frills right under my chin that made it difficult to move my head comfortably. My sleeves were long and fluffy, with more frills at the wrists. I picked up the blanket that was covering my feet, and to my great shock, I was wearing a floor-length skirt made of some very uncomfortable stiff fabric. The skirt's hem was slightly tattered. But for sure, this entire outfit was a crime against fashion.

While I was busy contemplating my surroundings and my outfit, the door opened, and three people walked in—a doctor, a nurse, and a young girl dressed in a long black dress with a white apron, looking every bit like a maid from an old television drama. The doctor approached me first, his demeanor polite and concerned. "How are you feeling, my lady?"

"I'm not sure. My head hurts. Do you have any aspirin?"

The doctor looked puzzled. "Aspirin, my lady? I am not familiar with such a remedy."

"It's for headaches. How can a doctor not know this?" I said, my head pounding.

Before I could question him further, the girl in the maid's outfit stepped forward. "Forgive me for interrupting, my lady, but everyone has prayed for your swift recovery."

"Recovery from what? Where am I? And who are you?"

She curtsied. "My lady, you are at the Candler Charity Hospital. Two nights ago, you suffered a stroke and have been unconscious for three days. Sir Bryant ensured you received the best care and summoned Doctor Candler to attend to you."

"Unconscious for three days? What are you talking about? And who is Sir Bryant? Also, what's with the maid outfit? Is this a prank?"

The three of them exchanged bewildered glances. The doctor then turned to the nurse. "It appears there may be complications from her stroke. We must inform Sir Bryant immediately. She might be experiencing unusual aftereffects."

The nurse nodded, and they quickly exited the room, leaving me alone with the girl in the maid's outfit. The room fell into a heavy silence, broken only by the dull throb in my head and the wooden ambiance around me.

The young girl sensed my discomfort and fetched me a glass of water. Her movements were graceful, as if she had been trained for such tasks from a young age. I hesitated but took the glass, feeling the coolness of the water through the delicate crystal.

After drinking the water, I took a deep breath. I needed to deal with this situation calmly. Panic leads to confusion, and confusion leads to chaos. I had to stay patient and calm.

"What's your name?" I asked, trying to keep my voice steady.

She smiled politely. "I am Violet Smith, my lady."

"Well, hello, Miss Violet. Nice to meet you. Who are you exactly?"

"I am your lady's maid, my lady. I have served in this position for the last three years."

This prank was getting better and better. "Lady's maid... I see. Can you call Olivia or Mateo?"

"Who is Olivia or Mateo, my lady?"

I sighed internally. She had no idea who I was talking about. "Never mind. Can you bring me my cell phone so I can make a call?"

She looked genuinely confused. "A cell phone, my lady? Do you mean a sound telegraph? I believe it is also called a telephone."

What in the world was a sound telegraph? Was this some elaborate prank show? Olivia and Mateo, if you were responsible for this... I swear I'm going to kill you when I find you. I tried to calm myself down. If this was their game, I might as well play along to get more information.

"Miss Violet, why don't you tell me what the doctor said?"

She looked nervous but replied quickly. "The doctor said you might have lost your memory after your stroke..."

"Lost my memory?" I interrupted. "I remember everything. Why do you think I have amnesia?"

"Amnesia? I am not familiar with that term, but the doctor believes the stroke caused some complication, something about the blood supply to your brain."

"A stroke? A blockage in my brain? I would have been dead if that happened."

"Please don't say such things, my lady. You are still recovering. The doctor has already informed Sir Bryant, and they will find a solution for your recovery," she said reassuringly.

"Who is this Sir Bryant that everyone keeps mentioning?"

She looked confused. "He is your father, miss. Do you not remember him?"

Now I was getting angry. Olivia and Mateo would never joke about my parents. "My father? I haven't had one since I was fifteen. You must be mistaken. My name is Aria Gibson. I live in apartment 24, Luxe Tower, Martin-Cross Street,

Portmaine City, Agnor. I work at PulseNova Media. I am a journalist."

Her face turned pale. "My lady, your name is Lady Ariadne Bryant, daughter of Sir Richard and Lady Laura of the House of Bryant. Your family runs one of the largest steel industries in Agnor."

"Yeah, sure. Why not..." I mocked her words with sarcasm.

Silence hung between us, thick and uneasy. She was either a very good actor or she truly believed her story. Yesterday night, I was at home in my bed, chilling with Olivia and Mateo, but now I am here. I know for a fact that I don't sleepwalk, and there was no way someone kidnapped me. It's too elaborate of a plot to fool me into thinking I am someone else.

Then it struck me. This was a dream. Of course! Now it made so much sense. A figment of my imagination. I looked around once again. It felt too real to be a dream, but the human brain is a very complicated thing. It does have the power to trick you into believing something that might not be real. Even John Nash believed that his hallucinations were real for the longest time. So, why can't it happen to me? I will wake up after some time, and everything will be back to the way it is supposed to be. My normal life.

The pulsing sharp waves of pain were back once again, making me feel so strange. So, I decided to lie down, hoping to find some relief. Before I knew it, I was asleep. It was a dreamless sleep, but it achieved its purpose.

And when I woke up, I felt better—more alert. The room was bathed in shades of deep red, casting a warm glow over the wooden furnishings. Violet was gone, leaving me alone. I walked towards the arch-shaped window and looked outside. The scene was serene, with no trace of city life. I couldn't see a single parked car, dangling wires, or even a streetlight. Instead, strange, dim lamps dotted the landscape, their faint glow barely cutting through the twilight. Beyond that lay a shimmering lake, reflecting the dark red sky like a pool of liquid fire. Domestic animals grazed peacefully on the expansive lawns, their silhouettes against the vibrant sky adding a touch of pastoral beauty. It was like stepping into a painting from history, where the world was more calm and simple.

I really should give my mind some credit for imagining and making up stuff like this. It's an underrated talent in this fast-paced world. While I contemplated my surroundings, I heard a knock on the wooden door. As a reflex, I immediately said, "Come in."

A tall young man, who looked to be in his early twenties, walked in. He wore a white shirt and black dress pants while he carried a stiff but worried expression. His dark ash-blond hair was neatly combed, and his angular face was framed by sharp features. He looked handsome, but his eyes also had an intensity that seemed unnerving. As he walked towards me, his movements were precise and graceful, each step purposeful. His posture was erect, exuding a serious, dominating aura. But he looked concerned—anxious—scared.

In a slightly hoarse yet deep voice, he asked with concern, "Hello, Ariadne. How are you feeling?"

"Hi there. Okay... I think. Sorry, but how can I help you?"

"So it is true. You don't remember anything," he said softly, more to himself than to me.

I gave him a polite smile and asked, "Am I supposed to know you, Sir?"

"Well, you should know who I am, for I am your brother."

This dream was just getting weirder and weirder. I tried extremely hard to control my expression, but it failed miserably. "Brother? Do you mean like a real biological brother?"

His brows furrowed. "Yes. Is there something wrong with that?"

"This is enough already. If this is a prank, it has got to stop. You know what, I admit defeat. I've been fooled. So, can I seriously go back home now? I really have work to get done and I am exhausted by all this," I exclaimed, half jokingly and half seriously.

"Ariadne, your behavior perplexes me," he said, a mix of frustration and concern in his voice.

I snapped in frustration. "For the last time, I am not Ariadne. My name is Aria. Like I said before, I am Aria Gibson. Why isn't anyone listening to me?"

His expression grew serious. "Calm down. Everything is fine, Aria..." He hesitated slightly as he said my real name. "The doctor told me that you fail to recollect your past memories. All this time I thought of it as an exaggeration, but I see now that it is true. Do not worry; everything shall be fine."

I sighed and earnestly asked, "Where am I truly?"

He replied softly, "Candler Charity Hospital. It's located on the outskirts of Portmaine city. Do you know where that is?"

"The same Portmaine city that I am from?" I questioned.

"Yes, what other city named Portmaine exists in this country?" He asked, his tone a mixture of confusion and impatience.

"Well, if we are in the very same city, then can I please leave? In fact, why don't you take me to apartment 24, Luxe Tower, Martin-Cross Street. I have been living there for the last three years," I asked in a firm voice.

His forehead crinkled and in a very soft voice, barely above a whisper, he mumbled more to himself, "Goodness, how should I deal with this hassle now? Why did father send me?"

How did I become the hassle? He had no right to judge me. It was this situation that was a hassle. Frustrated, I walked back to my bed and sat down on the edge, crossing my arms. He gave me one pointed look but didn't say a word. Instead, he sat down on the chair with a resigned sigh, his posture stiff and formal. The silence between us was thick and suffocating, each second stretching forever. I could feel his gaze on me, constantly questioning my every movement. I tried to avoid his eyes, focusing instead on the soft patterns of the wooden floorboards beneath my feet.

A few minutes later, Violet entered the room holding a candle stand in her hand, followed closely by the doctor. She gave both of us a small curtsy and then gently placed the candle stand on the table. The room had grown dark, and the glow of the candle was now the only source of light. It illuminated the room in a soft, warm glow, casting flickering shadows on the walls and highlighting the rustic charm of the wooden furnishings. The candlelight softened the room's starkness, creating a warm ambiance that contrasted sharply with the silence between us.

I sat quietly on the bed, watching the scene unfold. Violet moved efficiently around the room, following the low, commanding instructions of my so-called brother. His voice was firm yet gentle, a stark contrast to the tension that had filled the room earlier.

The doctor approached me and handed me a prescription. I glanced at it, feeling a wave of confusion wash over me. The names of the medicines were unfamiliar, and his handwriting was nearly illegible. Why didn't he print it? I thought, frustration bubbling up again.

I was about to ask the doctor some questions when my self-proclaimed brother snatched the prescription from my hand. "Thank you so much, doctor. I am sorry for any inconvenience caused. I know that she had to be brought here at the very last moment, and now we are taking her back suddenly. But it is my father's strong belief that her recovery alongside her needs would be taken care of a lot better back home instead of your humble hospital."

The doctor's face remained impassive as he nodded in understanding, "Please do not apologize Sir. It is my job to treat patients. Although, I am extremely sorry that I am not able to provide any more help. I would have insisted that Miss Bryant stay back here for a few more days but I know that she would be in far greater comforts back home. I will make sure to visit every day and check on her condition. Please do not worry. Whatever strange disease that Miss Bryant has befallen, we shall spare no effort to figure out a cure." To which both of them shook hands as if in agreement.

After that brief conversation, roughly an hour later, all my bags were packed and we were ready to leave. I was going to go home and according to what's been happening so far, this home was definitely not going to be my apartment. Despite all the strange events, I decided to stay quiet.

Whenever I spoke, it made my head hurt further. I had to come to the realization that this was not a prank. No prank could have been planned with so much precision or to such details. Nor was this an escape room game. Also, there was no reason for anyone to go to such lengths to fool me. This was a dream. I admit that it was extremely realistic but the human mind is very powerful. Also, there was no other explanation other than that. So yes. I was sure. This was a dream.

Chapter 2

A RIADNE
October, 1899

Descending three flights of stairs from my hospital room on the third floor felt like shedding layers of confinement. Each step echoed in the wide, empty corridors, the sound amplified by the hospital's sterile silence. The building's dull aesthetic and sparse furnishings spoke of functionality over comfort, yet there was an undeniable air of affluence. Spacious rooms and a well-kept lobby hinted at a place that could afford to prioritize health over hospitality.

A tall, bulky man in a doorman's uniform waited by the imposing door at the bottom of the stairs. His thick horseshoe mustache and the small mole under his left eye gave him an intimidating presence. As he opened the door, a rush of cold air greeted me, sharp and refreshing. The night sky stretched out, a crescent moon hanging like a silver jewel among countless tiny stars that twinkled faintly. The air felt unusually pure, almost as if the world had reverted to a time before humans began their slow destruction of it.

A dark black carriage with metal fittings approached, its silhouette a stark contrast against the dimly lit surroundings.

The coachman, standing tall, greeted us warmly. "Hello, Sir. I hope this is a pleasing day," he said before turning to me with a respectful nod. "Congratulations on your recovery, my lady."

My brother climbed into the carriage with a swift, practiced movement. When I hesitated, he extended his hand to me. It felt oddly formal, but I accepted it and settled into the carriage. The coachman and Violet, who had been with me in the hospital room, loaded the luggage. As we started moving, I felt a mixture of relief and anxiety.

"Where is Miss Violet? Isn't she coming with us?" I asked, my voice breaking the silence inside the carriage.

Eugene's response was curt. "Miss Violet? Who might that be?"

"The girl who was with me in the hospital room."

"She is sitting in the front with the coachman. Isn't that obvious?"

His tone grated on my nerves. "Sorry. I wasn't aware," I replied, my voice matching his straightforwardness. I muttered under my breath, "As if you deserve it."

"What did you say?" He shot back.

"Nothing."

"Why don't I deserve it?"

"I said it's nothing." I shrugged, realizing that arguing would only exhaust me further. "I am sorry but I seriously must ask... if you are my brother, what is your name? I am sure that the doctor informed you. I don't remember much."

He looked at me, suspicion clouding his eyes. "Eugene Bryant. Try not to forget it this time."

Ignoring him became a necessity for my sanity. Why was my brain conjuring someone so exasperating in this dream? It's my dream, so it should follow my rules. I just have to wake up, and he'll be gone. I turned my attention to the window. The dim gas lamps cast long shadows on the poorly made roads. The streets were mostly empty, save for a few horses and the occasional passerby. The silence outside was almost soothing, a stark contrast to the tension inside the carriage.

I shifted slightly, trying to make myself comfortable, when something caught my eye. A small metal rod in front of me bore an engraving in beautiful cursive: 'Clarence 1897'. The model of the carriage, perhaps? But 1897?

A sudden surge of realization hit me. "What's the date today?" I asked, louder than I intended.

For the past forty minutes, we had ridden in silence, except for our initial exchange. Eugene's reply was immediate, "02nd of October 1899."

"02nd of October 1899?" I repeated, my voice barely above a whisper. How is that possible? Why dream about this specific year?

He looked at me with a mix of curiosity and concern. "Why? What might be the problem with today's date?"

I was about to answer his question when the carriage came to a halt in front of a massive iron gate. The gate looked like it had been forged centuries ago, yet it gleamed as if it were brand new. Standing eight feet tall and painted a dark black, each rod twisted and curled into intricate designs, transforming something as mundane as a gate into a majestic piece of art. Within moments, two guards appeared and the gates swung open.

My intended reply vanished from my mind as wonder took over. The carriage moved through a breathtaking panorama of vibrant hues swaying in the breeze, leaves rustling gently. We followed a long, wide path flanked by an endless, perfectly manicured green lawn. The landscape was so picturesque that I could scarcely believe it was real. When the carriage finally stopped, I didn't wait for assistance. I flung the door open and stepped out, my heart pounding with a mix of excitement and disbelief.

"Ariadne!" Eugene's shout broke through my reverie. Even the coachman seemed startled by my sudden movement but quickly composed himself, announcing, "We have arrived at our destination."

I stood there, transfixed. Before me was a marvel of Jacobethan architecture—a castle. In an awestruck whisper, I asked, "This castle is my home? Bloody hell are we royalty?" If this dream involved a royal family, a castle, and life in 1899, then perhaps I could enjoy it a little.

Eugene's reply shattered every bit of my brief fantasy. "How do you regard this as a castle? It is but obviously a mansion. Our home since birth, Clairborough Manor. And why would we be royalty? Agnor is a democratic nation. We haven't served any monarchy since 1822."

"Ahh... that's true. Sorry. My imagination just ran a bit wild. But this looks just like a castle. What's the difference?" I asked with a grin, trying to mask my disappointment.

"Of course, they are different. How do you regard them as the same thing?" He looked at me with that suspicious stare again. "I know now with absolute certainty."

"Know what?"

"I may confirm the fact that you are, in reality, unwell. That it is the truth that you have forgotten everything."

Did he just realize that now? "So what did you think of me until this moment?"

"Isn't that obvious? You were lying. Another one of your silent rebellions to get some attention," he stated blankly.

I stared at him, a mix of frustration and sadness welling up inside me. What kind of person had I been in this life that my own brother thought so poorly of me? And why did my dreams have to include such exasperating people?

I stared at him in disbelief as he walked inside. Wow. Really? What a low opinion he must have of me. Despite my irritation, I followed him into the mansion, which was one of the most exquisite places I had ever seen. The corridors were illuminated mostly by candles, casting a warm, flickering glow, while occasional electric lights hinted at modernity.

As soon as we entered, a few servants approached us, their expressions a mix of curiosity and deference. Eugene wasted no time in addressing them. "Thankfully, due to the grace of God, Lady Ariadne has managed to overcome a serious medical condition, but she has had a very tiring past few days and is in a fragile state, both mentally and physically. I expect all of you to pay extra attention to her needs and care for her with the utmost diligence."

He then turned to an older man, whose bearing and demeanor marked him as someone of importance within the household. "Mr. Bailey, please ensure that a light meal is prepared for both of us and sent to our rooms. Also, here is a list of Lady Ariadne's medicines and dietary suggestions from the doctor. Make sure these are strictly adhered to. Two nurses will be arriving early tomorrow morning to take over her care. Until then, her lady's maid will tend to her."

The servants scattered, each taking on their assigned tasks with a sense of urgency. Eugene's orders were clear and precise, yet his tone remained cold and distant, devoid of any warmth or genuine concern.

Once the servants had dispersed, I turned to Eugene, demanding answers in a softer voice, "Mr. Eugene, why do you think I am in a fragile state? I am fine. I have barely known you for a few hours, but you've managed to irritate me to this extent. That's seriously some talent."

The corner of his lip curled into a sarcastic smile. "Dear sister, you just proved it by speaking to me like that."

Without another word, he left, leaving me dumbfounded. What the hell is wrong with that man? I glanced at Violet, who was barely suppressing a smile. After standing in the massive lobby for a few minutes, my annoyance turned into confusion. What was I supposed to do now? I looked at Violet, who was patiently waiting for my next instructions. "Miss Violet, what am I supposed to do now?"

She looked momentarily puzzled. "Are you asking me, my lady?"

"I don't see any other Miss Violet around here, do you?"

My sarcasm made her slightly nervous. "Umm... why don't we proceed to your resting quarters?"

"Okay. Sounds good. Lead the way."

Her eyes widened in surprise. "My Lady, you want me to lead the way?"

"Didn't you hear Mr. Eugene? I am in a fragile state, mentally and physically. So do you think I know the way?"

She looked flustered and immediately started walking She looked very flustered. She was not used to being teased. She immediately started walking and I followed her.

Calling this mansion huge was an understatement. It was a labyrinthine marvel of architecture, with rooms leading into other rooms, seemingly endless corridors, and a bewildering network of passageways. Left turns, right turns, stairs, and more stairs; we walked for what felt like an eternity—almost ten minutes, before finally arriving at my so-called bedroom.

The bedroom stood in stark contrast to the sterile, utilitarian hospital room I had left behind. It was a snapshot of timeless elegance, as if frozen in the grandeur of the past. At its center was a grand king-size bed, the focal point of the room, adorned with richly embroidered sheets and a cascading canopy. The bed's frame was embellished with delicate floral carvings and gilded accents, and the sheets displayed intricate patterns reminiscent of a bygone era.

Heavy curtains, draped in layers of lace, framed the large windows, barely visible in the moonlight that seeped through. The soft, dappled light from the setting sun had long faded, replaced by the gentle illumination of the moon, casting enchanting patterns of shadows. These curtains, with an air of regal refinement, seemed to whisper stories of the past.

In the left corner, an elegantly crafted dressing table of dark wood held antique perfume bottles, ornate hairbrushes, and delicate porcelain trinket boxes, each item embodying the grace and sophistication of the era. The dim glow of a candle flickered on the table, casting a warm, golden light that added to the room's nostalgic charm.

To the right, a spacious balcony beckoned, framed by tall, ornate doors. It featured two exquisite chairs and a small table, offering a breathtaking panoramic view of the moonlit landscape. The mansion's architect had ingeniously placed this sanctuary to allow the occupant to marvel at the natural beauty beyond the windowpanes, now bathed in silver light.

Every element in the room spoke of meticulous selection and refined luxury. It felt as if I had been transported to a world where the beauty of the past was preserved in every exquisite detail, the night adding a layer of serene mystery to the timeless elegance surrounding me.

"My lady, would you like to take a bath before dinner?" Violet asked.

"Yes, I would love to," I replied, welcoming the idea.

The bathroom was unique—ancient and a tad complicated. Violet insisted on helping me, but the thought made me shudder. There was no way I would let someone else bathe me. After persistent refusals, I finally convinced her to just explain the mechanics: which tap was hot, which was cold, which oil to use, and what soap to apply.

The water temperature was perfect, just between hot and warm. After the day I had had, the bath felt incredibly calming. Wrapping myself in a bathrobe, I moved to the dressing room, only to find Violet and two maids waiting to help me dress.

"What are you doing here? Get out!" I yelled, startled and embarrassed.

They looked taken aback. "My Lady, we are here to help you get dressed," Violet explained.

I felt a surge of frustration and near tears. Why was this happening? I tried to calm down, knowing that panic would only make things worse. "No! Please leave. I am completely capable of dressing myself."

Violet was about to argue, but I pleaded, "Miss Violet, I will do anything you want, but I cannot let you see me naked. Please, leave. Now."

Thankfully, she agreed, leaving me to dress alone. The clothes Violet had laid out for bed were simple yet elegant—a soft, silk nightgown that felt luxurious against my skin. By the time I was dressed, a servant brought in my dinner: a simple sandwich, cookies, and juice. Violet returned, handing me a small tray with various medicines.

"My lady, here are your medicines," she said, her voice gentle but with a hint of hesitation. "You should take these to aid your recovery."

I examined the assortment of pills and potions, their unfamiliar shapes and colors making me uneasy. Violet watched closely as I took each one, ensuring I didn't miss a dose.

Once satisfied, she checked my temperature and pulse with a practiced hand, her expression serious but tentative.

"You seem stable for now, my lady. Rest well."

I nodded, feeling a strange mix of gratitude and annoyance. As I settled into bed, exhaustion quickly overcame me. I was convinced that when I woke up, I would be back in my own world. But as I drifted off to sleep, the lingering unease whispered that this dream had no intention of ending just yet.

Chapter 3

A RIADNE

October, 1899

My morning routine was simple.

After last night's bathing incident, Violet mercifully refrained from insisting on helping me again. She laid out three full-length dresses for me to choose from. The first two were excessively adorned with lace and puffed sleeves, looking incredibly uncomfortable. The third, a light brown linen dress with straight white elbow sleeves, was much simpler and more appealing. I opted for the third choice.

I had just exited the room when Violet insisted on makeup. It felt absurd to wear makeup for breakfast, but since this was a dream, I decided not to fuss over these details. She adorned me with classic pearl studs, a touch of rouge on my cheeks, and baby pink lipstick, making me look presentable by her standards. She even suggested heels, but I firmly refused. I had no intention of torturing my feet in a house this big.

Once dressed, I stood before the mirror and for the first time, saw my reflection. This dream had just taken a surreal turn. Normally, I couldn't conjure up faces in my dreams, but now, my reflection was remarkably vivid. The young visage staring back at me had flawless skin, and instead of my familiar brown hair, I saw a lustrous shade of dark ash-blond. My eyes, usually a dark brown, were now a bright, captivating shade of hazel, framed by long, dark lashes. The face and body were entirely different, yet curiously, the skin tone and height were the same. It felt as if my soul was trapped in a stranger's body—a deeply unsettling sensation.

Tentatively, I touched my face. My cheeks felt warm, and I noticed the light tinge of freckles barely visible under the makeup. As I moved my hand, the reflection moved in perfect synchrony. This unfamiliar reflection was now moving according to my will.

I whispered, "This was a dream. It had to be. It definitely was!" The reflection mimicked my actions, whispering back the same words, adding to the eeriness.

"My lady, it's time for you to proceed for breakfast," Violet's words brought me back to my surroundings.

"Yeah... let's go. Please show me the way," I replied.

Just like yesterday, this house was a labyrinth. If Violet hadn't shown me the way, I would have been hopelessly lost. The breakfast hall was relatively smaller compared to the other dining rooms I passed, but it was still massive. Eugene was already seated, engrossed in a newspaper. I whispered to Violet, "Where should I sit?"

Before she could answer, Eugene interrupted, pointing to the chair beside him. "Sit there."

"Okay," I responded, taking my seat. The atmosphere was silent. Eugene continued reading the newspaper while I sat awkwardly, unsure of what to do.

"Where is the food?" I eventually asked.

"Have patience. We are waiting for them."

"Them?" I echoed, curiosity piqued. But he didn't answer and continued reading.

After waiting for almost ten minutes, a middle-aged couple entered the room. Eugene immediately stood up, and though I was a few seconds late, I followed suit. The man looked to be in his late fifties, with a proud, protruding belly and hair the same color as mine. When he saw me, a sense of relief spread across his face.

"Ariadne, how are you feeling?" he asked with great concern.

His question caught me off guard. With an awkward smile, I answered, "I am okay. Thank you, umm... for asking."

"I was planning to visit yesterday but thought it better to let you rest. I spoke to Doctor Candler. He updated me on your condition. My poor child, I can't imagine how terrifying this must be for you, but don't worry. We will find a solution. A team of doctors will be assembled to research your condition and figure out a cure."

He turned to Mr. Bailey. "Bailey, make sure the staff is extremely attentive to Lady Ariadne. All her needs should be met, and assist her in every way possible."

Mr. Bailey responded formally, "Indeed we shall."

"Have the nurses arrived?" he further inquired.

"Yes, Sir," came the prompt reply. "They have been attended to and will commence their duties without delay."

Then the woman spoke. She seemed younger, appearing to be in her late forties, though she exuded a youthful energy.

She possessed a slender figure and was impeccably attired, her ensemble reflecting refined taste. Thick makeup and exquisite jewelry accentuated her elegance.

"My dear daughter, how have you been feeling? Do you fail to recollect who I am?" Her tone put me on edge. How was I supposed to answer such a question without sounding rude?

"Um... I do feel better, but I must admit, I still can't recall any of you. I'm sorry," I replied, trying to convey my confusion gently.

She inquired, "What are we to make of this peculiar situation, and how should we handle the Cordinburg gala? Ariadne's current condition leaves her unable to attend."

Eugene interrupted, "Mother, the doctor mentioned that this is a temporary condition. She will get better soon, and as for the Cordinburg gala, there is enough time for her to prepare."

"Enough time? You foolish child. The gala is on the 21st of December during the winter equinox. How will she manage to learn everything in such a short span?" Was this lady in her right mind? Her only daughter had lost all her memories, and all she cared about was the gala and how I wouldn't have time to prepare. Prepare for what?

The old man interrupted in a firm voice, "Enough. Ariadne surviving this ordeal and coming back to us safe and sound is already a miracle. We should be grateful for that."

His conduct reflected a personality shaped by decades of experience. The moment he spoke, the room went silent. He asked Mr. Bailey to serve the food, and soon we all ate. No one uttered a word throughout breakfast. Despite the palpable awkwardness in the air, my hunger got the best of me. I indulged in a hearty meal of fresh-baked bread with creamy butter, a selection of cold meats and cheeses, a soft-boiled egg, and a bowl of porridge sweetened with honey. A side of fresh fruit and a steaming cup of rich, dark coffee completed the spread. As I savored each bite, I couldn't help but notice the lady's occasional glances in my direction. It seemed she had something on her mind, something she was holding back, perhaps an urge to correct my behavior.

Breakfast concluded swiftly. As everyone prepared to depart, the lady addressed me with a saccharine tone. "Ariadne, would you kindly join me after breakfast?"

I nodded and followed her into a room. The walls were adorned with a soothing pastel green hue, serving as a backdrop to the enormous paintings that graced their expanse. Like my bedroom, this room was adorned with curtains and upholstery that held an intriguing allure, exuding a sense of antiquated charm that defied modern fashion. The furniture, while undoubtedly outdated, possessed a timeless quality that was strangely captivating.

As I settled onto the plush sofa, her expression momentarily shifted. With a gentle tone, she remarked, "Ariadne, please, cross your legs and sit in a more ladylike manner."

Every word from her made me feel uneasy, but I did as she asked. "Now then, is it true that you fail to recollect anything, or is this another one of your ruses? Another attention-seeking tantrum?" Her directness was unsettling, her words laced with offense. I couldn't help but wonder what she truly thought of me.

"Excuse me?" I questioned, taken aback.

"Don't give me that look," she continued, unapologetic. "I had to ask. I've never encountered anything as absurd as this. Losing all your memories after a sudden stroke? You must understand why it raises suspicions."

"I am not lying. What benefit would I get from lying about something like this?" I was genuinely baffled.

"Let's not dwell on it," she replied curtly. "We need to take precautions now. My dear daughter, do you recall any of the lessons your governess taught you?"

"Governess?" I blinked in confusion.

She sighed, trying to maintain her composure. "I suppose not. I observed you at breakfast—it was quite a spectacle. It's evident you've forgotten dining etiquette entirely. Have you also forgotten the fundamental codes of polite behavior that women are expected to adhere to?"

I stared at her, feeling more confused by the moment.

"Judging from your expression, I guess not. What about your education? Do you fail to remember that as well?"

I tried to stay calm. I had no interest in starting an argument. "Can you be more specific about what education you are referring to?"

"I am referring to knitting, flower arrangement, formal dancing, piano playing, literature, French, etiquette, embroidery, calligraphy, history of fine art, and the art of conversation..." She recited the extensive array of traditional skills and knowledge expected of a well-rounded lady, each item on the list bearing the weight of societal expectations.

Before she could continue with this absurd list, I interrupted. "I do remember how to play the piano and speak fluent German, but would subjects like Mathematics, Economics, Physics, Chemistry, Biology, Political Science, literature, advanced cultural studies, or maybe a master's degree in journalism and mass media communication qualify as an education in your eyes?"

Her reaction was almost comical, as if she might faint at any moment. "My goodness! You truly are unwell, aren't you? Just look at the nonsense you're spouting." It took her a few moments to regain her composure before she continued, "My dear child, the Cordinburg gala is roughly eleven weeks away. I understand you're still in recovery, but there's much you need to prepare. I am summoning your governess immediately. You must reacquaint yourself with the basics, or you'll risk making a spectacle of yourself. I won't allow the Bryant household to be embarrassed in any way."

She was unbelievable. I was almost on the verge of laughing. "Mother..." The word felt strange, almost painful, reminding me of my real mother. I shoved that thought away. "May I know why the Cordinburg gala is so important to you? I can just choose not to attend. There is no way I can embarrass you then. That solves all your problems, doesn't it?"

"My dear, how can you even think like that? The Cordinburg Gala is not just an ordinary gala. It happens only once in five years and presents the ideal occasion for you to acquaint yourself with numerous new individuals. Many young ladies find potential suitors at such gatherings. It was at the very same gala that I met your father. The notion of you not attending is utterly inconceivable."

I cut her off. "Wait a minute! So, your intention for me to attend this gala is for me to find someone to marry?"

"My dear, you should never speak of such topics in such a direct manner. People might regard you as too forward. My intention is for you to meet many new people and hopefully catch the eye of some kind gentleman..."

Her delight at the prospect was infuriating. "And what! Marry a stranger?" I exclaimed, raising my voice slightly.

"Hush. How dare you speak to your mother like that?"

"How old am I for you to think of such things?"

"You are turning one and twenty soon. It is but natural that you start thinking of such things." she explained with conviction.

Wait, twenty-one? In reality, I am twenty-five years old and even then I didn't want to get married that early. So twenty-one... marriage? I knew this dream was not about being royalty and stuff, but it was still a dream. Why is it now turning into a nightmare?

"Are you insane?" I blurted out, unable to contain my disbelief.

"Preposterous. How dare you speak to your mother like that?"

"No... You are the preposterous one. Marry someone when I am not even twenty-one? That too a complete stranger. What is wrong with you?" Saying that, I walked out of the room, leaving her stupefied and speechless. What the hell was wrong with this place? Marriage at twenty-one? Utter nonsense.

Violet touched my elbow and, in the most polite tone, said, "My lady, please wait."

I jerked my elbow away. "Leave me alone!"

I knew how rude I was, but at that moment, my brain was firing on all cylinders. There were too many thoughts, and with each second, I felt more conflicted and confused. I walked out of that corridor. I had made a decision. I had to get out of this mansion. Despite its grandeur and archaic aesthetic, I felt suffocated. I wanted to leave. Get out of this place and just wake up. This dream was getting unnecessarily long and extremely ridiculous. I was just done with it. I craved the familiarity of my routine. I wanted to go back and live my life with my friends and family. I had no interest in living this life amidst this random bunch of strangers.

I continued to walk, taking random turns and stumbling through different corridors. After wandering aimlessly for almost fifteen minutes, I finally found a door that led outside.

The wide path cut through green lawns, the manicured grass stretching out on either side like a lush carpet. In the distance, a dense forest of towering trees began to come into view, their branches swaying gently in the breeze. The world around me was drenched in shades of red, orange, and yellow as autumn leaves fluttered down like confetti from the heavens.

Each step was accompanied by the satisfying crackle of dried leaves under my boots. The air was filled with the crisp scent of fall, and I could hear birds chirping softly in the distance, their melodies blending harmoniously with the rustling leaves. The trees stood tall and proud, their branches reaching out like welcoming arms, shedding their leaves in a beautiful, melancholic dance.

It was cold, but I had managed to grab someone's coat on my way out, the thick fabric wrapping me in a cocoon of warmth. After walking for almost an hour, the majestic eight-foot-tall gate finally appeared before me, its wrought-iron bars intricately designed with swirling patterns and ornate details.

I had decided. If this was a dream that did not want to end, then I was going to test my imagination to its very limit. It had to end sometime, right? So, let's at least enjoy it, exploring the deepest parts of my imagination instead of getting annoyed by the company of irritating people.

Chapter 4

A RIADNE
October, 1899

It took me almost an hour to reach the gate. The sheer size of this property made me shudder. It was enormous, with no modern transport to help me travel from one place to another. The walk helped me calm down. I was no longer angry, but I was still frustrated.

From a distance, I could see two guards at the gate. They hadn't noticed my presence yet. The trees provided good camouflage, and since it was 1899, there were no CCTV cameras. If they did exist, it would confirm that this was indeed a dream. I wanted to go outside, but I wasn't sure if they would let me pass through that easily. I was apparently the daughter of this household, but would they really let me go out unaccompanied? I wasn't going to take that chance.

As I glanced around, my eyes took in the imposing walls flanking the gate, rising high on either side. My attention was drawn to a distant glimmer along the rough clay surface, far to the right. It was a little far from where I was standing, and my peripheral vision was not that strong. Instead of confronting the guards, I decided to explore and find another path outside.

I walked to the right, following the source of the reflection, and found myself in front of a wooden door set into the towering wall. It looked like a piece of artwork, something you'd find in a museum. The door, made from weathered wood, showed the marks of time and history. Sturdy metal hinges supported it, their worn appearance adding to the door's rustic charm.

I tried to open the latch, but it was locked with a metal lock that glistened in the sunlight. The rest of the door was a blend of age and nature's influence, with patches of rust and moss forming intricate patterns across its surface. It felt like this small portal to an unknown world had become a canvas marked by the passage of time, creating a unique and enchanting piece of art.

There was no way I was going to be able to open the door unless someone brought me the key, the probability of which was negligible. I was contemplating returning to confront the guards when a cat suddenly jumped out from a nearby bush. It caught me off guard, making me lose my balance and tumble onto the soft grass.

This feline intruder was a creature of captivating beauty, boasting pristine white fur that shimmered like spun silk beneath the warm sunlight. Its gaze fixated on me with mesmerizing green eyes, seemed to be assessing whether I posed a threat or was merely a passerby. For a moment, we shared an unspoken connection, both trying to decipher the intentions of the other. But then, without uttering a sound, the enigmatic cat gracefully turned and strode away, swiftly vanishing from sight. Where did she come from? It was as if she had magically appeared from the lush surroundings.

The wall was too high for her to jump. It took me a few seconds to figure it out. I looked closely at the bushes. On one corner to the left, near the very bottom of the wall, I spotted a small hole. It wasn't conspicuous, just a humble gap in the wall's foundation. No one would find it unless they carefully inspected this never-ending wall. And with 2,000 acres of land, who was ever going to bother? I tried to crawl through it. The edges of the gap were rough, and the tiny stones in the soil pricked at my knees. I lacked the cat's agility and small size, but I somehow managed to squeeze myself through. Luckily, my dress or coat didn't tear, but they got a little messy.

Once I was done patting down most of the dirt, I stood up and looked around. The world around me looked rather captivating. Last night, I was a soul lost amidst the darkness, but that wasn't the case today. The path we traveled was dimly lit, with neither the moon nor the gas lamps offering a strong enough glow to reveal my surroundings. I could barely make out the path as the carriage structure was a major obstacle to the view, but now everything was crystal clear.

Clairborough Manor was located on a plateau, slightly elevated compared to its surroundings. From my vantage point, I could see a cluster of tiny cottages—signs of human civilization. It was the perfect destination to test my imagination, so I decided to walk down.

I was definitely not dressed for so much walking, but since this was a dream, a figment of my imagination, anything and everything seemed possible. 'I was so wrong about that!' By the time I reached those so-called signs of human civilization, I felt exhausted, and the cold made it a lot worse. Next time, I would definitely wear pants and not these horrible leather shoes, which were a terrible idea for any sort of physical exertion.

The sun was still high, but I had no wristwatch or phone. Figuring out the time or my exact location was impossible. The world around me was slightly different and yet the same. While randomly wandering around I passed this gigantic shade tree with vibrant orange leaves. Sitting on a bench, under the tree was a young couple. Despite the cold, they looked comfortable.

The town was surprisingly serene. A few people rode bicycles with large front wheels, while others strolled leisurely, tipping their hats in greeting. The sound of a distant blacksmith hammering echoed through the air, mingling with the soft chatter of townsfolk.

In one corner, a group of young men gathered. Their clothing showcased a blend of individuality and simplicity, with vests, suspenders, and flat caps that gave off an air of distinctive style. Nearby, petite ladies in ankle-length dresses adorned with intricate lace and delicate embroidery chatted and laughed. They carried small lace umbrellas, adding an extra touch of elegance to their appearance. Horse-drawn carriages occasionally clattered by, their wheels rumbling over the cobblestones, completing the picture of a bustling yet peaceful town.

Market stalls lined the main street, offering a variety of goods. The aroma of freshly baked bread mixed with the scent of leather from a cobbler's shop. Vendors greeted me with warm smiles, though their eyes quickly assessed the dirt-covered hem of my dress. The market was relatively small, a contrast to the sprawling, bustling centers of major cities. Eugene had mentioned that the manor was on the outskirts of Portmaine City, but I doubted that. Portmaine City was the epicenter of a fast-paced modern lifestyle, always bustling with people and commerce. This place, however, was silent, simple, and peaceful. It felt more like a village, a step back in time to a slower, more deliberate way of life.

One thing was for sure: my mind had conjured a very fine representation of the world in 1899. Astonishingly realistic. While trying to make sense of my surroundings, I saw a newspaper lying on the ground, gently moved toward me by the breeze. Out of curiosity, I picked it up. Written in bold letters on the front page was the headline: Parliament Refuses Appeals of the Slovain Community. The article continued:

"The Agnorian parliament abolished slavery in November, 1872. Despite this progressive step, the Slovain Community continues to suffer from widespread discrimination. Opposition party members have repeatedly appealed to the government for new laws on anti-discrimination and fair pay. However, the parliament has once again delayed action, citing 'the necessity for due consideration.'"

"The exact details of the appeal remain unclear, but a member of President Benjamin Henderson's ruling party stated that the appeal includes what he called 'irrational requests,' such as monetary compensation and public apologies from prominent figures for historical injustices. Members of the Slovain Community have remained silent, offering no comment on these accusations. It is evident that this issue has escalated into a significant political agenda for the opposition and a prominent debate topic among scholars."

The article continued for a few more lines, filled with political views, followed by information on groceries, farming tips, local markets, and theater performances. This newspaper was a stark reminder of Agnor's turbulent past. I recalled studying this period in middle school. It reminded me of a particular diagram from my history textbook that outlined Agnor's historical timeline—one which I had to cram intensively as it was a crucial part of the syllabus for my tenth board examinations. I aced that exam, thanks in large part to my father's incessant lectures on history when I was a kid. His passion for history was something he passed on to me.

I was lost trying to remember what happened next when my thought process was interrupted by the irresistible aroma of freshly baked bread wafting through the air. The scent was enough to make my mouth water, as I could distinctly pick out the inviting notes of yeast, honey, and the comforting warmth of wheat. It suddenly brought me back to my reality. I had no money and I was starving. The smell was very tempting but I continued to walk away until the smell disappeared. Shortly, I was once again in the presence of that familiar gigantic shade tree with its orange hues that covered this courtyard in its protective embrace from the sun.

The young couple was no longer sitting on the bench. Instead, a tall old woman had taken their place. Her pronounced wrinkles and dense curly grey hair were unmistakable. She had a very familiar face that tugged at my memory. As I walked closer, her features became clearer, and I was certain—it was her. The same old woman who sold me those so-called magical rings.

She smiled at me, a strange, knowing smile that sent shivers down my spine. I rubbed my eyes to confirm her presence, but when I looked again, she had vanished. Did I just hallucinate her presence? I walked closer to the bench, looking around, but there was no trace of her. The air where she had sat was cooler as if touched by a lingering presence. And then at that moment, I saw something that shattered all my conviction of this being a dream. Kept on the bench intentionally were one fifty-dollar bill, two ten-dollar bills, and a few coins that added up to seventy-three dollars and eighty-one cents. The exact change, the same notes, and coins that I paid her with. And that's when all my sense of reality vanished. 'This was not a dream!'

How did I forget about those so-called rings? Is this really happening because of that? Am I really trapped in someone else's body in 1899? Those rings were supposed to make the owner fulfill his or her destiny and I managed to open the box. So if I was the owner, what destiny was I supposed to fulfill in 1899 as some aristocrat's daughter?

The thoughts continued to circle. All my bottled-up feelings and subconscious suppression of emotions had now flooded into my consciousness.

Yesterday at the hospital, the reason why my head hurt like hell and my chest burned was not because of a hangover. It was because I was recovering from a stroke. The dizziness, the drugged effect... was all making sense now. Oh no... no... no! What the hell is happening? I need to go back. Am I dead in the future? Am I going to stay trapped in this girl's body forever? I pinched myself on my arm as hard as possible. It hurt. I hoped it wouldn't but it did. I could feel the sting on my arm as it turned red. It felt like time had stopped. I took a closer look at the money. The weight of the money felt real. It was definitely the money I paid her and then I was lost in a flurry of thoughts.

I sat down to process everything, staring at the notes and coins in my hand. Minutes passed, though it felt like hours, as the weight of my situation sank in.

It took me a long time to truly come to terms with what was happening. A rather normal response to the sudden change in one's environment, especially when this change involved my soul getting trapped in someone else's body in the late 19th century.

The weather was getting colder and the sky was now a light shade of orange. I had been aimlessly wandering across this random town for the whole day. Sitting on some random bench in 1899, cold, hungry, and full of exhaustion... I knew for sure. This was definitely... not at all a dream. All of this was real, which meant that the box did contain some magical items. Those rings were magical and I should have never touched them. I sat there for quite some time. Frozen with shock. Questioning every single thing that had happened. That's when an old man touched my shoulder and asked, "Dear child, what are you doing here all alone? It's getting late. Are you lost?"

I looked at him. Mustering up all my courage, I gave him the faintest of smiles. "No, I am not."

After that, I was walking again, back to the mansion. A house full of strangers. My unfamiliar new home. The walk was horrifyingly long. It took me hours to reach the convoluted black iron gate. I navigated through random streets and climbed a plateau as the sky turned pitch black. With no way to contact Eugene and no vehicle, I relied on my excellent memory and the dimly lit, curved path visible from a distance. That path led straight to the mansion, grim and frightening. My calf muscles screamed in pain. I was freezing, hungry, exhausted to my very limit, and mentally paralyzed with shock.

When I reached the gate, I saw relief flood the guards' faces. They opened the gate and rang the bell to alert others. A carriage arrived shortly, cutting my walk short. I got in, and the guards escorted me back.

The main door of the mansion opened, revealing Eugene—silent and stern. In an authoritative tone, he demanded, "Follow me!" I obeyed. We walked past a few rooms until we stood in front of a dark brown wooden door to his study. He opened it, and we walked in.

The room was illuminated by a softly glowing chandelier suspended from the center of the ceiling. The walls were adorned with numerous bookshelves, their wooden surfaces holding the faint, lingering scent of cigars. My gaze shifted to the desk, where a half-open ink bottle stood alongside a well-used pen, both resting atop a scattered arrangement of papers. A telephone, positioned within arm's reach, hinted at recent activity. Did he rush out in a hurry to see me?

"Sit," he commanded, and I did. He continued, "Ariadne, would you mind telling me where you were today?" His eyes blazed with intensity.

In a whisper, I answered, "Town."

"Speak clearly."

"I visited the nearby town."

"Why?"

"I wanted to leave. Explore... Just escape this mansion," I whispered softly.

"Look me in the eye and answer. Couldn't you have informed someone? Anyone? Do you have any idea how worried everyone has been?"

I took a deep breath. There was no way I was going to get away with this. Eugene was furious, and it was because of me. Initially, I thought of this as a dream. My attempt at exploration was a normal response, but he doesn't know that. To him, I am just his unwell sister who ran away. They will probably think of me as a foolish child throwing a tantrum, unaware of the harsh dangers of society. But I wasn't one. Despite the appearance of a soon-to-be twenty-one-year-old, I was a mature, intellectual woman who had graduated college, got a job, and even managed to buy her own apartment. A young woman navigating through life, tackling obstacles, and dealing with past emotional trauma with her therapist.

This was going to be the worst first impression. How had I transformed into a foolish rich girl trapped in the society of 1899, surrounded by strangers, in just one day? Right now, I had no clue what was to come next, and that thought terrified me. But the worst part was that I was alone. It felt just like the moments after my parents' death. But fortunately, this time, there was no grief of losing loved ones.

I looked him in the eye and answered clearly, "It was a momentary lapse of judgment. It won't happen again. I promise."

"What I want to know is why it happened in the first place. Do you have any idea how reckless this decision was? You were gone the whole day and no one knew where you were. Do you know what we went through? The entire staff searched the property twice but couldn't find you. How did you even leave? The guards never saw you."

Embarrassed, I admitted, "I used another way out. A hole in the wall."

He looked dumbfounded. "A hole? What hole? Have you seriously lost it?"

"Believe me, you have no idea what's happening to me. I'm handling this situation a lot better than you'd expect," I replied, his confusion deepening.

"Are you serious? You don't even feel guilty for making us go through all this, do you?"

"You wouldn't understand. It's nothing. Don't worry. I'll behave from now on. Isn't that what you want?" I said, my voice rising slightly.

"Ariadne Bryant!" His stern voice reverberated in the room, making me flinch.

"Don't raise your voice!" I glared back with equal intensity.

His sudden outburst unleashed a torrent of bottled-up emotions. Laughter and tears mixed uncontrollably. Despite my emotional turmoil, no one had the right to speak to me like that. My cheeks were moist, but I was laughing. What was happening? I must have looked insane. He just stared at me in disbelief, caught between frustration and worry.

Taking a deep breath, he softened his tone, full of genuine concern. "Why are you crying?"

"You wouldn't understand," I whispered.

He hesitated, clearly struggling with how to respond. "If it's nothing, you wouldn't be crying. Yesterday, you were calm and curious, not in blind disbelief and fear. What changed today?"

I chuckled through my tears. "I don't remember." I knew he wouldn't believe that I was from the future, but the 73 dollars and 81 cents in my pocket felt like tangible proof of my sanity. "I don't know who you are or where I am. I feel like a stranger, lost and suddenly relocated to this unfamiliar place. I want to go home."

"You are home. The doctor said you'd regain your memory. You didn't remember anything yesterday either, but you weren't acting like this. What's different now?" His voice softened further, showing genuine concern.

Mentally, I noted the change: knowing this was reality and not a dream had shifted everything. He continued, "If you don't remember old memories, make new ones. Is that so difficult? Do you know how much everyone adores you in this house? You might be pampered and spoiled, but you're also loved. Although I fail to see any shyness or obedience in you anymore."

My eyes were red and puffy. Did he say pampered and spoiled? I mentally rolled my eyes. Who have I become?

"Yes. Why would I lie about that?"

"But I don't know you. Everyone here is a stranger, and I refuse to get married."

He looked taken aback. "Married? How did that thought even—did Mother say something?"

My eyes widened. "Say something? She corrected my posture, criticized how I eat, and went on about some ridiculous code of polite behavior. Does that sound like someone who adores me?"

He sighed. "Ignore her."

"What?"

"Mother is like that. We can't change her, but she loves you in her own way. I'm sure of it."

"So, I don't have to learn all those ridiculous things or get married?" I stared at him, hardly believing his words. He, the cold, stern figure, was laughing. Today had been the most eventful day of my life, and here he was, finding my emotional turmoil amusing.

"No, you don't, Miss Ariadne Bryant. Though opposing Mother might make life difficult, you don't have to do anything you don't want to. Take your time adjusting, but don't do foolish things like running away through hidden holes in the wall."

I smiled, despite myself. He had a sense of humor. "I won't do it again. I promise. I'm not mentally insane, just homesick, anxious, and dealing with memory loss."

He ruffled my hair. "Good."

"Can I ask one more thing? What are our parents' names?"

"Let me reintroduce our family. Our father is Sir Richard Bryant, and our mother is Lady Laura Bryant. They have two children—me and you. You're younger by three years. We own a large steel industry now, but our grandfather used to forge swords for noble families. Originally, we came from a family of skilled workers, so the other aristocrats used to look down on us. But things have changed. Steel brings money, and money runs the country. So hold your head high when you meet the others. Even if you don't remember, you must try to get through this. You are the only daughter of the Bryants. Life has thrown a challenge at you. Face it with courage and spirit. Running away won't solve anything."

Wiping my cheeks, I whispered, "Yes."

"Now go rest and freshen up. You look like a mess."

He escorted me back to my bedroom where a red-cheeked Violet awaited my arrival. I immediately asked, "What happened to your cheek?"

No one answered. I asked again, more firmly. Another maid curtsied and replied, "My lady, her ladyship decided to punish her for not knowing your whereabouts."

I felt terrible. "What? That woman is seriously getting on my nerves. I'm so sorry, Violet. I promise this will never happen again."

She looked flustered. "My lady, you can't say such things about her ladyship. And please don't apologize. It was my fault. I failed to serve you properly."

"No, you didn't! Please don't think that way. As for Mother..." Just thinking about her irritated me. "Let me deal with her."

Our argument continued for a while, but eventually, we sorted everything out. The maids insisted I take a bath, and I agreed. Covered in dirt and dust, a hot shower worked wonders, helping me feel more at ease. The nurses checked on me, administered my medicines, and after my shower, I hid the 73 dollars and 81 cents inside a book on my bookshelf. Objects hidden in plain sight were the hardest to find.

After a satisfying meal, I opted for some rest. As soon as my head hit the pillow, my mind became a whirlwind of thoughts. Somewhere within that chaotic mental landscape, I drifted off to sleep, dreaming of my former life. It seemed like I slept for an eternity, but when I finally woke, I was in a terrible state. A splitting headache, a red, runny nose, and a body warmer than usual. I was sick, and this stubborn cold showed no signs of leaving anytime soon. Unfortunately, antibiotics were yet to be discovered.

In a husky, strained voice, I whispered, "Violet, I think it's time to call Doctor Candler. And could you please fetch me some warm water, along with a few more blankets?" I sneezed, not once but twice. And so, another day in this new reality began.

Chapter 5

ARIADNE

October, 1899

Spending the whole day in freezing temperatures in vintage leather shoes, wearing a thin dress and a coat, to explore a town until you are so physically exhausted that your legs refuse to walk was the perfect recipe for falling sick. When this is accompanied by the sudden realization that you are living in 1899 in someone else's body—that's how you achieve self-ruin, resulting in high fever, extreme cold, a sprained ankle, and mental paranoia.

I had to spend three days on complete bed rest because of all that. I slept for almost fourteen hours a day, and when I wasn't sleeping, I was lost in a never-ending loop of regret and confusion. The weight of my actions bore down on me, pressing my mind into a relentless cycle of self-recrimination. At first, I felt as if I were teetering on the edge of insanity. My sanity seemed to hang by a thread as I obsessively checked the 73 dollars and 81 cents I had left, over and over, almost every hour.

By the end of the third day, I realized I couldn't keep spiraling like this. I had to force myself to stop obsessing, to ignore the impossible reality I was now a part of. Moving on wouldn't be easy—I knew that. Every time I tried to accept my new reality, a dark pit yawned open in my stomach, swallowing me whole with fear and anxiety. Was this really the ring's doing? What kind of twisted fate was I supposed to fulfill in 1899?

I had read countless novels where a woman from the future dies and finds herself reincarnated in the past. Those characters always seemed to embrace their new lives, finding a strange joy and fulfillment. But that wasn't my story. I didn't want to stay here. The terrifying likelihood that I might never return home loomed over me, a constant shadow.

The thought of never seeing Olivia, my aunt, my uncle, all my friends—all my family—again was unbearable. Every single attachment and connection I had formed was severed. They were all gone. Every professional achievement, every aspiration, every dream—all dead. It was as if they had vanished in an instant, leaving me in a world where I had no place. Even if I lived for a century, everyone I knew and loved would be gone, not even born yet. The permanence of that loss crushed me. I had lost them... for eternity. Just like that, in one devastating moment, they were gone.

The gravity of my situation kept pulling me back into despair, pushing me toward the edge of an emotional cliff, testing me, 'When will she break?'

The mother of this human body visited me a few times to check on my condition. She seemed genuinely worried, but even my horrible state didn't stop her from lecturing me about my code of conduct and the foolish behavior I had demonstrated. In a weird, twisted way, that helped. My frustration with her relentless reprimands frequently overwhelmed my capacity to mourn and reflect on my loss, providing a strange, albeit temporary, distraction from the agony gnawing at my heart.

When Doctor Candler found out about my foolish escape attempt and all the strange behavior that came with it, he was quite puzzled. But this did not affect his polite mannerism. His very words to me were, "Miss Bryant, I understand that you are facing difficult circumstances, but your recent actions are cause for concern. Your body is already weakened due to the lingering effects of your stroke, the cause of which remains unknown. Your memory loss and current affliction of a severe cold and fever puzzle me. Do you realize how grave your condition has been? Surviving that stroke was nothing short of miraculous, and now you seem to be neglecting your health. Are you intentionally endangering yourself? There are many people in this world who genuinely care for you and love you. At this moment, you've been exceptionally fortunate not to develop pneumonia, which could have been fatal. Your well-being should never be taken lightly. Please keep that in mind, no matter what. Sir Eugene, I strongly recommend ensuring Miss Bryant receives absolute rest and refrains from any reckless actions, even in her dreams. I advise a complete avoidance of strenuous outdoor activities."

All of this resulted in a significant amount of monitoring and care. I couldn't even eat on my own, brush my hair, or adjust my blanket for sleep without someone's assistance. It was an unusual level of attention, but strangely, it didn't feel unwelcome. Given the emotional turmoil I was experiencing, the constant presence of these new people served as a welcome distraction. My new mother and Eugene visited me frequently, although, oddly enough, my father never did. Not that it bothered me; I had my own inner thoughts to occupy my mind.

Amidst the emotional turmoil, persistent cold and fever, attentive care, medical treatments, doctor's visits, and my own contemplation, time seemed to slip through my fingers, silently passing by. Before I realized it, a week had quietly unfolded since my arrival.

Then, one morning, I noticed a subtle shift. The fever had broken, and my body felt lighter. Embracing this little new energy, I decided to leave the confines of my room and have lunch in the dining room. Eugene was preoccupied with business matters, and my new mother had chosen to spend the day at the Fultons'. That left me alone with my father, which for sure was going to be an awkward encounter.

As I settled into my seat at the dining table, my father turned to me with genuine concern. His tall frame cast a shadow over the table as he asked, "My dear, how are you feeling?"

My voice was husky and muffled, but I tried to smile as I answered. "I am much better. Still recovering." This was followed by three consecutive sneezes.

His face fell, and I could see the frustration in his eyes. "I still fail to understand why you decided to run away. Why would you do that? Look at the condition you're in."

I had heard these words of disappointment from everyone, including Violet. "I'm sorry. I truly am. It was a momentary lapse of judgment." Although he was not my real father, for some reason, I truly felt guilty.

His voice softened as he asked, "Were you uncomfortable? Did someone say something to offend you? Because in all honesty, I fail to understand why you would do something so foolish."

How could I tell him that I wasn't his daughter, that I didn't even know him or anyone in this mansion? Everyone was taking care of me as if I was part of their family, but I wasn't. So all I said was, "I am sorry."

My throat felt sore, and I started to cough. He got up and walked towards me, gently patting my back. His face was pale, and his jaw was clenched. I could see how horrible he felt seeing me like this. The nervousness and worry in his eyes were so evident—an unconditional love of a father. He reminded me of my dad, whose voice I had almost completely forgotten.

"It's okay. Calm down," he whispered, his voice trembling slightly. "My dear child, there is nothing you can ever do that I won't be able to forgive. But don't ever make me go through something like that again. You have no idea how horrible it feels when someone so precious to you is sick or hurt."

His words felt like a punch to my stomach. I did know how it felt when someone precious to you was hurt, and it was worse when you could never see them again. Although I didn't know this man, he was this girl's father—the girl I was currently living as. He had just gotten his daughter back from the clutches of death, but instead of celebrating her survival, he was stuck with a daughter who didn't even recognize him. Someone who was just causing more trouble. But although she didn't remember him, she was alive, and I knew I would have done anything in the world to see my real parents like that... alive.

All these emotions suddenly exploded, and my eyes became moist. I wasn't exactly crying; I was just overwhelmed. The moment he saw me like that, he sat down beside me and hugged me. His hand gently patted my back, and at that moment, I felt this was what I needed. He softly whispered, "It's going to be okay," and I hugged him back.

At that point, I realized why he'd never come to my room when I was sick. It hurt him to see me in a weak condition, and that made me see the depth of his love—a parent's unconditional love. Despite my constant sneezing and husky voice, he was very patient, and we talked the whole afternoon. He told me about his tricks for tolerating Mother's temper and Eugene's cold nature, revealing the softer sides of their personalities.

"Your mother," he began, "is stubborn and rigid. She's abrupt and often harsh in her manner, but beneath that exterior is a woman of strong principles and a deep sense of duty. She expects a lot because she believes in our potential. And although I don't wish to push you, there is nothing wrong with finding a partner."

He continued, "And Eugene—well, he might seem cold, but he cares deeply for this family. He's like a fortress, protecting us in his own quiet way. His aloofness is just a shield."

Then, with a fond smile, he spoke of Mr. Bailey. "Ah, you also need to know about Mr. Bailey. He's the backbone of this mansion. As the head butler, he's strict but kind, meticulous and precise in everything he does. Without him, everything would descend into chaos. He keeps the household running like clockwork, yet always finds time to offer a kind word or a helping hand."

Our conversation flowed seamlessly to the most random topics. I expressed my interest in subjects like economics, politics, literature, and journalism. I told him how I admired people who could uncover stories and give a voice to the voiceless, which seemed to intrigue him. I shared my food preferences and my views on marriage, which astonished him. The list went on and on. By the end, he was quite shocked by the sudden change in my personality, but he wasn't critical of it. Compared to the rest of this family, this man was different. He was understanding and easy to talk to. He had a strong sense of authority in this house, and I had seen it before, but despite that, he was just... nice.

That afternoon, for the first time, I sensed a glimmer of hope. Perhaps the people I was going to share my life with—this new family, these unfamiliar faces—might not be so terrible after all. Maybe, just maybe, they would make this entire adjustment a little easier.

Three weeks had whizzed past since that conversation, and now it was already the 6th of November. My rather foolish escape attempt and the subsequent ordeal left me in a sorry state, prompting my father to make a couple of decisions. Firstly, it was pretty much expected but I was under house arrest. Secondly, to my new mother's dismay, he had chosen to postpone all my lessons with my governess. I could only resume them when I felt mentally and physically ready, acting of my own accord. However, my free will had only managed to delay this decision until now.

Basically, the point was that I had some time to figure things out. A sort of buffer period for this miraculous lifestyle transition. I had never really bothered to imagine what life would be like in 1899. What was I to do with the knowledge of the daily lives of aristocrats and common people in a time period etched in history textbooks? I did know some historical and political nuances about this time period. But I also knew only one-line summaries of events that occurred around these years.

It wasn't relevant, so I didn't care. It wasn't like I expected to miraculously get my soul trapped in a twenty-one-year-old's body living in 1899 due to some magical rings that were apparently supposed to help me fulfill my destiny.

The days passed, and slowly, I began to find a rhythm. It was not an easy transition, but with each passing day, I grew a little more comfortable in this borrowed life. Even as I adjusted, everything still felt incredibly unfamiliar, and I often felt like a puzzle piece that just didn't quite fit into this new reality. But gradually, things were starting to change—just a little.

In my twenty-five years of life, I had traveled across Asia and Europe. Yet, nothing prepared me for the sheer splendor and grandeur I encountered at Clairborough Manor. Its beauty took my breath away, leaving me in constant awe, as if I were wandering through a living museum. Despite the initial confusion, I gradually memorized its intricate layout, growing to admire every exquisite detail, even if some corners still left me feeling lost.

But none of this stopped me from missing my old life. I missed my apartment—the comfort of my familiar bed, the scent of my own bedsheets, and the familiarity of my wardrobe. Fashion in this era was, to put it mildly, a bit of a nightmare. The corsets, the layers of skirts, the high-necked blouses—all of it felt restrictive and foreign to me.

Above all, what weighed heaviest on my heart was the absence of Olivia and her parents. They had been my unwavering support system after my own parents passed away, offering their love without any expectations. They cherished me as if I were their own daughter. It was incredible how I had somehow ended up with three sets of families in one life.

But what made life here particularly challenging was the way people perceived me. They didn't truly know me; they knew the old Ariadne Bryant, who was seen as an extremely shy young woman who rarely voiced her opinions and obediently followed her mother's lead. A little attention-seeking sometimes but she was a pampered aristocrat of the 19th century, content to stay in her own lane, and somewhat oblivious to the real world beyond her sheltered existence. They all loved her, for she was family, but her relationship with Eugene was distant. While he occasionally indulged her wishes, her reserved nature made communication difficult. Knowing Eugene's personality, it made sense too. Her father spoke with her at times, enjoyed dancing with her, and readily spoiled her whenever she asked. But overall, the old Ariadne always yielded to her mother's dominant nature, which confined her further into her shell.

Given the stark contrast between the old Ariadne and myself, people often found themselves confused when interacting with me. Whenever I tried to express my true preferences and be the person I had always known myself to be, I was met with comments like, "You weren't like this before," "Why are you behaving so unnaturally," or "Don't worry, once you remember, you'll return to your old self." It served as a constant reminder that they didn't truly love or cherish me; it was the owner of this body they cared for. While I didn't seek their attention or affection, it felt like I was constantly being compared to a shadow of who Ariadne was versus who I am. This slightly hurt, but it was best that I did not delve into it too much.

The good part was, while there were occasional moments of disappointment, no one was overly critical of my choices or actions, except my new mother. She was a woman of strong principles and a deep sense of duty, but her rigid, abrupt manner often clashed with my modern sensibilities.

Each day was a balancing act between adapting to this new world and clinging to the remnants of my old life. I found solace in the small routines I established—morning walks in the garden, reading in the library, and writing in my journal—preferably alone. The historical texts and newspapers became my tools, helping me piece together the social and political landscape of 1899.

Every morning, I would scan the local newspapers, noting the headlines and trying to discern the broader implications of the events reported. The issues of the day, from local politics to international affairs, fascinated me. I would cut out articles, jot down notes, and cross-reference them with the history I knew, searching for patterns and understanding.

For instance, President Benjamin Henderson's efforts to uplift the Slovain community might have seemed like a positive step. However, historians from my time found no evidence of their impact. Henderson's administration was largely known for its incompetence, a major factor contributing to Agnor's political turmoil and eventual loss of independence. As a result, the effectiveness of his policies was often dismissed. Understanding these historical nuances became a strange comfort, bridging the gap between my past and present.

Chapter 6

A RIADNE
November, 1899

My days in this new household were a journey of discovery. Understanding the household's dynamics, the roles of my family members, and my place in this world was a constant challenge. Adapting to society's norms of this era and deciphering my identity here was no easy task, but it was gradually becoming more manageable.

Engaging in intriguing conversations with my father felt natural and easy. However, my interactions with Eugene were often fraught with disagreements over minor matters. But the one person I had completely given up on was my new mother. She was hopeless. Her bones were deeply infused with archaic patriarchal notions and she refused to have it any other way. She hated the way I spoke, the way I walked, how I ate, or even how I slept. She demanded nothing less than perfect manners, believing that I should conform to societal expectations in every way. All of this made her very trying as an individual.

So after numerous arguments with my father and brother, my new mother won and it was eventually decided that I would resume lessons with my governess starting tomorrow. While I wished I could have a say in this matter, I understood that my voice held little sway. I also recognized that if I resisted her wishes any further, she would likely make my life even more challenging, and I already had enough on my plate.

Hence, the next day, I was forced to wake up at the brink of dawn, followed by a frigid shower that left me shivering. By a quarter to nine, my governess arrived. Miss Mabel, an intriguing yet intimidating figure, made her entrance with an air of severity that filled the room. Her light brown eyes were sharp and unyielding, her petite face heavily adorned with makeup that did nothing to soften her harsh expression. Her long, crooked nose only enhanced her intimidating demeanor. Jet-black hair was pulled back into a tight bun, not a single strand out of place, reflecting her icy formality. At thirty-two, she moved with a precision and strictness that made her seem unapproachable.

"Lady Ariadne, first and foremost, my sincerest congratulations on recovering from your illness and my deepest sympathies for its aftereffects," she said in a cold, monotonous tone. "Since my elder sister is currently engaged at another household, I have been asked to assist you upon the ardent request of her ladyship." Her face remained hard and expressionless, making her words sound rehearsed and devoid of genuine sentiment. Every syllable dripped with false courtesy, her presence as frigid as the shower I had just endured.

In just ten minutes, I knew I would despise every second of this. A cold shiver ran down my spine when our eyes met; her gaze was like ice. Her words, thinly veiled in politeness, subtly stripped me of my pride. She embodied judgment, and every glance and phrase confirmed it.

The atmosphere in the tea room quickly became suffocating. My new mother launched into a never-ending rant about my behavior and the conduct expected of me, speaking as if I were invisible. Miss Mabel responded with a simple, "I see," to every complaint, her tone dripping with condescension.

Then, they decided to test me. Miss Mabel instructed in her cold tone, "Please sit down. Now stand up. Pour me a cup of tea. Now pour yourself one. Please go ahead and drink it. Can you take a stroll around the room? Now please do this. Can you do that?"

This went on for quite some time before she handed me a novel and stated, "Please read Sonnet 18, page 42."

I complied, reading aloud, "Shall I compare thee to a summer's day? Thou art more lovely and more temperate: Rough winds do shake the darling buds of May, And summer's lease hath all too short a date; Sometimes too hot the eye of heaven shines, And often is his gold complexion dimm'd—"

She interrupted abruptly, "Please explain what you just read."

I resisted the urge to snap back and explained the sonnet's meaning, thanks to my middle school English teacher's love for Shakespeare. Miss Mabel's expression remained unchanged, but my new mother's smile suggested I had passed this part of the test.

Next came French. I struggled miserably, barely managing a few words. My basic knowledge from middle school was no match for her complex, archaic vocabulary. After this, she had me write a few sentences and solve basic arithmetic problems, which were easy. But then, she quizzed me on knitting, flower arrangement, and formal dancing—subjects I knew nothing about.

As if that weren't enough, Miss Mabel then tested my musical abilities. She led me to the piano and asked me to play a classical piece. My fingers fumbled over the keys, producing a discordant melody. She sighed, noting my lack of skill, and moved on to vocal exercises, where my off-key singing confirmed her low expectations.

Throughout, Miss Mabel scribbled notes, her icy gaze never wavering. After three dreadfully long hours, my new mother declared in exaggerated disappointment, "Do you now realize what I have been dealing with?"

Miss Mabel gave her a sympathetic look. "I indeed do. We have much work ahead, your ladyship. It will be difficult for Lady Ariadne to relearn everything before the Cordinburg Gala, but I promise to spare no effort. If worst comes to worst, we might need to keep her out of society for a year on grounds of medical recovery."

"Absolutely not. She has already made her debut. We cannot delay this. Do your best to ensure she at least appears satisfactory."

I was speechless. They truly despised how I behaved. I wanted to lash out but held back, knowing this wasn't the right moment.

Miss Mabel continued, "Lady Ariadne, your English and arithmetic skills are exemplary, but your sentence structuring is often misleading, and your handwriting is poor. You've forgotten coherent French, lack vocabulary, and display no knowledge of classical music, dance, or flowers. Your posture is ghastly, and you lack dining etiquette. Attending the Cordinburg Gala in such a state will be disastrous."

I struggled to grasp ancient French and classical music's intricacies, subjects I had never explored. "I admit my handwriting isn't pretty, but it serves its purpose. If these lessons are to prepare me for the gala, why not provide a list of do's and don'ts and show me? I'm a fast learner. Also, let's focus on my strengths. Learning an entirely new language in weeks is improbable."

They stared at me in silence, frustrated by my reasonable argument. They shifted the conversation to lecture me about societal perception. By four in the evening, it finally ended. Leaving the tea room, I felt liberated, albeit briefly. This freedom would only last until tomorrow when I'd relive this ordeal again.

A few days later, I was walking through one of the corridors in our mansion when I heard familiar voices. It was mid-afternoon, and lunch had ended sometime back. I was on my way to fetch one of my father's books from the study when I overheard Father and Eugene talking. Both of them were sitting in the study, drinking tea. I was about to enter, but I stopped when I realized they were discussing me. Although eavesdropping was not morally right, I couldn't help myself.

"I can't even recognize her anymore," my father said. "Not that this change is bad, but she's too different. I'm glad she's not acting as her extremely shy self anymore, but now she's just so firm in her thoughts. It's too drastic of a change."

Eugene added in a straight tone, "I agree to a certain extent. She's a completely different person—very vocal and quite rebellious. Even Mother is having a hard time reining her in with those lessons."

My vision was blocked by the door, so I couldn't see their faces clearly. "Hmm... I do like the sound of Ariadne being rebellious, but I'm not so sure. I do not dislike these changes. It's good that she is standing up for herself and finally holding her ground in front of Laura. She was always too submissive before, but those governess lessons have become such a headache. Even the servants are gossiping about it all the time. They make it sound like some sort of match, and clearly, Ariadne has been winning most. Did you hear about the bets?" He laughed.

"Of course I have. Who hasn't? Honestly, I have mixed opinions about all of this. On one hand, I cannot comprehend what she goes through every day without any memories of her past. I still cannot forget the look she gave me when I first saw her. She looked at me as if I was some stranger trying to hurt her. But now that she is finally adjusting, I'm not sure. I don't want to push her to the extreme and make her revert to how she was. She was difficult to talk to before—always so timid and hesitant about everything. Now, although she challenges me far too often, I like this version of her better. She seems more rational and smart. Some of her ideas and thoughts are truly remarkable. I just hope she learns to behave better in front of others and stops challenging me all the time."

"Son, I think that's because you've never had your sister challenge you like that before. I argued with my brothers all the time. Your sister was always very timid and aloof, which worried me. How was she going to survive all alone in this world?"

"What's there to worry about? She has us," Eugene stated confidently.

"Don't assume that. After she got married, how were you planning on protecting her? It would be your wish against her husband's or in-laws'. She would have had no choice but to comply with their whims."

"Don't make it sound so harsh. Do you think I'd let her marry just anyone? Her husband has to be a decent person. I'll make sure of that."

"Sometimes you cannot protect your loved ones. It's a harsh lesson you learn as you grow up," my father said, his tone heavy with past experience.

They went silent. I was about to knock when the half-open door swung open and Eugene said, "How long are you planning to stand there, Ariadne?"

Eugene's presence made me flinch. I felt foolish for eavesdropping, and my ears burned red. I walked inside and greeted Father politely.

"Eavesdropping is not a good habit," Eugene mocked.

I was embarrassed but tried to hide it. "I agree. It isn't, but why the sudden talk about moral codes and etiquette? I have Miss Mabel and Mother reminding me of those every day."

"Please don't start on that again. We've heard enough arguments about it. Is it really that bad?" Father asked.

I covered my face with and with a long sign, "Yes! It's horrible. Can we please cancel it indefinitely?"

"When your mother permits it, I'll be extremely glad to do just that."

Both of them laughed. Eugene sarcastically commented, "It wasn't I who told you to forget all your past lessons so you could go through that hell all over again."

"Well, it wasn't me either. Those lessons are dreadful enough to make me wish I could control this memory issue."

"Oh come on, dear. Don't be so harsh on them. Your mother is only doing that because she's worried and cares for you," Father interrupted.

"More like she cares about my behavior and what people would think if I presented myself at the gala like this," I grumbled.

"Don't be like that..." There was a moment of silence. Then, trying to change the topic, Father asked, "Anyways, Eugene, are you all set for tomorrow?"

"Yes. I'll be heading out early and will be back in three days. I've already booked my accommodation at the Hugh Grand Hotel and informed Mr. Bailey to prepare the carriage," Eugene answered promptly.

"Where are you going?" I asked.

"I'm heading to Restersburg city for some work."

Restersburg City was one of the most happening places in Agnor. Seeing it in its archaic form sounded incredible. I immediately asked, "Can I come with you?"

He looked confused. "I mentioned I was going for work. What would you possibly want to accompany me for?"

I rolled my eyes. "Oh please. I have zero interest in your work."

His forehead crinkled at my tone. "Excuse me?"

There was no point arguing if I wanted to get out of this mansion. I took a deep breath and confessed, "I just want an excuse to skip some lessons. We're going to be learning about different postures, dancing, and flower arrangements. Even your company would be more tolerable."

He looked at me suspiciously. In less than a second, he stated firmly, "Absolutely not. You are not coming."

"Oh come on. I'll behave," I pleaded.

"You're still recovering. Going out of town is out of the question. Also, you're grounded."

"Don't use my health as an excuse. I'm perfectly fine. And it's high time my grounding ends. I've been well-behaved for weeks."

The casual conversation had turned into an argument. Eugene was annoyed, and I was irritated. Father seemed to find this amusing. He suppressed a smile as I looked at him and asked, "Please, can I go? I'll behave and take care of myself."

Then I looked at Eugene. "I won't interfere with your work. It'll be as if I'm not there. I promise."

"And who's going to convince your mother?" Father asked, the humor still in his voice.

"I was hoping you would. Who can refuse the head of the household?"

Father's expression softened. "Fine. Do what you want..."

Eugene was still hesitant, but he had no choice but to agree. It was decided. I was going to skip that miserable lecture with Miss Mabel and visit Restersburg city. The idea sounded exciting in the living room, but lying in bed, I wondered... was Restersburg a thriving city even in 1899? The thought of witnessing history was thrilling. For the first time since arriving here, I looked forward to the next day, eager for a change from my constant wishing and praying to wake up home.

Chapter 7

ARIADNE

November, 1899

Despite the last-minute notice, Violet efficiently packed my bags well ahead of time. I was going on a two-night, three-day trip, and Eugene had made it abundantly clear that our departure was set for 5:00 a.m. sharp. He had even warned that if I were even a minute late, he'd leave without me. I couldn't help but wonder about the urgency surrounding this trip. After all, Restersburg was merely a two-hour drive from my previous residence, and Clairborough Manor was situated on the outskirts of Port Maine City. How long could the journey possibly take? Little did I know that this day would teach me the value of modern transportation networks—one should never take the convenience of modern roads and highways for granted, given the significant reduction in travel time they afford.

The journey began with a carriage ride to the nearest railway station, followed by a four-hour train ride. Afterward, there was another hour-long carriage journey to reach our final destination, Hugh Grand Hotel. In total, it took us seven hours of travel to reach our destination. It was undoubtedly an exhausting trip, but it was worth it. The change of scenery was so refreshing, and my room at the hotel was a true marvel. The high ceilings were adorned with intricate plasterwork, and richly patterned wallpaper added a touch of opulence. Heavy brocade curtains framed tall windows, offering a view of the bustling streets below. The spacious room featured polished mahogany furniture, including a grand four-poster bed draped in luxurious fabrics. A crystal chandelier cast a warm glow, illuminating the room's delicate antique details and subtle modern comforts. It felt like stepping into a bygone era, where every element exuded timeless charm.

Despite Violet's company, I cherished the privacy. She had her own separate living quarters, leaving me with a massive room to myself where I could do as I pleased without any external interference—no servants, no family, no Miss Mable, no one at all. I was so used to living all alone, being just by myself, I had forgotten what living with so many people felt like. And although I did like it, I had missed this sort of privacy.

After quickly changing into more comfortable clothes, I headed downstairs to the hotel's restaurant, where Eugene was already waiting patiently. The food at the restaurant was decent, though nothing particularly exceptional. I was savoring my steak when Eugene broke the relative silence between us. "So, you got what you wanted. You're in Restersburg City."

I looked at him blankly. "Yes, I know. What about it?"

"What are you planning to do here?" he asked, raising an eyebrow.

"I'm not entirely sure yet. Maybe explore the city," I replied casually.

A wry grin crept across his lips. "Explore? Since when did you become a fan of exploring?"

My fork clattered onto the plate, rattling loudly. Annoyance flashed in my eyes. "Why are you always trying to pick a fight? I know I'm behaving differently now, but I think that's perfectly fine. So yes, maybe I do enjoy exploring now."

Eugene quickly raised his hands in defense. "Relax, Ariadne. I get it. Do as you please. I won't interfere."

"Thank you," I said, returning to my meal. After a few bites, curiosity got the better of me. "So, what's your purpose for coming here?"

"I'm here to buy an automobile," Eugene declared proudly.

My eyes widened slightly. "A car?"

"Yes. If my memory serves me right, they're called cars in the United States," he said, taking a bite of his bread.

I nodded, trying to suppress a laugh. "I guess so. Anyway, which automobile are you planning to buy?"

"Probably a Rolls-Royce Model B. They can travel up to 20 miles per hour, which is pretty fast."

I struggled to stifle my amusement. "That sounds nice. But do you even know how to drive?"

A glimmer of excitement appeared in his eyes. "Not yet. I'm planning to start lessons soon."

"Would it be alright if I learn how to drive as well?" I inquired casually.

Eugene was in the middle of taking a sip of water when my question caught him off guard, causing him to cough. "Are you alright?" I asked immediately.

"I'm fine," he replied after a moment. "But why would you want to learn to drive?"

"Just because I can. It would be rather convenient for traveling."

He looked at me skeptically. "We'll have a chauffeur. And learning to drive an automobile is quite complex. Someone like you couldn't possibly manage it."

I gave him a suspicious look. "What do you mean by 'someone like me'?" A playful idea struck me. "How about a bet?"

"A bet?" he echoed, intrigued.

"Yes. We both start taking driving lessons at the same time, and whoever learns to drive first wins. If I win, you help me convince our parents to let me do something I want—no questions asked."

He looked curious. "And if you lose?"

"I'll do whatever you want, as long as it's reasonable and doesn't undermine my rights or cause harm. And no forcing me into marriage."

"Doesn't that rule out a lot of options?"

"It does, but the same conditions apply to you. I won't ask for anything absurd, just something within the realm of possibility."

He appeared intrigued but agreed to discuss it further later. Eugene had a meeting with the automobile dealer at three in the afternoon, so he left shortly afterward. I decided to explore the city, with Violet insisting on accompanying me, leaving me little choice but to let her tag along.

Restersburg City surprised me with an aura of opulence and exclusivity I hadn't expected. Unlike the rustic cottages and charming brick roads near Clairborough Manor, this place boasted impeccably constructed streets paved with smooth cobblestones worn down by years of use. The towering townhouses and grand mansions lining these streets bore intricate architectural details that whispered of affluence and history.

Every road seemed to converge at the grand city center, a bustling hub where modernity and tradition met head-on. Here, tall buildings reached for the sky, their facades blending ornate masonry with expansive glass windows. It was a place where past and present harmoniously coexisted, showcasing the evolution of architecture and design.

Amidst this urban landscape, opulent residences were framed by lush, manicured gardens. Sculpted hedges and winding stone paths added a touch of nature's grace to the heart of the city, providing a perfect setting for leisurely strolls on sunny days.

The city's markets were a lively hive of activity and commerce, with street vendors offering fresh produce, fragrant flowers, and handcrafted treasures. Overhead, the azure sky stretched expansively, framed by the silhouettes of historical and contemporary structures. The air was filled with the hum of conversation, the occasional laughter of children playing in nearby parks, and the distant sounds of carriages and early automobiles traversing the streets.

Despite the chilly weather, the sun beamed brightly as I strolled along, casting long shadows on the cobblestone paths. As I continued to explore, the rhythmic 'click' of the heels Violet had insisted I wear accompanied every step. They were quickly becoming my nemesis, but I pressed on, feeling as if I had stepped into a vintage black-and-white film.

As I wandered through the streets, my attention was drawn to a bustling crowd in the far corner of a street. Unlike the more polished areas I was exploring, this part of the city had a suburban and crowded vibe, teeming with sounds, sights, smells, and flavors that piqued my curiosity. It was a stark contrast to the sophistication of the other side of Restersburg.

Here, the streets were narrower, the buildings leaned closer together, and the architecture bore the wear and tear of time. The laughter of children echoed through the air as they played games on the cobblestone streets, and the enticing aroma of street food wafted from small stalls that lined the sidewalks.

Merchants in this part of town set up shop in colorful tents, their wares spilling out onto the streets. It was a place where you could find everything from vibrant textiles and handmade crafts to exotic spices and tantalizing street snacks.

The atmosphere was one of camaraderie and community, a stark contrast to the distant formality of the wealthier districts. Here, people knew their neighbors and greeted strangers with warm smiles. Despite the lack of sophistication, there was a vibrant and unbridled joy that permeated every corner of this side of the city. The sounds of chatter, laughter, and music blended into a symphony of noise, occasionally rising to a rowdy crescendo as people celebrated life with fervor.

There were times when certain streets seemed better left unexplored, especially during those rowdy moments when it was wiser to steer clear. Yet, despite the occasional uproar, this side of the city exuded an infectious energy that was hard to resist. It was a place of vibrant life, where every corner held the promise of adventure and every encounter was a story waiting to be told.

Despite my desire to explore this lively corner, going there dressed as I was would have attracted too much attention. I had the basic common sense to know what was safe and what wasn't. So, I continued to explore random shops and streets on the more polished side of the city. After walking around for some time, I came across a boutique that specialized in clothing for men. The display window beckoned with an array of sophisticated garments. It was at that moment that a daring idea began to take shape in my mind.

Leaning closer to Violet, I whispered, "Violet, can you keep a secret?" Her response was immediate and reassuring, "Of course, my lady."

"Great. Follow me," I said with a hint of excitement. She trailed behind me as I led her into the men's boutique. The moment we stepped inside, we were greeted by an elderly gentleman who exuded an air of formality but wore a warm smile. He had the aura of an experienced shopkeeper who had been in the business for generations.

"Welcome, madame. What might you be looking for this evening?" he asked courteously.

"Hello, good Sir. I was wondering if you have a casual suit that's in trend lately," I said in a more cheerful tone than usual.

He could sense a potential purchase but remained calm. "Ah, indeed, madame. Do you happen to know the size of the lucky young gentleman who will be wearing this suit?"

"Unfortunately, I do not. It's for my younger brother, and he's very similar to my height and build." At this point, Violet tugged at my coat, clearly curious about which younger brother I was referring to. I chose to ignore her and continued my conversation with the elderly shopkeeper.

"He is one lucky brother to have such a caring sister," he said, employing a typical marketing approach, but I played along.

"I agree, but he just doesn't know how to appreciate my love," I replied with a coy smile.

We continued to explore the boutique, and eventually, I found the perfect attire: plain black trousers, a crisp white shirt, a matching jacket, and a stylish tie. It felt more formal than my usual preference, but my earlier city exploration had shown that this was the prevailing fashion among men. Although it was a bit on the expensive side, the generous allowance Eugene had granted me easily covered the cost.

As I perused the shop, I also came across a rather decent-looking handkerchief. It was made of fine material and featured exquisite embroidery with dark, contrasting shades—a style that would suit Eugene perfectly. Perhaps it was my mood or a genuine desire to be a caring sister, but I decided to purchase it for him. If I was going to play the role of a doting sister, it made sense to add a touch of truth to the act.

The moment we stepped out of the shop, Violet grabbed my hand and stopped me. "Who is that suit for? My lady, have you found yourself a beau?"

I responded with a teasing smile. "No, of course not. Who do you think it's for when it's clearly my size?" It took her a few seconds to make sense of what I was saying, and then she exclaimed, "My lady, you absolutely cannot!"

I continued to play dumb. "What can't I absolutely do?"

She was flustered and even a bit annoyed. "Lady Ariadne, you will get yourself in trouble again, and Sir Eugene will be really furious. Please do not do this."

I enjoyed teasing Violet. Her reactions were adorable at times. "And here I thought I was the one giving orders."

She immediately became extremely rigid and formally apologized, "I am so sorry. I didn't mean to offend you, my lady."

I grinned, urging her to loosen up. "Come on, Violet, no need to be so stiff. I was just having some fun." I wasn't a fan of her apologizing or blindly obeying my every command; it felt weird to assert ownership over another person, and that wasn't my style.

"So, the suit isn't for you?" she inquired.

"It is for me, but I was joking about ordering you," I said.

She continued to try and convince me how foolish my idea was, but all she managed to do was motivate me further.

The next day, Eugene left immediately after breakfast. Purchasing an automobile in 1899 turned out to be far more intricate than I had imagined. The process involved extensive paperwork and detailed negotiations with the dealer, a man named Morris Emmerson. There were also considerations about fueling the vehicle, as well as learning to operate and maintain the newfangled machine.

After Eugene left, I quickly changed into my new suit, relishing the newfound comfort. It was a far cry from the dresses I was expected to wear. I missed the familiar feel of jeans, and these trousers were the closest I could find in this era. Yesterday, I had deliberately chosen a jacket and shirt that were one size too large to help conceal my feminine features, much to Violet's disapproval. With a bit of makeup, I managed to craft the early stages of a fake mustache. By the time I was finished, I looked like a young adolescent boy—short and petite, but undeniably a boy. I persuaded Violet to ditch her formal attire and go for something more casual. It was a tiny act of defiance, but it brought a sense of freedom. By the end of it, Violet and I looked like siblings. Two short, petite youngsters enjoying the city.

Today, my goal was to delve into the suburban parts of the city, a stark contrast to the sophistication of yesterday's areas. Here, the streets were less clean, bustling with crowds and small vendors selling all sorts of items. I could easily purchase fresh bread or even a pack of cigarettes. I also enjoyed watching street performances, from dance to theater, and observed a few gambling sessions. It was a lively neighborhood filled with proud, mostly working-class youth.

Despite the challenges of their lives, the people here seemed genuinely happy.

It was not like the fake reality I was participating in—the opulent households with grand facades, the massive accommodations surrounded by manicured gardens, the armies of servants catering to every whim, the strict protocols governing every interaction, and the ridiculous façade meant for others to witness. In those affluent districts, wide boulevards were lined with perfectly trimmed trees, and horse-drawn carriages glided smoothly over pristine cobblestone streets. The air was filled with the subtle scent of blooming flowers from the carefully tended gardens, and the sound of refined laughter and polite conversation echoed from the terraces of elegant cafes.

In contrast, the suburban side of Restersburg was alive with raw, unfiltered energy. The buildings leaned closer together, their worn facades telling stories of decades past. Children played freely in the narrow alleys, their laughter mingling with the calls of street vendors hawking their goods. The aroma of sizzling street food wafted through the air, mingling with the earthy scent of the cobblestones underfoot. Here, the vibrancy of daily life was palpable, unmasked by the veneer of propriety that cloaked the wealthier parts of the city. Despite opposing my dressing as a boy and exploring the backstreets of Restersburg City, even Violet had to admit how much fun it was.

Standing at the corner of a bustling street, I watched as Violet made her way to a nearby stall to grab us some hot coffee. Today had been an absolute blast, a mini-vacation where I could indulge in my whims and escape the rigid expectations of my daily life.

As I soaked in the lively atmosphere, the street performers, the chatter of the crowd, the scents of street food wafting through the air, I casually checked the date on my pocket watch. The realization hit me quite suddenly—it was the 2nd of November. One month gone.

I stood there, absorbing the weight of that thought. A whole month had passed since I first set foot in Clairborough Manor in 1899. A wave of emotions washed over me—nostalgia, amazement, even a bit of disbelief. I was here. I was fine. I was living this life. I had managed to carve out a place for myself in this foreign time.

I knew how to approach this life now. The initial confusion and anxiety had dwindled. I was more confident, more used to it all. I wasn't just surviving—I was thriving, adapting, and even enjoying the unexpected twists and turns that each day brought.

Just as I was reflecting on my newfound sense of belonging, I heard the distant sounds of hundreds of people cheering and booing. Out of curiosity, I walked in the direction of the noise. Like me, many other curious onlookers had gathered around. I stood at the corner of one street, observing the scene.

In the very center of it all was a local minister giving a speech using a microphone. He was part of the current ruling party and worked under Benjamin Henderson. It was a political rally—election season must have been starting, and Henderson's campaign was in full swing. Knowing what

I knew about the future, how I wished he could just lose and disappear. It would have been perfect to have a good leader in this time period who could make a real difference.

The atmosphere was charged, with flags waving and people holding up signs. The minister's voice boomed through the speakers, his words met with alternating cheers and boos. I listened to his speech for a few minutes, and in that short amount of time, he managed to convince me how extremely backward his thinking was. In a very overt but subtle manner, he supported the subjugation and mistreatment of the Slovain community.

Frustration bubbled within me as I watched. It was infuriating to see the crowd's mixed reactions, knowing the dark path history would take. How different things could be if only people could see through the rhetoric and choose leaders who genuinely cared about progress and equality.

I listened to his speech for a while and then decided to go back. Violet must have been awaiting my return. I was about to head back to where I was previously standing when suddenly, multiple groups of people who were mixed with the political rally's crowd started shouting in unison:

"Every man is equal, for we all are children of God!"

"Slovain rights are human rights!"

"Break the chains of inequality!"

"Don't let the rich get richer and the poor get poorer!"

"The Slovain community is not your slaves. Get us equal rights! Get us equal rights!"

It was a powerful moment, and I couldn't help but stand there for a while, taking in the spirit of those demanding justice and equality. Even a few people around me started shouting. It only took me a few seconds to connect the dots. This was what the newspaper article was talking about.

In 1872, slavery was abolished in this nation, a monumental step forward. But despite this progress, the communities of former slaves continued to face mass discrimination. Employers were reluctant to hire them, leading to widespread poverty and resentment. This tension erupted into severe riots in 1883, resulting in the deaths of hundreds of thousands of people.

Realizing the gravity of the situation, the President at the time introduced various schemes and initiatives aimed at improving the living conditions of these marginalized communities. From 1880 to 1907, Agnor's laws evolved to embrace the ideals of liberty, equality, and fraternity—concepts first championed by France and later adopted into Agnor's society. These ideals slowly gained popularity, offering a glimmer of hope for a more inclusive future.

However, the dawn of the 20th century brought new challenges. After 1901, the nation was dragged into the great war against Britain, a conflict that plunged Agnor into ruin. The war devastated the economy and led to the fall of the current government, overshadowing the social progress that had been made.

As I stood there, absorbing the fervor of the crowd and the weight of history, I felt a deep sense of frustration and helplessness. The rally was a stark reminder that the fight for justice was far from over. How different things could be if only people could see through the rhetoric and choose leaders who genuinely cared about progress and equality. The shouts of "Equal rights for all" and "Break the chains of inequality" echoed in my mind.

But I let it be. What change was I supposed to bring? Knowing the future was useless. I barely had the power to help myself, let alone prevent the dark future ahead. Besides, there was another reason why I couldn't take things too seriously. This was history. This was the past. This was not my time period. All these things I was witnessing didn't make a difference to me. I was just a visitor, and one day—hopefully soon—I would be back in my own time. Once again, these stories would be lines on a paper, sources of inspiration and lessons to learn from, so the future generations wouldn't repeat the mistakes of the past.

Chapter 8

ARIADNE
November, 1899

The sharp blare of a megaphone cut through the market's usual hum.

Without warning, chaos erupted. People were running and screaming, their panic palpable. Police arrived, their mechanical voices booming through megaphones, "Protesters, surrender peacefully. If not, we will have to retaliate." The words were lost in the din. The bustling crowd I enjoyed had transformed into a frantic stampede. Identifying protesters among the civilians was impossible, plunging the peaceful rally into further chaos.

Trapped in the human stampede, I sprinted, my heart pounding. Escape seemed impossible, though my suit thankfully allowed for movement. Just as I thought I might break free, a strong hand seized mine. An officer barked, "You're under arrest for inciting violence and protesting against the government. Come with me."

"I'm not a protester," I protested, my voice drowned in the uproar. "I'm just a civilian." My words were useless; the officer's grip tightened, dragging me through the chaos. Panic surged through me. Getting arrested would mean disaster. Eugene would be furious, and Violet would most likely be fired. I couldn't afford to be caught.

I stopped resisting and let him pull me, jostled by the crowd. Being short was a disadvantage; I could only see shoulders and chests squeezing their way out.

Then, unexpectedly, a powerful stream of water shot from a cannon, drenching me and everyone nearby. The force left me coughing and struggling for breath. But it was my chance. The officer, caught off guard, let go of my hand.

I hunched and tried to find my way out. In the chaos, being short turned out to be an advantage. The bodies around me acted as shields as I crawled through narrow gaps, fighting for freedom. After what felt like an eternity, I reached the edge of the road, where the crush of people was thinner.

I spotted a familiar alley to my right, one I had passed earlier. There were fewer officers and protesters here, making it a safer route to escape. I was about to run when I saw a skeletal lady with a knife, just a few feet away, poised to stab a man whose back was to her.

The man had black, curly hair that resembled Olivia's. Before I knew it, my hands moved. I grabbed a police baton dropped in the chaos and aimed at her shoulder. My aim was perfect. The baton struck her, and she lost her balance. I ran to the man, grabbed his arm, and yelled, "Run!"

He didn't hesitate. His grip was firm. As the lady lunged to stab me, he twisted her hand with surprising strength, making her scream. We shoved her away and took off without missing a beat.

The path was still congested with people, some possibly her accomplices, trailing us. We didn't look back; we just ran. Navigating the intricate network of small roads and cramped alleys was challenging. We darted through narrow passageways, the maze of houses and alleys endless. Finally, I saw the market square's center. I was about to run straight ahead when the man pulled me into a very narrow alley, crushing me between the wall and his body.

"What are you doing?" I hissed, my voice barely above a whisper.

He pressed his palm against my lips, his breath warm on my face as he whispered, "Shush... They're close." The alley was suffocatingly narrow, our bodies forced together, his heartbeat a frantic rhythm against my ear. He towered over me, his presence both protective and overbearing. His eyes suddenly widened with shock. "Holy shit, you're a girl!"

I shoved his hand away. "Yeah... what about it?"

He stared, flustered but undeniably intrigued. "Nothing. Just... why is someone with a pretty face like yours dressed like a man? Mustaches don't suit you."

I rolled my eyes. "Are you seriously complimenting my looks right now?"

His deep ocean-blue eyes sparkled with a mix of mockery and curiosity. "There's nothing wrong with admiring beauty, even in a situation like this. Have we met before? You look familiar."

I almost laughed at the absurdity. "Shut up. It's cramped enough in here without you making it worse." His gaze held that infuriating, teasing grin, and despite the danger, he seemed to find our predicament amusingly intimate.

We stood there in that cramped alley for a few minutes. When the distant clamour finally subsided, we exchanged a nod and decided it was time to move, to find a safer refuge than the dark, exposed alley. We had to find a place to hide. We ran and walked from time to time. Constantly looking back and making sure that no one was following us. The winding alleys and crooked streets of this unfamiliar part of the city seemed like a labyrinth, and we had no idea where we were heading.

After wandering around for some time, I spotted a door in some narrow upward sloping alley. He let go of my hand. I completely forgot that all this time, we were holding hands. I tried to push it open but it was locked. Then I saw him trying to attempt something foolish. Wrapping a few rocks in his handkerchief, he broke the glass of the window located above him in a few swift motions.

"It won't work," I said. "That window is too high. You'll never make it."

"Relax. A man can always try," he mocked. I worried the noise would attract attention, but we were lucky so far. After several failed attempts, he sighed and looked at me.

"Guess it's too high," he admitted.

"Told you," I said with a smug grin.

He suddenly turned to me. "How much do you weigh?"

"Excuse me?" My eyes widened.

"If I lift you, can you reach it?" he clarified.

I hesitated. "Maybe..."

In one swift motion, he crouched down and lifted me onto his shoulders. I found myself straddling his neck, my legs dangling down his chest. It made me feel like a child, a sense of both vulnerability and unexpected camaraderie washing over me. He was surprisingly strong, his hands steady as they held my thighs for support.

"Hold still," he muttered, his voice vibrating against my calves. I reached for the handle but it was still a few inches out of reach.

"Can you lift me a bit higher?" I whispered, trying to keep the frustration out of my voice.

He adjusted his grip and straightened up slightly, pushing me closer to the window. "Hurry," he urged, his breath coming in controlled gasps. "You're heavier than you look."

"Charming," I shot back, focusing on the task at hand. After a few seconds of straining, I managed to unlatch the window. Carefully, I climbed through, ensuring I didn't slip or fall on the broken glass. The room inside was dark, lit only by the small window I'd entered through. I carefully moved towards the door and opened the latch. The door was a bit heavy and it took some effort to pull, but it opened slightly and he managed to enter.

Each and every one of his movements had a unique grace. All this time, my mind was in a state of confusion and panic. Too many things were happening at the same time. I didn't get a chance to really look at him, but now that he was standing in front of me, I could see his face dimly lit by the light coming from the window.

His features were striking: a perfectly angled nose, strong jawline, and a cascade of black curls that framed his face, just brushing his ears. He stood just under six feet tall, his white shirt and dark blue trousers clinging to a frame that spoke of hidden strength even in their disheveled state. But it was his eyes that truly captivated me.

A deep ocean blue, they held an intensity that sent shivers down my spine. I found myself unable to look away, lost in their depths despite the surrounding chaos. His gaze was both piercing and mysterious, drawing me in with an almost magnetic pull. His hair, now drenched from the water cannon, added a rugged charm to his otherwise pristine appearance.

In that moment, even amidst the chaos and danger, I couldn't ignore one undeniable truth: this man was strikingly handsome, and I could stare into those eyes for a long-long time.

"What?" he asked, his voice pulling me back to reality. His eyes held a hint of suspicion.

"This is not the time to focus on how someone looks," I reminded myself. We found a small staircase leading to the first floor. After climbing the stairs, we realized it was an abandoned house, dust covering everything. There was little inside besides some furniture draped in long white sheets.

I moved towards the window that overlooked the main market square. Peering outside, I saw the chaos was still unfolding—protesters and policemen were mixed among the citizens, some fighting, some struggling, and others running.

"I think it's best if we stay here for a while. There's still a lot of tension outside," I suggested.

He nodded and pulled a white sheet off a sofa. Dust swirled around us, making us both cough. Beneath the sheet was an old, torn, and ragged sofa with a few insects scurrying away.

"Guess we're sitting on the floor," he said, a hint of childish disappointment in his voice.

I tried to suppress a smile but couldn't help it when he began folding the sheet and laying it neatly on the floor. As I sat down, exhaustion washed over me. I hadn't realized how long I'd been running. The support of the wall against my back was a relief.

I closed my eyes, savoring the peace, until I felt his gaze on me.

"What?" I asked softly, opening my eyes.

He looked a bit awkward, scratching near his left eyebrow. "Nothing..."

We both fell into silence, the creaking of wooden boards under our weight the only sound. After a moment, he whispered, "Are you okay?"

I hadn't expected him to care. "I'm fine," I replied softly.

His eyes sparkled with curiosity as he immediately asked, "Why are you dressed like this?"

How was I supposed to answer that? Should I tell him that I wanted to explore without catching too much attention, have a good time without etiquette lessons, and just be myself? "No particular reason," I said with a casual shrug. "I just like wearing trousers. They're comfortable."

He didn't seem convinced, but before he could ask another question, I said, "Why was she trying to stab you?"

He stared at me, his gaze unwavering and serious. Then, in less than a second, his seriousness vanished. "Who knows? Actually, who cares?" he said half-jokingly.

"Listen, someone was trying to stab you. That's attempted murder. It's reasonable to be concerned," I retorted, trying to mask my worry with sarcasm.

He dismissed the gravity of the situation again. "Guess I'm not sane then. Happy?"

I was getting annoyed. "Do you think I didn't notice that they were targeting you?"

His eyes narrowed as he focused on me. "What do you mean?"

"That woman was trying to stab you. There were plenty of people around, but she aimed for you. And those people in the alleys—they were all following you. Specifically you."

He was silent for a few moments, then sighed. "Yes, they were following me, and that lady was trying to stab me. But I don't know why. There are too many reasons why someone would want me dead."

"And?" I pressed.

He gave a wry smile. "For someone I just met, you sure ask a lot of questions. How do I know you're not with them?"

"Why would I save you then?" I shot back.

"Maybe to gain my trust, get some information, and then kill me?" he suggested, half-joking.

I almost laughed. His self-importance was absurd. But at the same time, I wondered about the life he'd lived to make him so suspicious of everyone. And what was with his mood swings? One moment deadly serious, the next cracking jokes. "Forget I asked anything," I said, shaking my head.

He rested his head against the wall behind us, and I joined him, staring out at the mid-afternoon scene. The irony of the situation wasn't lost on me. In just a month, I had gone from hanging out with friends and dealing with routine office work to etiquette lessons and running from officers and protesters in the city of Restersburg in 1899. Lost in my thoughts, I closed my eyes.

When I woke up, the sky was still bright, and judging from the sun's position, we had only been there for about an hour. Glancing outside, I noticed fewer people around.

"I think the situation has calmed down. Should we head out?" he asked.

I nodded. "Yeah, let's go."

We hurried down the stairs and into the alley, my once-immaculate suit now creased and smeared with dirt, looking utterly shabby. We twisted and turned through a maze of tiny streets, but I could sense my luck running out.

Little did I know, our desperate escape was leading us straight into another perilous situation—one that would bring me face-to-face with death once again.

Chapter 9

XAVIER
November, 1899

It's amusing, in a darkly ironic way, how I always seem to get entangled in problems that aren't of my own making. Problems born from his conflicts, his issues. Is it too much to ask for one day in this world where I am not dragged into this mayhem that stems from his actions, his desires—his insatiable greed?

Four weeks ago, a group of local ministers decided to organize political rallies across major cities in Agnor, all aimed at addressing the growing uncertainty and troubles linked to the Slovain community. Troubles that had once tainted and caused turmoil during my father's time in office. I was instructed to attend all political rallies, a duty meant to signify the president's family's support, a role usually reserved for the First Lady of Agnor. But following what happened to my elder brother, the ugly confrontation between my parents, and the ever-widening chasm between them, there was no chance my mother would fulfill any of her obligations. This included every single one of her responsibilities.

The evening before the political rally at Restersburg Market Square, the phone rang, slicing through the quiet of my room. I picked up, already knowing who it was. My father's voice came through, cold and devoid of any warmth.

"Stay off the stage at the rally tomorrow. The OSE might retaliate. Be prepared."

His words, though expected, sent a chill down my spine. "Understood. I'll inform the others and cancel the rally."

"You fool!" he snapped, his tone icy and sharp. "We are not cowards. Don't take such drastic steps unless absolutely necessary. Just heighten security."

"But there will be civilians," I protested, my voice rising with urgency. "What if people get caught in the crossfire?"

"Then you know who to blame," he retorted, his voice hardening further. "Don't act like a child. Do what you must, and this time, catch them." The line went dead before I could respond.

The Order of Slovain Extremists, or OSE, had been a thorn in the government's side for over a decade. They fought relentlessly for the rights of the Slovain community, a group persecuted and marginalized since the mass genocides of the late 1880s. While they publicly claimed to avoid civilian casualties and positioned themselves as avengers of injustice, their actions told a different story. Their violent uprisings, illegal activities, and targeted assassinations had surged in the past twelve years, creating an atmosphere of fear and instability.

As I hung up the phone, I couldn't shake the heavy weight of my father's words. He demanded results, regardless of the cost. The OSE's campaigns, often seen as a verbal assault on the government, had grown more extreme. They didn't hesitate to stockpile firearms, bribe ministers, or eliminate those who stood in their way.

I sat back, running a hand through my hair, my mind racing. I had to act, fast.

Barely thirty minutes after the call with my father, there was a sharp knock at my door. The deputy commissioner strode in, offering a brisk salute.

"Sir, welcome to Restersburg. I've been informed about the potential OSE movement at tomorrow's rally. The president has instructed me to ensure your safety and assist you in any way necessary. My officers are ready for your further instructions."

Why couldn't rigid, upright officers like him learn to relax from time to time? Hadn't he received the message? Officially, I wasn't supposed to make decisions or issue commands, but that never seemed to matter. Just because I was my father's son, every top officer or minister seemed to follow my orders. It was not how things were supposed to be. I wasn't their superior, nor did I possess the qualifications for such a role. I was simply another tool in my father's arsenal to achieve his objectives—a puppet incapable of independent thought or action. Every decision in my life stemmed from his actions or his thoughts, and any unofficial authority or power I held was solely because of my status as his son.

"Thank you, Deputy Commissioner," I replied, masking my frustration with a tight smile. "Heighten the security and keep your men alert. We can't afford any mistakes."

The entire night, the police patrolled the area with unwavering dedication. Security measures were heightened, and we meticulously cross-checked all common public places, but there was no trace or evidence to suggest any potential OSE activity. The following day, security was at its peak, yet apart from the deputy commissioner, myself, and Chris, who was another high-ranking officer and one of my only good friends, no one else had been informed about the potential OSE threat. We were in the dark about what might happen, and it was already well past noon. If my father's intel, as reliable as it usually was, held true, the OSE would make a move soon.

When no one was around, I turned to Chris, my frustration bubbling over. "Is my father's intel even accurate? Can't that old man deal with his own problems for once?"

Chris sighed, a familiar weariness in his eyes. "Xavier, your father—the president—has a multitude of pressing matters to contend with. Other issues, not just political."

"Other issues?" I scoffed, feeling the weight of sarcasm in my voice. "It's all political nonsense. The rally is about to start, and we have no clue how to stop them when we don't even know what they're planning or who they are."

Chris mirrored my frustration. "Believe me, I'm well aware of that. If we can't catch them or prevent their actions, my position will be on the line."

I pondered the situation for a moment. Catching them before the rally seemed highly unlikely, and identifying them in the midst of the event would be a daunting task. "Our main objective is to apprehend a significant OSE member, right?" I asked.

Chris appeared puzzled. "Yes, but what's your point?"

I explained, "We can set a trap, and I'll be the bait."

Chris stared at me as if I had lost my mind. "Xavier, you realize that keeping you safe during the rally will be incredibly challenging. You're talking about risking your life for the sake of just one high-ranking OSE member. We have no idea what they're planning, and it will be their territory."

"Exactly, that's why they won't expect it. We'll have a team nearby, and as soon as they make a move, we'll apprehend them. This is our best shot."

I laid out the plan. "Listen, playing it safe won't work. We need to lure them out. As soon as there's any sign of OSE activity, have the police intervene and reduce security around me. If things escalate, use water cannons on the crowd to disperse them, but ensure the officers use batons, not guns. We need to minimize harm to innocent civilians. The key is to keep a close eye on anyone targeting me and prevent them from disappearing into the crowd. Block most of the exit points, leaving just one open, and lead them to an area where we can apprehend them."

Chris frowned deeply. "This is not what your father wants. His strict orders were to keep you safe and arrest OSE members. Not dangle you as bait and endanger your life."

"It's either this or nothing. You know better than anyone that my life is constantly in danger. This is the best I can come up with given the situation."

Chris looked torn, his brow furrowed in concern. "Alright, but if something happens, you'll have to take the responsibility. And no matter what happens, I am going to be right beside you all the time."

Which didn't really matter as, in the end, my father would find a way to hold me accountable for something regardless of the outcome.

When the clock struck one, the rally began. Initially, everything went smoothly; people gathered, listening attentively. Then, a sudden shift. Multiple groups started shouting, their voices rising above the crowd. They were mixed with the citizens attending the rally, scattered everywhere, chanting in unison:

"Every man is equal, for we all are children of God!"

"Slovain rights are human rights!"

"Break the chains of inequality!"

"Don't let the rich get richer and the poor get poorer!"

"The Slovain community is not your slaves. Get us equal rights! Get us equal rights!"

Each slogan hit like a hammer, exposing the deep-rooted biases, self-serving interests, and greed that plagued society. This society favored the wealthy and discriminated against the poor, especially the Slovain community. The mass chanting continued, creating a powerful, resonant wave of discontent.

That's when it hit me. This was exactly what they wanted. If the government retaliated against a group of unarmed protesters simply for speaking up, it would cause major trouble and cost my father a lot of supporters in the upcoming elections. Even a peaceful protest would create buzz and spark conversations, but a violent crackdown would be disastrous.

Oh shit! We cannot get the police involved and shoot the water cannons. Not now, because then we would be responsible for turning a peaceful protest into a violent confrontation, endangering the locals.

Chris stood beside me, dressed inconspicuously, guarding me as I played the role of bait. I urgently shouted to him, "We have to stop the police and prevent the use of water cannons!"

"What?" he yelled back, the noise and crowd making it difficult to hear me.

I raised my voice even louder, practically shouting, "We must prevent the police from interfering and using water cannons!"

"Why?" Chris questioned.

"Because right now, it looks like a peaceful protest led by the local Slovain community, not the OSE," I explained. But it was too late. The officers engaged, using their batons and resorting to violence, arresting protesters indiscriminately.

"Shit!" Chris immediately sprinted away from me, heading toward the deputy commissioner to halt the intervention. I attempted to follow him, but in the chaos of the crowd, I lost sight of him within seconds. All around me, police officers were forcefully dragging people and striking them with batons, while protesters shouted slogans and expressed their grievances. It was only a matter of time before the water cannons would be deployed, and just as I had predicted, mayhem engulfed everything.

People were running, and I was getting crushed from all sides. I was trying to find my way back to Chris or the police when a ragged-looking middle-aged man grabbed me by my collar and yelled, "You're Xavier Henderson! You and your kind have oppressed us for too long. My parents, my brothers, my sisters—they were slaughtered in the mass genocide! And now, you want to arrest us just for demanding our rights? You deserve to die!"

Suddenly, a group of individuals began pursuing me, their intentions clearly hostile. I was supposed to be acting as bait to draw out any attackers, but in the midst of the chaos, I wondered if any officers were actually keeping an eye on my safety. It seemed they were all too preoccupied with beating unarmed protesters.

About six to eight people closed in on me. I tried to fend off a few, but it was a futile effort. Fortunately, three local officers noticed what was happening and rushed to my aid. However, we were still outnumbered four to seven. They instructed me to run, and without hesitation, I complied. The crowd provided some cover, allowing me to gradually distance myself from my pursuers.

As I headed toward the group of officers, a baton suddenly whizzed past my face, striking an elderly, frail-looking woman who had been standing behind me. Just perfect. Was I on the brink of getting stabbed... again? Suddenly, a young adolescent boy ran towards me and grabbed my hand. "Run!" she yelled, and grabbed my arm. I followed instinctively. The woman we had left behind tried to fight back, but I managed to twist her hand and break free. In a matter of seconds, we managed to push her away.

We continued to sprint through a labyrinth of narrow streets, the persistent voices of our pursuers not far behind.

We darted through narrow passageways, the maze of houses and alleys endless. Finally, I saw an open area ahead. Before I could make a move, she pulled me into a dark alley, crushing me between the wall and her body.

"What are you doing?" she shouted, her voice high-pitched with panic.

Why was she overreacting? Hadn't she noticed their ominous presence trailing us like shadows? I placed my palm firmly over her mouth and whispered, "Shush... They're right behind us." Her unease was palpable, her breathing ragged. I guessed she wasn't accustomed to being chased, but then again, who really is?

She was shorter than me, barely reaching my shoulder, and I could sense her heart pounding through her chest. Her voice, when she spoke, had an unusual pitch, too high and tense. That's when I noticed her chest. It was bulging, and before I knew it, I blurted out, "Holy shit, you're a girl!"

Her reaction was immediate. She flushed red with embarrassment and then glared at me angrily. When I looked closely, I could see the poor attempt at a mustache. She looked uncomfortable, and now I knew why. I tried to create some space between us, but the alley was too cramped. Why is it that I always manage to attract danger?

She stood there, drenched and covered in dust, an enigma in the midst of chaos. Despite her disheveled appearance, there was something oddly familiar about her. In an attempt to break the tension, I cracked a joke, hoping to ease the situation. It didn't have the desired effect, though it did elicit an angry response, which, strangely, I found rather cute.

"Nothing. Just... why is someone with a pretty face like yours dressed like a man? Mustaches don't suit you."

"Are you seriously complimenting my looks right now?" she hissed.

"Shut up. It's cramped enough in here without you making it worse."

She reminded me of the cat I had as a child, always quick to scratch when I petted her. But what was someone like her doing in a place like this? Her attire, though now soiled, had an air of expense about it. Was she a thief? No, that didn't seem plausible; she lacked the finesse for such a profession. She appeared healthy, as if well taken care of. Perhaps she was a high-ranking servant from some noble family. But then, why would a servant go to such lengths to disguise herself as a boy and attend a political rally on her own?

Sometime later, we managed to find refuge in a random abandoned house. The crushing guilt flooded every inch of my body. Anyone who got injured today was due to my fault. I had failed. My plan would have worked had it been the OSE, but now I had made things so much worse. Why did the police even engage? It was just a local protest. I can only imagine what the newspapers will say tomorrow. That old man is going to blame me for everything, but there's no point in overthinking it now.

I needed to locate Chris as soon as possible, but venturing out alone, especially with her, was a dangerous proposition. It would only jeopardize her safety further. Exhaustion washed over me; I had hardly slept for an hour the previous night. But this girl. She had questions. A surprisingly large number of questions. She definitely was the curious kind.

Approximately an hour later, I looked outside. There were relatively fewer people, but it still looked like a mess. I had to find Chris as soon as possible and do some damage control. Get people to stop talking and bury this incident. At least lighten the severity of the upcoming backlash.

"I think the situation has calmed down. Should we head out?" I asked.

Luckily she nodded without any complaints and said, "Yeah. Let's go."

Both of us climbed down the stairs and started walking down the alley. I tried to retrace our steps, but it was too confusing. These alleys were a maze. We took multiple turns amidst this twisted, complicated web of tiny streets, but soon we were lost. After wandering around for a few minutes, suddenly I heard a deafening gunshot. I started running toward the sound. It was either the police, the local protestors, or the OSE. But if this was the police, this was going to become a horrifying civil rights disaster.

Out of nowhere, she suddenly grabbed my elbow, her breathing ragged and eyes filled with fear. "Where are you going? We need to run. Now!"

I yanked my elbow free from her grip, exasperation evident in my voice. "You have no idea how disastrous this whole situation can become. I need to go before they overcomplicate everything."

I could see the anger boiling inside those clear brownish-gold eyes. "Overcomplicate what? Are you insane? This whole situation is already completely disastrous. We just heard a freaking gunshot. This is already beyond repair. If we go there now, we're only inviting more trouble and danger."

I yelled in frustration, "Then don't follow me!" And with that, I turned and left, abandoning her in the midst of chaos.

Chapter 10

XAVIER
November, 1899

I didn't mean to sound so harsh, but sometimes my temper got the better of me. This was definitely one of those moments. I sprinted through the dimly lit alley, my heart pounding in sync with my steps. The echo of the gunshot still rang in my ears. As I rounded the corner, a pool of blood came into view, dark and foreboding. An old man lay on the ground, his blue shirt soaked in crimson.

I knelt beside him. His eyes fluttered open, dazed but conscious. "You're going to be okay," I whispered, noting the bullet wound in his hand. The exit wound was visible, which was a small mercy. I grabbed him under the arms, dragging him toward the shadowy corner, trying to shield him from whoever had done this.

Minutes passed, each one stretching longer than the last. I began to assess his injury, but the moment I touched his arm, he screamed, the sound piercing the silence and revealing our location.

Footsteps echoed in the alley. I looked up to see a young man, maybe in his late twenties, sprinting towards us. His brown hair clung to his forehead with sweat, his black eyes wide with panic. He was well-dressed, tall but disheveled, as if he'd been running for his life. Was he fleeing the police, or was he just an innocent caught in the chaos?

As soon as he spotted us, he pulled out a gun. Instinctively, I did the same, both of us now locked in a deadly standoff. Why did he have a gun?

He seemed bewildered. "Mr. Xavier Henderson! What are you doing here? What have you done?"

My gun was aimed at his heart. "Nothing! I could ask you the same question..."

He glanced at the old man and then back at me, eyes narrowing. "Did you shoot him?"

"Of course not! Did you?"

"Are you insane? What would I gain from that?"

Tension crackled in the air, both of us knowing that if either of us pulled the trigger, it would be the end for both. My mind raced, searching for a way out of this infuriating predicament. Why did this have to happen now?

Then she appeared, sprinting towards us with a police baton in hand. She skidded to a halt, taking in the scene in a heartbeat. Two men, guns drawn, and an old man bleeding on the ground. Her wide eyes darted between us, her face a mask of shock and disbelief.

"What the hell happened here!" she snapped, her voice cutting through the tension like a knife.

Both of us spoke at once, pointing fingers. "He did this!"

She hesitated, clearly unsure who to believe. Taking a deep breath, she steadied herself, though I could see her left leg shaking. "Okay, listen. Both of you said you didn't do this. Lower your guns. Let's help this man and go our separate ways..."

Had she lost her mind? "What if he shoots?"

The young man echoed my thoughts. "Same goes for him. And who are you anyway? How can we trust you?"

Her face twisted with frustration. She threw off her jacket, showing us her empty pockets. "Do I look like I have a gun? You two are the ones holding weapons. And if you keep delaying, this man will die from blood loss. So, stop acting like idiots and help me get him to a hospital!"

Our eyes locked in a silent agreement. Slowly, we both inched our hands away from our guns, the tension easing but not disappearing. On the count of three, we holstered our weapons. The old man's condition was worsening; we had no time to waste.

The woman took charge, her voice calm but firm. "Apply pressure here. Use this water to clean the wound." She knew what she was doing. Was she really just a civilian?

Moments later, officers arrived, drawn by the commotion. They quickly took over, and we were led to their base. Doctors rushed to treat the injured, including the old man. The officers wrapped us in blankets, offering hot tea to fend off the cold.

In the chaos, she and I exchanged a glance. Her eyes still held a mix of fear and determination. "What a day," she muttered.

The young man and I responded in unison, "I wonder myself." The unexpected synchronization in our responses caught us both off guard. Everything had been unfolding so rapidly, and this day had been nothing short of eventful. However, it wasn't over yet.

Shortly after, a group of reporters infiltrated the police base. I found myself surrounded by officers trying to shield me from the press. Cameras flashed with deafening clicks, and questions flew at me from all directions.

"Mr. Xavier Henderson, can you tell us what happened at the political rally?" one reporter shouted above the clamor.

"The government will issue a detailed statement soon," I responded quickly, trying to maintain composure.

"Is it true that the president has decided to reinstate the positions of the Slovain community back to its 1885 standing?" another reporter blurted out.

"Absolutely not! Please refrain from creating any speculations based on groundless rumors," I retorted, hoping to quell any misinformation.

The questions showed no signs of abating, a relentless torrent. They scarcely allowed me to respond before firing the next one.

"How is the government going to take responsibility for today's situation?"

"The government is against the upliftment of the Slovain community, isn't it?"

"The OSE was involved, wasn't it?"

"How many people have been injured? Any deaths so far?"

"What is the government going to do to compensate the victims for this mistake?"

"There have been rumors that your father would be retiring before his term due to old age. Is this true?"

The reporters were relentless, their inquiries like a storm, and I did my best to provide measured responses amidst the chaos.

Then, a small hand tapped my shoulder. The young woman, still dressed like a boy, pulled me behind her tiny frame. She stood in front of me, facing the reporters with surprising confidence. She took a deep breath and exclaimed, "Can all of you shut up for heaven's sake and at least give the man a moment to answer?"

A deafening silence fell over the area. The reporters, startled by her boldness, were momentarily at a loss for words. She continued, this time more softly, "Don't you have any integrity as reporters? Mr. Xavier Henderson clearly mentioned that the government will issue a statement soon and explain the whole incident. So, how can you keep on asking such leading questions? You are all journalists for reputable newspapers, not backstreet gossipers or paparazzi. Stop asking biased questions and cooking up stories based on groundless rumors. Instead, seek the truth and report it accurately, for heaven's sake."

Out of nowhere, a reporter jeered, "And who are you to speak for him, young lad?"

With unwavering authority, she responded, "A bystander and aspiring journalist who is horrified at a bunch of respectable professionals working on an agenda to paint the government in a bad light without knowing the full story. Any journalist who writes a story without verifying their facts will suffer major consequences in court on grounds of defamation of the government. Isn't that correct, Mr. Henderson?" She turned to me for confirmation, and I could only nod, still stunned.

She had managed to silence them all. She grabbed my hand and led me into one of the empty rooms, followed by Chris and the brown-haired young man. The tension in the room was palpable. I had never seen anyone shut reporters down like that. They all looked at her with shock and awe, clearly taken aback.

Chris broke the silence. "You did quite a number on all of them, young man."

She smiled. "They deserved it, but I really hope you have some answers for them soon. This is just a momentary silence."

Chris turned to me. "Are you okay? I should have never left you. I'm so sorry. I tried to find you, but..."

I reassured him. "I'm fine. How's the situation?"

"Seventy-three local civilians and thirty-six officers suffered minor injuries, but one man was shot in the hand. No one knows by whom. We managed to arrest sixty-four protesters."

"Is anyone from the protesters injured?"

"Almost all of them. The officers got a little violent, but no one died. It's mostly a few broken bones and bruises."

"Did they get access to doctors?" He didn't respond immediately.

I yelled in frustration. "Are you insane? Get all of them some medical help right now."

"I tried, but the officers kept interfering. You know how much stigma exists against that community. Some people even refuse to touch them."

"I don't care. Give the order. You are the highest authority here, after me from the center. Please don't make this into a civil rights disaster."

He immediately left to get things done properly, and I turned to the other two. "I'm sorry you had to witness that."

"No issues. It's nice to meet someone who at least cares. It's not always that you get to see how the government deals with a crisis on the inside," the brown-haired man stated.

"This time, in the worst way possible," I added. He gave me an apologetic smile. "By the way, I just realized, I don't know your names." I commented.

The brown-haired man answered first. "I am Demion Marshal. I work at a private law firm. It's an honor to meet you, Mr. Henderson."

"Wait a minute? Are you seriously Demion Marshal!" the girl interrupted, her voice filled with shock and awe.

He looked confused, but she continued. "Did you write the paper on how Agnor's economy could be improved by making the middle class stronger and incentivizing policies that induce purchasing power to reduce income inequality?"

Now he was visibly shocked. "How are you aware of my university research paper? I'm sure only a few people actually managed to read it as it was banned twenty-three days after being published."

A slight excitement spread across her face. "Who doesn't know about it? I mean, my dad always loved talking about it.

He was a huge fan." She fumbled to find the right words, then took a deep breath and spoke quickly, "I was lucky enough to read it before it was banned. Your views on Agnor's economic policies are groundbreaking. Way ahead of your time. The methods and steps you suggest to tackle income inequality and your vision of transforming Agnor into a superpower that can stand proudly beside the United States and other developed nations are truly incredible. I've studied every one of your suggested reforms in-depth. It's an honor to meet you, Sir."

He looked flattered, even a little shy. The overwhelming praise from this young boy—or rather, this girl—made him blush. He tried to maintain his composure. "You overpraise my work. It was rather average, and even my professors at Agnor University deemed it a vain attempt of a foolish young man meant to fail. A common man's pipe dream."

She replied calmly, "Ignore those fools. They are stuck in a time period that rejects modernity and equality. They were the same people who opposed abolishing slavery, and just two decades later, everyone knows what a revolutionary step it was."

"Ahem..." I interrupted. "Are you really that famous? Unfortunately, I've never heard of your name or these papers that she... I mean, he mentioned."

"I'm sure you haven't. Actually, no one has. That's why I'm so astonished that this young man has actually read them. My views on certain topics were deemed too revolutionary and borderline blasphemous by some people." Then he looked at her and asked, "May I know your name, Mister?"

The girl looked nervous for a fraction of a second but quickly recovered. She didn't make any eye contact with me but in a confident voice told him, "I am Luca Everett. Nice to meet you. It's truly an honor to meet so many great people in one day." The man was about to ask her a few questions when she said, "I'm really sorry, but it's getting late. I think we've already answered all the questions from the officers, and I really need to go or else I might lose my job. It was nice meeting both of you. Is there any other way I can leave, Mr. Henderson? The front entrance will be crowded with too many people, including those nosy reporters."

"You can take the back entrance. Follow me," I said quickly.

She did, following close behind me as we navigated the dimly lit corridors of the police base. The hum of activity and distant murmur of voices faded as we moved further away from the main area. After a few minutes, we reached a heavy door marked "Exit." I placed my hand on the doorknob, ready to open it, but paused. I turned around, blocking the only way out.

"Who are you really, Miss?" I asked, my voice low but firm.

There was no way for her to leave or dodge the question. It was just us in the narrow corridor. She looked flustered, but her eyes didn't waver as she stared into mine. "No one that the son of the president should bother with." But still, she had tenacity.

"I'm not asking as the son of the president but as just me. Even I deserve to know the name of my savior."

"Mr. Xavier Henderson, let's just say that we both helped each other out and call it a day."

"You really won't tell me your name?"

"I don't think it's of any importance. If one day we meet again, I shall tell you, but I highly doubt we will. Also, I'm seriously late. If I don't reach my hotel in time, I'm going to get in some real trouble with my brother. So, can you please not block the door and let me leave?"

She mentioned her brother, so not a thief indeed. "Sure. If you ever need a favor, do not hesitate to ask." This time I truly opened the door. She was gone before I could finish my sentence, running and rushing toward somewhere. I really hoped I could meet her again. But I had other matters to look after, and that was how I met her for the first time. As she left, a strange mix of intrigue and a sense of loss washed over me. Questions flooded my mind. Who was she? Why was she here? What was her connection to all this chaos? Her presence left me with a burning curiosity, and I couldn't help but wonder if our paths would cross again.

My father, Benjamin Henderson, was first elected as the 20th president of Agnor in 1890. Since then, the Agnor House of Parliament had become my home. He won the consecutive election in 1895 and now aimed for his third consecutive victory next year. But unlike the last two elections, this time, his biggest obstacle towards victory was the Slovain community and the rising interests of citizens in modernization. The citizens no longer craved a traditional leader like him. They wanted a charismatic leader full of revolutionary ideas. Someone who was willing to embrace modernity. But my father was now an old cog stuck in outdated rusting machinery, trying to run towards the future with his head stuck in the past.

Both Chris and I stood quietly in the waiting room, a place that often haunted my dreams. The walls were adorned with portraits of past leaders, their eyes seeming to judge us. Time seemed to stretch interminably. After what felt like an eternity but was only seventeen minutes, Mr. Joey Randolph, the chief of staff, exited his office and gestured for us to go in. As we entered, Chris promptly gave the old man a salute, and I stood at attention. We greeted him in unison.

My father stood still, staring out of the window, his hands clasped behind his back. Without turning to face us, he said, "Do you think of this morning as good, Mr. Jefferson?"

Chris remained silent, his expression unreadable.

"I find it stinking of failure," my father continued, his voice cold.

Chris responded in a firm voice, "Sir, we arrested 64 protesters. They are currently being investigated, and I am positive we will find some connection to their ties to the OSE. We are sparing no effort."

My father turned around slowly, his gaze cold and hard. "Mr. Jefferson, sparing no effort would lead to success, not failure. Everything was supposed to be handled silently. Why did it have to be so overt? Do you have any idea how the press is spinning this?"

"Sincerest apologies, Sir. We tried our best to track down the OSE members before the rally, but there was no evidence indicating any potential move from their side," Chris stated, his tone rigid and genuine.

"Excuses! Not only are we now unsure whether the protest was organized by the OSE, but we've also given the opposition more grounds to undermine us publicly." His voice grew louder, the familiar refrain of ceaseless criticism echoing in the room. He demanded perfection in every facet of life—not that he was perfect himself, though I was sure he thought he was.

Then, he turned his attention to me, his gaze piercing. "And you, where were you when all this was happening? How foolish are you to risk your life and act as bait for a few terrorists in a minor rally? Is your life that expendable?"

I stood still, my posture unwavering. "I got caught up amidst the water cannons and the protesters, separating me from others. It took me some time to get to the police base because I ran into a gunshot victim."

"Is that so? Was a gunshot victim that important in a political situation that was escalating with every wasted second?" He advanced slowly, his tone unrelenting as he locked eyes with me. His gaze was as cold-hearted as ever. "You're a disappointment. I assigned you a single task, and once again, you've come up short. How is it that I've raised such a fool?"

As he spoke, memories of past criticisms flooded my mind. His disdains always cut deeper than any wounds. Why couldn't he see that the world was changing and that his rigid ways would only lead to his downfall. I had a lot to say, but as always, I forced myself to remain composed. A man like him didn't listen. Especially when it came from me. "I apologize, father." My gaze fixed firmly on the ground, I braced myself for the familiar sting of his words. This was routine, an expected outcome of any action, success or failure. Apologies were a constant in my life, typically accompanied by some form of physical punishment. Thankfully, it didn't sting as deeply as it once did during my younger years.

Chris interjected, his voice measured. "But Sir, we did prevent the media from creating a civil rights issue. If I may be bold enough to make a suggestion, the next time the opposition brings this up, please reiterate the fact that everyone who was injured, irrespective of the community they originated from, was treated with dignity and equality."

"And what good would that do, Mr. Jefferson?" my father asked loudly, his tone dripping with disdain.

Chris stood his ground. "It could enhance your public image, Sir. It would present you as a leader committed to the safety and well-being of all citizens, one who doesn't discriminate. You could highlight how your own son risked his life to protect the people, emphasizing that the police's reaction was due to the imminent risk posed by the OSE. With strategic leaks about the OSE's potential involvement, we can influence public opinion in our favor."

My father turned his icy gaze to me. "Perhaps you can learn something from him, you fool." After a brief pause, he added, "Now, get out. Mr. Jefferson, stay behind. I require a detailed report of the events."

I nodded and exited the room, leaving Chris to provide my father with the requested account.

I could finally breathe. The rich red carpet underfoot muffled the sound of my footsteps as I walked purposefully across the room, each step bringing me closer to the exit.

Emerging into the open air, I took a deep breath. I needed a break. I continued to walk for a long time, the cold wind constantly caressing my cheeks. Today, the wind had an icy chill while the sun shone brightly, illuminating the blue sky. This contrast had made the weather rather peculiar.

As far as my eye could see, naked branches stood tall, surrounding the expanse of blue that lay before me. A thin layer of ice had started to form over it, but the rays of light continued to dance delicately across the water, making the entire lake shimmer and sparkle like crystals.

Despite the freezing temperature, there was not a single snowflake to be seen. Although momentarily, the cold had managed to clear my head of any unnecessary thoughts. I was conscious of my every breath and the silence around me had brought a unique sense of peace. Some time passed, and then a voice interrupted this peace.

"I knew you would be here," Chris remarked as he settled down beside me on the bench. His concerned eyes met mine, and he inquired, "How are you holding up?"

"It's fine," I replied with a shrug, attempting to downplay the situation. "Nothing new. I've grown accustomed to it."

"It's only gotten worse since your brother," he observed, and I nodded in agreement. Trying to shift our focus, he continued, "What are you doing here anyway? It's freezing." I glanced at him for a second and then continued to stare back at the serene landscape before me. "You won't get a chance to look at this tomorrow. This beautiful lake will be gone. Covered under a thick layer of ice."

He quipped, "Really? Since when can you control the weather?"

"Since I was born, didn't you know?" I joked back, followed by a mischievous grin.

He raised an eyebrow in mock seriousness. "Oh, of course. You're a weather wizard."

I chuckled, appreciating the humor. "It's just a hunch, buddy. Get the joke."

After a few moments of companionable silence, I inquired, "So, what did he say? What new tasks have we been assigned?"

In a calm tone, he said, "You are going to help your father out by strengthening the foundations of his campaigns. Some negotiations with the Britishers and political campaigning, I guess. Randolph will help you with everything. You'll be involved in events, visits to key locations, meeting influential people, and adopting the right demeanor. Essentially, you'll serve as his representative whenever necessary—campaigning for him."

I couldn't help but laugh. "Don't you mean acting as his puppet? I'll follow his orders and do his bidding while he pulls my strings from the shadows, all under Randolph's watchful eye, of course."

He immediately refuted, "Don't say that. It won't be that horrible. Although he calls you a fool, he recognizes your popularity. The people like you, and he knows how that benefits him. Also, I clarified how all of this was your idea. Why didn't you speak up? You always let him take you for granted."

I let out a resigned sigh, my voice carrying a touch of frustration. "Chris, it's just not worth it. You know the kind of leader he is. Yes, he was an excellent military strategist who brought Agnor glory a few years ago, but that doesn't mean he's qualified to lead a country indefinitely. He's stern, uncompromising, and he always prioritizes Agnor above everything else, including his own family. But running a country is not the same as commanding an army. Politics is a delicate dance, not a battlefield. He still sees everything in black and white. Diplomacy, compromise—these are concepts he just can't grasp."

I paused, feeling the weight of my words. "He'll never understand why I did what I did. To him, there's only ever one right way: his way. Even if I follow his orders perfectly, he'd still find something to criticize, some fault to blame me for. My so-called popularity is meaningless to him. It's not about being liked or admired; it's about control.

He believes in leading through dominance, and that's just not me. I can't pretend to be something I'm not. I don't have the stomach for the lies and the facades, for making decisions that put people's lives at risk. I see politics as a game, one that requires a cold heart and a willingness to sacrifice others for the greater good. I'm not built that way. Whether he wins or loses the next election doesn't matter to me anymore. I'm tired, Chris. Tired of the constant pressure, the scrutiny, the never-ending cycle of trying to meet expectations I never agreed to. I just want to breathe, to live my life on my own terms. I want to find out who I am, not who he wants me to be."

Chris leaned in slightly, his expression cautious. "You're not just criticizing your father, Xavier. Remember, he's the president. You could get into serious trouble for speaking like this."

"Trouble or not, it needed to be said. We need a leader who understands the complexities of modern governance, not just a military mindset. Agnor deserves better," I stated firmly.

Trying to lighten the mood, I added with a smile, "Oh come on. Relax. It's nothing new, and it's not that bad. At least we can suffer through all this together."

Chris stared at me, a serious look in his eyes. "Xavier, there's something I need to tell you." The atmosphere around us shifted, growing heavier. In a soft voice, he continued, "I've been posted at the border. British troops have been showing some signs of suspicious activity. I have to go deal with that situation. You know how your father is. The one thing he takes most seriously is external threats."

"Hmm." There was an awkward silence. Then, after a few moments, he said, "I'm leaving the city in five days."

My eyes widened, shock coursing through me. "Five days!" I blurted out, my voice tinged with surprise and concern. I couldn't help but ask the inevitable question, "How long?"

"At least a year. Maybe more."

He was leaving... soon. Suddenly, I could feel a deep, dark pit forming in my stomach. Out of nowhere, an old memory of my brother resurfaced. Images of those days flashed in my head—the pressure, the expectations, the constant criticism. It had driven my brother to a point where he could no longer take it, ultimately leading to his tragic end. The pain of losing him still lingered, a haunting reminder of what this life could do to a person. I had a strong urge to run away from reality, but I managed to suppress it. I pushed all of my overwhelming emotions as deep down as possible. In a soft, heartfelt whisper, I uttered, "Stay safe and come back home... alive."

Chris patted my shoulder reassuringly. "Of course I will. Now, get up! It's one of my last few days in Portmaine City before I'm stuck in those boring suburban villages surrounding the national border. Let's go have some fun."

I stood up, determined to lift our spirits. With a mischievous grin, I took off running and called out, "What are you waiting for? Come on. The first man that reaches the gates gets to choose where we go and what we do." Soon, Chris joined in the race, our steps filled with the promise of shared moments before his departure.

Chapter 11

A RIADNE
November, 1899

How did I manage to run into Xavier Henderson and Demion Marshall at the same time while exploring suburban streets? And how did I end up being chased by people with knives, dealing with gunshot wounds, and lecturing reputable journalists in 1899? My life was starting to resemble those side characters in movies who always get killed for knowing too much or interfering too much.

Everyone in the future knows who Demion Marshall is. His name appears in every textbook, museum, and media related to the freedom struggle. We Agnorians take immense pride in our history and bravery. My father could never stop talking about him. All my childhood, I heard stories of how he became the leader Agnor needed, how he struggled, how he did what he had to do, and the sacrifices he made to unite Agnor and secure our freedom.

Demion Marshall was more than a leader; he was a revolutionary icon. Born into a humble family, he rose through the ranks with sheer determination and when our nation was drowning, he had a vision for a free Agnor. He was known for his strategic brilliance and his ability to inspire the masses with his fiery speeches. His most famous address, "The Spirit of Unity," was credited with rallying disparate factions into a cohesive force against oppression. He was not just a soldier on the battlefield but also a scholar who penned numerous treatises on freedom, justice, and economic independence. His dedication was absolute, often at great personal cost.

I had studied his research papers on Agnor's economy in great detail during my university days. His insights into economic resilience and sustainable development were ahead of his time. Although I wanted to interact more with him, to ask him questions that had intrigued me for years, I was running really late. I had to go back.

So after slipping out of the police base through the back entrance, I walked swiftly to the main market square. The clock across the street showed a quarter to five. The sky was darkening, and the temperature had dropped significantly in the last hour.

My heart raced with anxiety. I had to get back to my room and change before Eugene returned. The thought of getting caught sent shivers down my spine. A lifetime of grounding in this era was terrifying. No smartphones, no streaming services, no social media, and no access to my favorite authors. That was a fate I absolutely dreaded.

It took some time, but I eventually reached Hugh Grand Hotel. In the lobby, I saw Violet, looking panicked and pacing. When she spotted me, she rushed over, grabbed my arm, and practically dragged me into my room.

"My lady, where have you been?" she exclaimed, her voice trembling with anxiety.

I sighed, weariness weighing me down. "You have no idea what kind of day I've had."

"I told you, all of this was a terrible idea," Violet said, her anxiety intensifying.

I started rummaging through my luggage for clean clothes. "Stop talking for now and help me. Is Eugene back?"

"Yes, my lady," Violet replied, her nervousness palpable. "But I told him you weren't feeling well and decided to take a short nap."

"Smart thinking. Let me quickly change and then we'll rush downstairs for dinner."

Violet grabbed my arm, her expression filled with concern. "You can't just change clothes. You'll get caught."

Confused, I asked, "What do you mean?"

"Lady Ariadne, look at yourself. Your clothes are a mess, your hair is all over the place, and you're covered in dust and dirt. You need to take a shower. Immediately." She then noticed the red stains on my white shirt. With a horrified expression, she exclaimed, "Is that... blood? Are you hurt?"

I grabbed Violet by her shoulders and whispered urgently, "Calm down! It's just juice that spilled on me. Okay?"

She nodded, still pale and panicked.

Just then, there was a knock on the door, and my brother's voice came through. "Ariadne, are you ready? We need to head downstairs for dinner."

"Brother!" I tried to mask my nervousness. "I'm still getting ready. I'll need twenty more minutes. Can you please go ahead?"

With a sigh of impatience, he replied, "Ariadne, do hurry up." But thankfully, he left, and Violet and I could breathe a sigh of relief.

I quickly took a shower, combed my hair, and dressed as presentably as I could manage in such a short time. There was no way I was getting caught today. By then, Violet had calmed down.

I rushed downstairs for dinner, famished and drained from the day. Eugene was already seated, and we chatted as we ate. He updated me on his automobile deal, and soon, we headed back to our rooms for some much-needed rest. Tomorrow would be another long day as we returned home.

These past two days in Restersburg were finally over, but I had mixed feelings. I enjoyed my freedom, but almost getting killed had taken most of the fun out of it. On the other hand, I dreaded more lessons and rules. Honestly, I didn't know what was worse: getting chased by people with knives or staying trapped with lessons and rules without any freedom. I was surprised at how conflicted I felt.

Over the next few weeks, the whole Restersburg debacle faded into the past. Thankfully, I didn't get caught. The political rally gone wrong came up at dinner the next day, but Eugene didn't pay much attention, and I feigned ignorance. Our parents were concerned about our proximity to danger but relieved that we were safe.

Soon, the conversation drifted back to my lessons with Miss Mable, and everything returned to normal at home. Despite the brief excitement, life settled back into its usual routine, leaving me to grapple with my yearning for freedom and the constraints of my new life.

Today was an exciting day at Clairborough Manor. An all-new Rolls-Royce Model B had been delivered early in the morning. Automobiles were rare... very rare. It was the 'innovation' of the future. Eugene was thrilled, practically bouncing on his heels. My new mother, however, looked as if the devil himself had entered the house.

"An automobile," she muttered, her voice tinged with disdain. "Machines should be driven by men or horses, not by themselves."

Eugene brushed off her concerns with a laugh. "Mother, it's the future. You'll see, soon everyone will have one."

The next day, our chauffeur, Mr. Peter Dudley, reported for his first day of work. At twenty-two, he was among the early adopters of driving. Eugene briefed him on the situation: he was to teach us both how to drive and judge who learned the fastest. He was also aware of the bet between us.

For his first lesson, he gave both of us a joint lesson on the mechanics of the automobile, its various components, and its distinctive features. Eugene was the first to undergo his driving lesson, but it proved to be a challenging endeavor. Everything was new and confusing and he was trying his best to stay calm, but every now and then I could see some irritation evident in his eyes. I overheard him reassuring Eugene, emphasizing that feeling utterly bewildered during the initial lessons was entirely par for the course. According to him, this machinery was remarkably modern and operated in an unconventional manner. Thus, it would require a span of two to three months to become acclimated and eventually attain mastery.

Once Eugene concluded his lesson, it was my turn to step into the driver's seat. Eugene looked at me with vexation and said, "Are you sure you want to do this? It is far more difficult than I expected."

"Yes, brother. I'm sure," I replied politely, though inside, I felt a pang of guilt. Back home in the future, I was a veteran driver.

As I sat inside the car, it felt both familiar and alien. The controls were odd—primitive compared to the cars I was used to.

"Lady Ariadne, are you sure you want to learn how to drive? As Sir Eugene mentioned, it won't be easy." He mentioned, very politely. Although he had no opinion about the bet or my driving lessons, he did find the idea of a young noble lady learning how to drive, astonishing.

I responded with a small smile, "I am sure, Mr. Dudley. Shall we begin?"

"As you wish. To recap our earlier discussion, there are three pedals. The middle pedal is for reverse, the left pedal is the clutch, and the right pedal is the brake."

I inquired about the gas pedal, to which he looked puzzled and asked, "What exactly is a gas pedal?" I realized my mistake – this car didn't have a gas pedal. It was a vintage model, and I needed to adjust my thinking. I rephrased, "I mean, how do I make this car move?"

Mr. Dudley pointed to a hand throttle beneath the steering wheel and explained, "This helps you adjust the speed. Press the clutch – I mean, the left pedal – with your foot and push the hand throttle down for slow speed. You can also press the clutch and pull the hand throttle up for faster acceleration. Do you follow, my lady? Should I repeat?"

"No need to repeat," I replied. "Would you mind demonstrating how to drive?"

"Indeed I shall." He ignited the ignition, and the car started. After carefully paying attention to how he takes his turns, uses his breaks, and in general drives, I said, "Mr. Dudley, I think I would like to give it a try now."

He looked at me nervously. "Are you entirely certain, my lady? This machinery is exceedingly intricate. It could pose considerable difficulty if, inadvertently, you press the reverse pedal or the clutch instead of the brake. Might I propose a more gradual approach? It would be prudent to proceed cautiously, concentrating primarily on the theoretical aspects before delving into practical lessons."

"Trust me. I believe I will manage quite well," I assured him. Despite his reservations, he reluctantly relented. Prior to entrusting me with the automobile, he subjected me to three rounds of basic tests. However, eventually, he had no choice but to concede. I proved to be a quick learner and an exemplary student, compelling him to grant me the opportunity to drive.

Roughly forty-five minutes later, we returned to the mansion. The entire family had gathered in the tea room.

Immediately Eugene asked with a smirk on his face, "Given up so soon, sister?"

"What do you think, brother?" I raise my eyebrows.

His silence spoke volumes. The notion of me potentially failing brought a rare sense of joy to his usually composed demeanor, almost childlike in his excitement.

Interrupting the moment, Dudley interjected, "She is a natural, Sir." His genuine awe was evident as he lauded my driving skills in front of everyone. "Lady Ariadne handled the automobile with absolute ease. Honestly, I don't believe she requires any further instruction from my side."

Eugene scoffed in disbelief, exclaiming, "That's impossible."

"Not anymore, brother. It took me a few minutes to figure out how the automobile really moves, but I did. So, do you admit defeat?" I asked proudly although I did feel a bit guilty. I had definitely cheated but who was ever going to know?

"Mr. Dudley, are you being entirely serious? How is it possible for Lady Ariadne to master something as complex and intricate as driving in under an hour? You explicitly mentioned that it would take me at least two to three months to acquire these skills. This sudden development raises considerable suspicion, does it not?" Eugene inquired.

"It is indeed a peculiar turn of events, Sir," Mr. Dudley replied. "I am at a loss as to how Lady Ariadne accomplished this feat so swiftly, but occasionally, certain individuals do possess a natural aptitude for such tasks."

"Stop being a sore loser brother. I won. Fair and square." I interrupted.

Eugene composed himself and responded calmly, "I am not being a sore loser, Ariadne. I just find this rather peculiar." He couldn't help but see the situation as highly implausible.

Even my new mother found it odd. She was one of the few people, who told me again and again how stupid it was of me to try and learn how to drive—Especially because I was a woman. She was clearly not comfortable with modern innovation and she found the idea of her daughter driving even more revolting. But on the other hand, was my new father. Sitting in one corner of the room, this middle-aged man was smiling. Clearly proud of my absolute victory.

Later that evening, I found Eugene alone in his study, the room dimly lit with candles. "Brother, as you've seen, I won the bet," I said plainly.

He looked up, barely hiding a smirk. "I'm well aware. No need to gloat; it's unbecoming of a young lady."

"You even insisted that I show you how I drive," I teased, still amused by his earlier skepticism.

He sighed, a mix of frustration and admiration. "I'm sorry for doubting you, but it was surprising."

"Yes, I understand," I replied. "Anyway, as the winner, you need to help me convince our parents, especially Mother, to allow me something permanent."

He leaned back in his chair, eyeing me warily. "Yes, but it has to be sensible. I'm not a miracle worker."

"Of course. It's simple. A free day every Wednesday. No lessons, no rules. I can do whatever I want."

Eugene raised an eyebrow. "You talk as if you have no freedom. Since your memory loss, has there been anything you haven't done because others didn't want it?"

"That's not the point," I shot back. "Every decision I make is questioned. I want freedom without criticism."

He studied me for a moment. "And there's something more, isn't there?"

I nodded. "Yes. Are you familiar with the AHA?"

"Agnor Hunting Association? What about it?"

"I want permission to go there, preferably on those free Wednesdays."

His confusion was palpable. "Why? You know it's outside a forest. People go there to hunt animals. I never took you for someone who would like to hunt."

"I don't. They have a shooting range there. Specifically, a trap and skeet range. I want to learn that."

I took a deep breath, trying to gather my thoughts. How could I explain this to him?

Back in my own time, I had a few things I truly loved: books, shows, running, and shooting. Running gave me an adrenaline rush like no other. The surroundings would blur into a haze, my heart pounding against my rib cage, music blasting in my ears, making all thoughts vanish. Although I wasn't naturally athletic, I trained hard to run full marathons.

But here, running wasn't the same. I couldn't just go running; people would think I was crazy. The one thing I truly learned through all those lessons with Miss Mable was that I had to find a balance between what I liked and how people saw me. If I was too pushy with my ideas, I would face too much resistance. So I needed something else, something familiar and enjoyable, but not too foreign to this time period.

After my parents died in that horrible car accident, everything in my world shattered. The loss plunged me into a darkness I could hardly describe. Anxiety and depression took hold, and I spent nearly two years in trauma counseling. Concentrating on school became impossible, and I couldn't even enjoy time with friends or family. Nightmares of the accident haunted me every night, leaving me emotionally numb and disconnected from the world.

Shooting had truly helped me then. It was an unusual choice of therapy, but my counselor suggested something extreme to help me channel my negative emotions better. Trap and skeet shooting was perfect. It was a popular sport, helping people to improve their hunting skills, and though few women participated, it wasn't unheard of.

Taking another deep breath, I met Eugene's gaze. "It's not about hunting. They have a great library, and many aristocrats visit regularly. It's a perfect place to make new friends and expand my social circle. I can't just sit at home all day, Eugene. I need something meaningful to do."

Eugene looked thoughtful, then nodded. "Alright. I'll help you. It's quite a practical wish."

"Thank you, brother."

As I left the room, I felt a surge of relief. I had finally voiced my desire, and Eugene had agreed to help.

Chapter 12

A RIADNE
December, 1899

Eugene was true to his word. At the very next dinner, he broached the topic. "Father, Mother, I have a small request."

My new mother gently patted her lips with her napkin, her eyes sharp with curiosity. "What is it, my dear?"

Eugene glanced at me briefly before addressing her. "Would you consider excusing Ariadne from all her duties and lessons every Wednesday?"

She looked at Eugene, surprised, then quickly masked her shock with a steely resolve. "That's absurd. Ariadne is far behind in her lessons and has much to learn. Absolutely not."

An awkward silence followed, the clinking of silverware against plates the only sound. Eugene cleared his throat, his voice steady but insistent. "Mother, don't you think you've been too harsh on her lately?"

Her eyes shot up to meet his, narrowing. She didn't like being questioned, especially by her son. "Excuse me?"

Eugene pressed on, undeterred. "After she traveled with me to Restersburg, Miss Mable gave her many more tasks than usual. Despite the increased workload, Ariadne has managed to keep up with her lessons. Quite well, considering she has no knowledge or memories of her past."

She turned to me, her tone accusatory. "Was this your idea? Getting your brother to intervene whenever things don't go your way?"

I took a deep breath, keeping my voice steady. "No, Mother. It's not about avoiding responsibilities. I simply want a day off every Wednesday. No lessons with Miss Mable, no early mornings, no strict rules. Just one day where I can experience a bit of freedom and choose how to spend my time."

My father, who had been silently eating his dinner, finally looked up. His eyes met mine, a flicker of sympathy in them. "Just one day, every week."

"And what do you intend to do every Wednesday?" she asked, turning back to Eugene.

He cleared his throat again, more awkwardly this time. "Nothing bad. Just some leisure activities, spending time with friends, maybe participating in some sport hunting."

"Friends? Friends she doesn't even remember? And hunting? Only daughters of foreign ministers hunt. What is Ariadne going to do amidst them? This is absurd." She turned to my father, her voice rising. "Honey, do you have anything to say, or will you keep eating as if none of this concerns you?"

My father sighed, putting down his fork and knife with deliberate care. He looked around the table, taking in the tension. "Ariadne, do you really want to go hunting and have leisure excursions that badly? Is it worth your mother's peace of mind?"

"It's not about the activities, Father. I want the freedom to decide without always asking for permission. There is a difference."

He sighed again, deeper this time, rubbing his temples. "Fine. You have my permission to do as you wish every Wednesday, but you must promise to stay safe and out of trouble. I trust you, but if you break that trust, there will be consequences. Also, finish your lessons with Miss Mable as soon as possible. I want peace between you and your mother."

"Thank you so much, and I promise I won't get into any trouble."

A few moments later, Eugene interrupted with a teasing grin. "Miss Ariadne Bryant, are you forgetting to thank someone?"

He clearly wanted me to acknowledge his help, but I decided to play along. "I sincerely thank you, brother, for not being able to drive and letting me win the bet."

As expected, he looked annoyed, but then he laughed, and soon my father joined in. My new mother, her tone slightly frustrated but resigned, declared, "If Ariadne makes a fool of herself at the gala or fails to find a suitable suitor, don't blame me. All three of you must share the responsibility."

She wasn't happy, but she wasn't shouting either. In her own way, she was starting to accept these small changes. For the first time since I arrived, this dinner table didn't feel strange. Instead of silence, it was filled with chatter and laughter, making it feel a bit more like home. A home where I was no longer a stranger, but a family member. Not one where I am trying to play the role of their real daughter, but rather just as me. They were slowly starting to see me for who I was, not the Ariadne they knew.

Dressed in my new custom-made hunting outfit, consisting of a tailored olive-green jacket with brass buttons, a high-collared white blouse, fitted riding pants, and sturdy leather boots, I was ready for my first 'do whatever you want' Wednesday at the Agnor Hunting Association (AHA). Today there was no Miss Mable, no mother, no Violet—simply no one to bother me.

The drive to the AHA was filled with anticipation. I wasn't sure what to expect, but as we approached, I was taken aback by the grandeur of the place. Nestled amidst rolling green hills, with manicured lawns and a cobblestone path leading up to an elegant, ivy-covered mansion that served as the main lodge. Ornate wrought iron gates opened to reveal sprawling grounds dotted with ancient oak trees and meticulously maintained gardens.

Stables and kennels lined one side of the property, with well-bred horses and sleek hunting dogs visible from a distance. On the other side, there were several state-of-the-art shooting ranges, each designed to cater to different aspects of the sport. The centerpiece was a grand lake, its glassy surface reflecting the autumn sky. Apparently it was founded in 1759 as a means to attract foreign delegates and ministers who relished the sport.

The moment I entered the reception area, the scent of polished wood and leather greeted me. The interior was just as impressive, with dark wood paneling, antique chandeliers, and plush carpets. A middle-aged man in a crisp uniform approached me with a warm smile.

"Good morning, madame. We've been expecting you."

"You have?" I asked, a hint of doubt in my voice.

"Yes, indeed. Your father informed us of your visit. Everything has been arranged to ensure you have a seamless experience here."

I marveled at how privilege opened doors in this time period. After some polite conversation, he gave me a quick tour of the facilities.

"Madame, today we'll begin with some fundamental shooting techniques. As you get more comfortable with our facilities over the coming weeks, you'll be able to explore them more independently. Does that sound agreeable to you?"

I wanted to tell him that I already knew how to shoot but it would have looked suspicious. How was I supposed to explain all this sudden knowledge? So, I just let him give me a run-through of the basics.

"There are three primary types of competitive shooting: Rifle, Pistol, and Shotgun. For bird hunting, shotguns are preferred due to their spread pattern. Today, we'll be using a double-barreled shotgun, which allows for two shots in quick succession. Since your father requested something straightforward and effective, I've set up trap and skeet shooting to sharpen your skills. Everything is ready."

At the range, I was equipped with a double-barreled shotgun. Luckily, the weather today wasn't freezing, just a bit chilly but still bearable.

"To improve your aim for bird hunting, we use clay targets as stand-ins. These targets are mechanically launched into the air at high speeds, simulating the flight of birds. Since you're a beginner, shall we start by getting you acquainted with the shotgun?"

After what felt like an eternity of theory lessons, I began to feel impatient. The slow, meticulous pace at which this man explained the mechanics of shooting indicated that I might be stuck in these lessons for weeks, and I had no interest in that. The air in the shooting range was thick with the scent of gun oil and freshly cut grass, mingling with the distant chirping of birds.

I interrupted, "I apologize for the interruption, but I already possess some knowledge of shooting. My brother taught me some basics. I would greatly appreciate the opportunity to practice with clay targets instead. Might we proceed with practical lessons and forgo the theory?"

He regarded me with a questioning expression, clearly doubtful. "Are you entirely certain, my lady?"

"Yes, I am," I replied, trying to keep my voice steady and polite.

He appeared hesitant, but he didn't voice any objections. I confidently walked over to the designated shooting area, feeling the gravel crunch under my boots. The sun was high, casting sharp shadows on the ground. He handed me a finely crafted double-barreled shotgun, a work of art that felt perfectly balanced in my hands, the polished wood smooth against my palm.

With a practiced ease, I loaded shells into the empty chambers, the metallic click resonating in the quiet air. The cool metal of the shells was a familiar comfort. I took a deep breath, the scent of gunpowder already in my nose. I shouted, "Pull," and in response, the clay disk target launched from the right, cutting through the open blue sky.

The world seemed to narrow to just me and the target. My heart pounded in my chest, each beat echoing in my ears. I felt the stock of the shotgun press firmly against my shoulder as I aimed. My fingers squeezed the trigger, and the first shot echoed through the air like a crack of thunder. My ears rang from the sound, reminding me that electronic noise-canceling earmuffs didn't exist in this time period.

In that split second, I witnessed the satisfying sight of the clay disk disintegrating into a tiny pink cloud, the shards catching the sunlight. The moment of impact sent a thrill down my spine. Without missing a beat, I tracked the second target and fired again. The deafening sound rang out, followed by another pink cloud as the second disk shattered.

After two consecutive shots, I opened the shotgun, the warm metal releasing a faint wisp of smoke. The finely crafted lever moved smoothly under my thumb, and the gun broke open with a satisfying click, revealing the spent shells. I efficiently popped the shells into the basket beside me, the hollow clang echoing slightly, and then turned to him. He stood behind me, his expression a mix of amazement and respect.

His astonishment was palpable. "My lady, your skill is remarkable."

I smiled, feeling a rush of pride mixed with relief. "Thank you. As I mentioned, I have some experience."

The tension that had been building in my chest eased slightly as I saw the respect in his eyes. For the first time in this strange new life, I felt a sense of accomplishment. Once he was sure that my initial shots weren't a fluke, which they certainly weren't, he left me to my own devices. For hours, I continued to engage with the clay targets, the repetitive nature of the activity oddly soothing. The sharp crack of each shot echoed in the crisp December air, blending with the distant rustle of wind through bare branches. Despite the chilly weather biting at my cheeks and the incredulous glances of any passerby, I paid no heed to their opinions. This was pure, unadulterated fun, and I reveled in every moment of it.

The scent of gunpowder lingered around me as I meticulously deposited the used shotgun shells into the nearby basket. The rhythm of the action—load, aim, fire, reload—was comforting in its precision. Just as I was settling into a steady cadence, a voice behind me, soft and accented, broke through my focus. "Gut gemacht, mein Lieber." (Well done, my dear.)

Startled, I turned to face the source of the unfamiliar voice. Before me stood an intriguing figure, a stark contrast to the predominantly English and French-speaking individuals I had encountered thus far. She was a woman in her early thirties, her blonde hair slightly disheveled beneath her cap. Her cheeks were pink from the cold, and her breath was calm, a shotgun resting casually on her shoulder. Her grey eyes, sharp and inquisitive, scanned me with curiosity. She wore a hunting outfit covered in mud, grass, and even traces of snow, indicating she had been high up in the mountains—a seasoned hunter.

Despite her rugged appearance, there was an undeniable air of sophistication about her. Her beauty was striking, a testament to the elegant charm of the era, but what intrigued me most was that she spoke German. Agnor had minimal interactions with Germans during this time period. Most of our trade was with the British, not because it was mandated, but because trading with anyone else was prohibitively difficult—a fact our politicians rarely discussed, as it allowed them to line their pockets. But recently, things were changing. Specifically due to the escalating tensions at the border.

"Hallo, wer bist du?" (Hello, who are you?) I responded, my own German slightly rusty but serviceable.

The lady before me exclaimed in shock, "Du sprichst Deutsch!" (You speak German!)

"Ja," I replied with a smile.

Her face lit up with excitement. "Ich bin Petra Maybane. Es ist so selten, jemanden zu treffen, der Deutsch spricht." (I am Petra Maybane. It's so rare to meet someone who speaks German.)

"Ariadne Bryant," I introduced myself. "Es freut mich, dich kennenzulernen, Petra." (It's a pleasure to meet you, Petra.)

And that's how I made my first friend.

Chapter 13

XAVIER

December, 1899

A few weeks had passed since Chris left for his station at the border. My days blurred into a relentless grind of work and scrutiny. Mr. Joey Randolph, my father's meticulous chief of staff, seemed determined to drive me to the brink of madness. His watchful eyes monitored every move I made, reporting back to my father as if I were still eleven. Shadowing Randolph, following his instructions without question, smiling on command—it was painfully clear that no one wanted me to express any opinions or thoughts. Without my elder brother—my pillar of support—navigating the mundane and sticky situations that my father's role often entailed became a daily struggle. His absence was a void I felt acutely every single day.

Recently, I had noticed how my father kept meeting this prominent British minister to discuss Anglo-Agnor trading relations. The treaty negotiations were completely stagnant. Both sides were stubborn, refusing to yield, and the rising tensions at the border only made matters worse. All I had realized so far was that these meetings were useless.

Progress was nonexistent. Each session ended in frustration and unresolved tension from both sides.

That made the invitation in my hand extremely strange. Minister Hector Maybane wished to meet me informally—alone. Rumors whispered that his true aim was to annul the trading treaty, but these were vague and unreliable. Still, the request was too peculiar to ignore. On the appointed Wednesday, I arrived at the Agnor Hunting Association. The sun shone brightly despite the cold, casting long shadows over the frost-covered ground. The crisp air carried the scent of pine and burning wood from the nearby fireplace. The choice of location seemed odd. I doubted Maybane had any fondness for hunting, especially in the chilly month of December. The whole setup felt off, and a sense of foreboding settled in my gut.

As I walked through the entrance, the brisk air nipping at my skin, I spotted Maybane seated adjacent to a roaring fireplace, the warm glow of the fire dancing in his eyes. The crackling logs sent occasional sparks flying, adding a sense of coziness to the otherwise tense atmosphere.

"Hello, Mr. Henderson. A pleasure to meet you once again," he greeted me with a diplomatic smile, his eyes sharp and assessing.

"The pleasure is all mine," I replied, shaking his hand. His grip was firm, his skin cool to the touch. We sat down, and he ordered tea for both of us.

"Interesting choice of location, Mr. Maybane," I commented, taking in the serene ambiance. The walls were adorned with hunting trophies, their glassy eyes watching over us.

Our conversation was conducted with an air of calm and politeness, though beneath the surface, we both knew it was a facade.

"It was my wife's choice. She likes such places. But I must thank you for accepting my invitation and coming all the way here."

"That's not an issue. Although, I was caught a bit off-guard by the sudden invitation." I stirred my tea, watching the steam curl upward, mingling with the smoky aroma of the fireplace.

He leaned in slightly, his voice lowered. "I wanted to speak with you, preferably in a setting free from external interventions." By 'external interventions,' he meant Randolph, the ever-watchful shadow who seemed to follow my every move, even attracting the notice of a foreign minister.

"May I ask what this is about?" I asked, trying to mask my growing unease. My fingers drummed lightly on the armrest of my chair.

"You don't beat around the bush, do you?" He smirked slightly, the lines around his eyes deepening. "I heard that the OSE has been creating many problems and your father has been losing his popularity among the masses. What do you think is the probability of him winning the coming elections?"

"I am not sure. He has been losing a few supporters here and there, but it's nothing major enough to start a serious conversation. He has a very strong base of supporters. I think he shall just be fine in the upcoming elections."

"Of course, I know that. It's just that I have recently come across a few people who have been slightly critical of your father's leadership."

"Could you clarify the purpose of this meeting, Mr. Maybane?" I asked seriously, my tone a little harsher than expected—but necessary to not be looked down upon.

Maybane's words carried a certain weight as he continued, "If, for any reason, your father were to lose the elections, it could pose a significant challenge for all of us. As you've likely observed over the years, our queen has shown a particular fondness for your father's leadership. So, should the need arise for additional assistance, please don't hesitate to contact me. I trust you'll remember our conversation, and if circumstances require it, you can convey this message to the appropriate party."

I couldn't help but feel the weight of his implications. Queen Victoria was not our sovereign. We were an independent nation, and yet the British continued to meddle. Maybane's message was clear: he wanted me to act as an intermediary for my father, possibly to facilitate illegal funding. It was a dangerous proposition, and I understood why he had insisted on this discreet meeting. His words were meant for my father's ears, and I was merely a messenger caught in the middle of political maneuvering.

"I appreciate your concern and your offer of assistance," I began, choosing my words carefully, "but I must emphasize that my father's position is not as fragile as it might seem. Opposition and political rivalries are inherent to the democratic process, and while there are critics, his leadership remains stable. As for how Agnor's historical stances go, Agnor has never functioned according to the British Monarch's preferences, have they? But I know your intentions weren't bad, so I will keep your words in mind. I would also like to ask you about the trading treaty. Do you still plan for it to be stuck like this in the future too?"

He maintained the perfect demeanor of a diplomat, smiling politely. "As I and my colleagues have reiterated before, we are more than happy to trade with Agnor if they lower their import taxes on all British goods."

"And as we mentioned before, that doesn't benefit our economy. We do not want British goods to be sold at the cost of our local producers' interests," I stated back, keeping my tone civil but firm.

"Then I guess we are back to square one," he said, his smile never wavering, but his eyes narrowing slightly.

"Minister Maybane," I said, leaning forward, "I hope you understand that my father's resolve on this matter is as unyielding as ever. Any attempts to undermine his position will only strengthen his resolve and, by extension, mine."

Maybane's eyes narrowed further, the smile becoming more of a mask. "I see. Well, it's good to know where we stand. But remember, Xavier, in politics, the winds can change swiftly. Flexibility can be as much a strength as steadfastness."

"Thank you for the tea, Minister. I will convey your concerns to my father."

I was just about to rise from my seat, feeling the tension in the room reaching a palpable peak, when I saw her enter alongside another woman. I recognized her in an instant. They were dressed in hunting gear. The tailored olive-green jacket with brass buttons, a high-collared white blouse, and sturdy leather boots suited her well. She looked captivating—powerful and not to be underestimated.

Mr. Maybane raised his hand and signaled to one of the women. They both spotted him and made their way to our table. He stood up and greeted one of the women with a kiss on the cheek as she inquired, "Hallo Schatz. Wer ist das?"

I recalled hearing about Mr. Maybane's beautiful German wife also being in town. In response to her question, he explained, "Das ist Xavier Henderson. Präsident Benjamin Hendersons Sohn. Er spricht kein Deutsch, deshalb ist es besser, auf Englisch zu sprechen."

I didn't understand a word of their German conversation. However, I did catch my name and my father's name being mentioned, so I assumed it was an introduction of some sort.

And that's when she noticed me. The shock on her face was evident. Her eyes widened, and her lips parted slightly. All she could say was, "You?" Her reaction confirmed any doubt or suspicions I had. It was indeed her. And all thoughts of escaping this table left my brain.

I had replayed that day in my mind countless times, wondering what could have been done differently. But no matter how much I wanted to change things, the one thing I didn't want to change was meeting her. Her behavior, her movements, and every word we exchanged were etched into my memory. I found her intriguing.

But now, seeing her here with Mr. Maybane's wife raised even more questions. This was not company to be messed with. Her cheeks were still rosy from the cold, and she seemed to be shivering slightly. Her eyes darted from me to Mrs. Maybane and back, as if calculating her next move.

Mrs. Maybane immediately asked, noticing our locked gaze, "Do the two of you know each other?"

"We are acquainted, I guess," I replied politely, my gaze never leaving her's.

Mrs. Maybane, with her thick German accent, introduced herself, "That's interesting," and extended her hand to me. "Apologies for the late introduction. I am Mrs. Petra Maybane. Nice to meet you, Mr. Henderson." They both took their seats, and she directed her attention to the girl, asking, "So, Lady Ariadne, how do you know Mr. Henderson?"

She hesitated, a slight furrow appearing between her brows, but she managed to lie her way through the conversation. She was good at this game of lies. "We ran into each other a few weeks back. Also, how can I not know Mr. Xavier Henderson," she replied with a touch of humor, her blush and ladylike demeanor somewhat out of character.

I continued to look at her. A wry smile passing my lips. She looked at me for a brief second as she lied her way through, our eyes locking for a moment. There was an unspoken understanding between us as if she were whispering, 'Play along.' So I did.

Turning to Mrs. Maybane, I inquired, "How was your hunt today?"

She responded, "Quite successful. And how was your meeting? I hope it was more productive than the previous ones. My husband mentioned a bit about it. The trading treaty seems to have everyone in a difficult position."

I replied, "It's a work in progress. Both parties hold valid points and strong convictions. We are striving to find common ground."

Then Mr. Maybane introduced himself. "Hello, Miss Ariadne. Nice to meet you. I am Hector Maybane. The foreign minister of the British Empire. I handle Anglo-Agnor trading relations. Sorry for the late introduction."

Even she could notice the sharp, piercing gaze accompanied by his well-groomed appearance, exuding an air of authority. To any random person, one would flinch in his presence. Get intimidated. But no—not her. She was calm. Absolutely calm.

She replied with utmost politeness and the sweetest, politest smile, but a gaze as unnerving as his, as if telling him, 'Don't look down on me.' "I am Lady Ariadne Bryant. Daughter of Sir Richard and Lady Laura of the House of Bryant. Nice to meet you, Mr. Maybane."

The moment I heard her introduction, I knew why she looked familiar. She was Eugene Bryant's sister. If my memory served me right, he had once described her as an ignorant, shy, and timid child. But looking at the way she conducted herself, all on her own, both during our last encounter and now, I highly doubted that was true.

Mr. Maybane commented, "Oh really. I have had the opportunity to meet your father once. A very excellent man indeed.

How do you know my wife? I have never heard her mention your name before."

She smiled. "Actually, I just met her a few hours back, and we started talking, and now here I am. I hope it isn't a hindrance. I don't want to interrupt anything important."

Mrs. Maybane immediately said, "Of course not. We are friends, and a friend of mine is always welcome at our table." She looked at her husband and continued, "My dear, she is an amazing sharpshooter. Barely missed any of her targets, and such a sweet girl."

That's when Lady Ariadne said, "Sie schmeicheln mir. Sie war die echte Scharfschütze und ich muss nicht einmal erwähnen, wie großartig sie ist."

I looked at her in surprise. Seriously... who is this girl? First, I find her lurking around in Restersburg disguised as a boy amidst a political rally. Then she saves my life and manages to shut down veteran reporters. Now I learn that she is a sharpshooter and that she also speaks German. How did Eugene end up with a unique sister like her? How in the world could he describe someone like her as a shy, timid brat?

Suddenly, both the ladies said in unison, "Wir mussten nur Freunde werden."

"Did something interesting happen?" I asked, raising an eyebrow.

Lady Ariadne looked at me and said politely, "I was just complimenting Petra. Please excuse my manners. I wasn't trying to leave you out of the conversation."

"Don't worry. I am not petty enough to take offense to something like this." I gave her a polite smile. We had some talking to do. As if both of us realizing it at the same time, she said, "I am so sorry, Petra, but it seems I must be on my way. I have a curfew and I need to leave now. However, I would love to meet you once again."

Mrs. Maybane added, "Yes, indeed. And it was a delightful surprise meeting you, Miss Ariadne. We shall have to do this again sometime. Will you be here the coming Wednesday?"

Lady Ariadne nodded with a warm smile. "Yes, I will. I would look forward to that."

Just as she left, even I bid my farewell. It might have come across as unnatural to leave so abruptly, but I didn't care. She waited for me outside. And the moment she saw me, I could see the impatience bubbling. "What are you doing here?" she asked, her breath visible in the cold air.

"I could ask the same question, Lady Ariadne—Eugene Bryant's sister. Missed out on mentioning that tiny detail, now did you?" I commented, raising an eyebrow.

"You know my brother?" she asked in surprise, her expression shifting to a more serious one.

"A little," I admitted, watching her closely. She looked up, her lips curling into a hesitant smile.

She sighed, and her shoulders slumped slightly, but her voice was firm. "Please don't tell him about that. I will get in a lot of trouble."

"Don't worry. You saved my life. It's the least I could do. But may I ask you a question?"

"What do you want to know?" she responded, her guard slightly lowered.

"Why were you with Petra Maybane?" I inquired, concerned.

Her lips moved in thought, and she glanced down at the ground. Her fingers traced the edge of her hair as she casually explained, her voice sincere, "Didn't I just mention on the table, we ran into each other and she was really sweet."

"Don't get offended, but be careful. Her husband is Hector Maybane. It's better to be cautious around them," I said gently.

She nodded, her brow furrowing slightly. "I know. I didn't like the way he looked at me. Too domineering."

"You handled it well. That was a tricky situation," I remarked, meeting her eyes. Her gaze was steady and thoughtful, a silent acknowledgment passing between us.

At that moment, our surroundings seemed to fade into the background, leaving just the two of us.

Later, we walked to the parking lot, the gravel crunching softly under our feet. Her chauffeur arrived promptly, and she offered a brief, warm smile before leaving. That was the last I saw of her, for that week at least.

I wasn't aware of it then, but this girl was going to change my life in ways I couldn't yet imagine. Though it was only our second meeting, something about her intrigued me deeply.

As I watched her automobile disappear into the distance, I couldn't help but think back to our encounter in Restersburg. The more I saw her, the more I realized there was this depth to her that I was only beginning to uncover.

Chapter 14

A RIADNE
December, 1899

I once read a quote, "Technology makes this world a very small place." But was that due to technology, or was the world genuinely small? When I reached home, I couldn't resist asking Father if he had ever met Benjamin Henderson and his family. I secretly hoped he hadn't. How does one casually end up knowing the president and his family?

"Father, have you ever met President Henderson and his family?" I asked, trying to sound nonchalant.

He looked up from his newspaper, raising an eyebrow. "Yes, we have. Our families have moved in the same social circles for years, long before Mr. Henderson became president."

I felt a knot tighten in my stomach. "Really? And what about his son, Xavier?"

Father nodded. "Eugene has worked with him on some recent government policies. Our steel industry may play a modest role in the economy, but it's quite influential in the private sector. Eugene and Xavier often collaborate on such matters."

Father nodded. "Eugene has worked with him on some recent government policies. Our steel industry may play a modest role in the economy, but it's quite influential in the private sector. Eugene and Xavier often collaborate on such matters."

This new information made me grateful for saving Xavier's life; I hoped it would ensure his silence regarding the Restersburg incident. But another question lingered—how would meeting all these people change the history I know? Also, what kind of family had I been thrust into?

But another question lingered—how would meeting all these people change the history I know? Also, what kind of family had I been thrust into?

The following days passed in the same mundane routine. Then, on one particular evening, the Fultons graced our estate with their presence for dinner. My mother and father had occasionally mentioned a girl named Nora, but I hadn't bothered to inquire further. It often irked me how my mother constantly pestered me about finding a suitor while never uttering a word to Eugene. Now, I understood why. Eugene had experienced the same torment as I did, and that realization brought a sense of contentment.

The Fultons arrived at our estate a little after four in the afternoon. Their family consisted of three children: one daughter and two sons. Nora, their second child, was to be married to Eugene in June. I took a moment to process this new information about Eugene having a fiancée. After some obligatory small talk, I seized the opportunity to escape the rather dull drawing room, citing the need to show Nora my new dress for the Cordinburg gala.

As soon as we entered my dressing room, I noticed how Nora's dark black hair, styled in an elegant chignon, framed her soft features. Her light brown eyes were filled with a depth of understanding—something that immediately set her apart. She began recounting nearly every detail of her life, her voice a constant stream of vivid descriptions and insightful observations. Despite her enthusiasm, she maintained a level of maturity that made her easy to listen to.

What perplexed me was that Eugene had never mentioned any of this before. I contemplated asking Nora why she had chosen to marry someone like my brother. Eugene was just so rigid and annoying sometimes. But then my curiosity shifted towards him. Why would he agree to marry her? She is definitely a really sweet girl, but I highly doubt Eugene would like her. Their personalities are almost the opposite. They would drive each other insane and in the end, it would be a boring marriage with absolutely no love. Unless this is the opposites attract kind of situation.

However, I decided to keep these questions to myself. It wasn't my place to pry, and I didn't want to disrupt what seemed like a final decision. However, I did have a hunch that both of them barely had a say in this matter, especially when I observed her father's authoritative demeanor. He radiated an aura of strictness, making me wonder if he was even more demanding than my own mother—and that was quite the statement.

During our conversation, Nora turned towards me, her eyes filled with genuine concern. "Ariadne, I must tell you, I was terribly worried when I heard you were ill. If I hadn't been in France for the past six months, I would have rushed to your side. I hope you can forgive me for not being there."

I responded with an awkward smile. "No, that's perfectly fine. Thank you for your concern."

Her enthusiasm was infectious, but most importantly, I could see that she was kind—someone who truly believed in what she said. She knew exactly how to behave, the ideal way a woman should according to my mother's standards.

I wondered if she used to be close with the real Ariadne. Was that why she felt so comfortable? It made things a little awkward for me because I didn't know her as well as she seemed to know me. Perhaps she thought I was stressed about the upcoming Cordinburg gala and my prospects for finding a suitor during my second season in society. But the truth was, I didn't care about any of that.

She seemed to sense my hesitation. "Don't worry, Ariadne," she reassured me, her voice filled with empathy. "I'm sure you'll find a suitor. After all, I found your brother, and I'm really happy about that. I understand how stressful it can be."

Her words were well-intentioned, but I think she was misunderstanding something. I guessed it would be best to be honest with her, even if it went against the traditional expectations of our society. "Umm... Nora," I said, choosing my words carefully, "I'm not actually that excited about the gala or the prospect of marriage right now. My mother talks about it all the time, but to be honest, if I could skip it, I would.

I know it's not the traditional view, but I want to focus on myself for now. I'm still recovering, and I need that time. And although Mother is pushy, Father and Eugene are currently being really understanding. I hope you are too."

Nora's eyes widened slightly in surprise. Clearly, she hadn't expected such a candid response from me, especially considering the societal pressures that often surrounded young women of our station. "I see," she said, her expression thoughtful. She didn't press further, respecting my honesty, but she was definitely slightly confused.

Before she could start a new topic, Violet interrupted our conversation to announce that dinner was ready. Suddenly, Nora, with a grace that seemed effortless, rose from her seat and extended her delicate arm towards me. Her sea-blue dress flowed elegantly as she did so, and her formal manners caught me by surprise.

With a polite nod to Nora, I rose from my seat. I tried my best to be as graceful as her. She was the perfect example of how Miss Mable would want me to behave. But I was a bit unsure why she was offering her arm. I mean, why would someone need to escort me in my own house to dinner? All these formal mannerisms were so brain-draining and rigid. I mentally rolled my eyes. How did I end up here? I really missed Olivia at times like these. However, Nora, with a perceptive glance, realized my hesitation and confusion. She didn't say a word. Instead, she gently took my arm and placed it upon hers, a reassuring smile on her lips.

With her leading the way, we made our way to the dining room. I think if I am ever in a situation where I don't know how to behave, having Nora around would help. At least she would know what to do and how to behave, and I guess I could just mimic what she does. And so, the rest of the evening unfolded, a curious blend of polite smiles and hidden questions.

The 21st of December in 1899 marked the day when the Cordinburg gala, a dreaded event in my life, had finally arrived. Oh, the relief that it had come at last! This gala had been my living nemesis, causing an ungodly number of problems. Miss Mable had driven me insane over the course of the last two weeks with her endless stream of commands.

"Lady Ariadne, please do this..."

"Keep your posture firm while dancing, Lady Ariadne."

"Remember, Lady Ariadne, graceful moves..."

"Don't eat like that, Lady Ariadne."

The never-ending, excruciating lectures! I swore to myself that as soon as this gala was over, I would cancel them forever. But for now, I had to put up with it and be on my best behavior. If anything went wrong tonight, my mother would make my life a literal living hell by incessantly grilling me about it.

After three painstaking hours of styling hair, makeup, shoes, and the never-ending tiny details, Violet and two other maids were finally done dressing me. I had been a bit reluctant about the 1899 fashion sense, but thankfully, I was proven wrong. The gown I was wearing was nothing short of fabulous. As I gazed at my reflection in the mirror, I was truly shocked at how stunning I looked—nothing like my usual self.

The black halter neck ball gown I wore was a true masterpiece. The halter neckline drew attention to my shoulders and neck, accentuating them with a touch of modern elegance. The gown featured a dozen fine layers of fabrics that cascaded elegantly, each layer adding a touch of glamour. A delicate black net was tied like a bow at the back of my waist, continuing to flow gracefully until it reached the floor. The entire gown was adorned with thousands of tiny crystals, each hand-stitched in an intricate and mesmerizing design that caught the light with every step I took, creating a shimmering effect that was nothing short of enchanting.

A meticulously crafted bun was fastened at the nape of my neck, with loose tendrils of hair framing my face and neck in a style known as a "tendril twist." The overall effect was one of timeless beauty and sophistication, highlighting the elegant contours of my face.

The entire look was enhanced with long black satin gloves that extended gracefully up to my elbows, their smooth fabric adding a touch of elegance to my attire. Adorning one of my fingers was a striking crystal ring, its intricate design shimmering in the soft light of the dressing room—although it was a tad too large for my slender finger, it held a captivating charm.

In my ears, I wore larger silver crystal stud earrings, their weight a testament to their undeniable presence. They harmonized perfectly with my intricately styled hair, catching the light in dazzling bursts. And, of course, my choice of footwear was, as expected, heels—however, this time, they were even higher. Isn't that just the perfect recipe for discomfort and foot agony? I mentally sighed in exhaustion. The gala hadn't even started, and yet I was already done with it.

I descended the grand staircase with deliberate grace, the layers of my gown flowing elegantly with each step. The soft rustling of the fabric accompanied my movements, adding to the sense of occasion. As I approached the bottom, I saw Eugene and Father waiting at the foot of the stairs.

Father's eyes widened slightly, and a proud smile spread across his face. "Ariadne, you look absolutely stunning," he said, his voice filled with genuine joy.

Eugene's gaze traveled from the hem of my gown up to the halter neck and then met my eyes. He gave a small, appreciative nod, his usual stoic expression softening into one of admiration. "You've outdone yourself, sister," he remarked, his tone warm.

I felt a blush creep up my cheeks, flattered by their reactions. "Thank you," I replied, smiling. "Mother chose the gown."

Father chuckled warmly. "She always did have impeccable taste."

I glanced at Mother, who had just approached from the other side of the room. She wore a wry smile. "It was more like I was chosen as his wife because of such qualities," she said, playfully nudging Father.

Father leaned in to kiss her cheek affectionately, saying, "Indeed you were, darling."

The exchange was sweet and genuine, a moment of affection that contrasted with the grandeur of the evening. Despite being such contrasting personalities, I could see the affection between them—more like the bond of good friends rather than a passionate love. Maybe Nora and Eugene would end up like this after some time. With a final glance at my family, I took a deep breath. It was time to proceed to the castle for the highly anticipated Cordinburg gala.

We stepped outside, the crisp evening air brushing against my skin and filling my lungs with its fresh chill. The carriage ride to the castle was filled with a quiet anticipation, the rhythmic clatter of the horses' hooves adding to the sense of expectancy. As we approached our destination, the grand silhouette of Cordinburg castle loomed into view. The intricate architecture, a testament to the craftsmanship of the late 1700s, stood imposingly against the night sky. The castle's majestic charm seemed to emanate from every stone, each one whispering tales of history and grandeur.

Banners adorned with intricate symbols fluttered gently in the evening breeze, adding a touch of color to the grand façade. My eyes were drawn to the old version of Agnor's national flag that proudly unfurled at the top. Though it was a bit too far for my naked eye to discern all the details, the flag loomed with a historical significance that demanded respect. In the days when Agnor was ruled by a royal family, the Cordinburg castle had served as their primary residence—a symbol of their authority and power.

However, history had its way of reshaping the world. The great revolution of 1822 saw Agnor's transition into a constitutional republic, marking the end of the royal family's prominence and position in society. Castles like Cordinburg were now often rented out by the government to nobles or officials to host grand galas and gatherings, the remnants of a bygone era still visible in the architecture and the legacy they held.

As our carriage drew to a halt, Eugene's expression turned serious, his eyes filled with genuine concern. "Ariadne, listen carefully. I know that you have no memories of your past, but over the last three months, you've worked very hard to adjust to this life. After the stroke, you've changed... a lot. It's evident to me, and to everyone you've met during this time. It's quite obvious. But at the gala, you'll encounter many people you were acquainted with in the past—people you might fail to recognize. So please try to adjust a little."

I looked at him suspiciously, arching an eyebrow. "So, dear brother, what you're trying to say is that I can do whatever I want as long as I don't get caught?"

He sighed, rolling his eyes. "That is not what I said. Don't twist my words."

"I'm joking. Relax," I teased, giving him a light nudge. Eugene tried to hide a smile as we proceeded inside, but then Mother's sharp gaze fell upon us.

"Behave yourself, Ariadne," she warned, which only made Eugene's smirk more pronounced.

"Typical Ariadne. Doesn't Mother adore you so much?" Eugene added with a touch of sarcasm, clearly trying to push my buttons. I chose to ignore him, taking the high road this time.

We joined a small queue leading to a massive door, left completely open, with light spilling out invitingly. Ahead of us, various couples and families waited their turn. The butler announced each name and title with practiced precision as they gracefully entered the gala. It wasn't long before our turn came.

Father handed our invitation to the butler, who in turn announced, "Sir Richard, Lady Laura, Sir Eugene, and Lady Ariadne of the House of Bryant."

I held onto Eugene's elbow as he slowly escorted me inside. Despite my disdain for the endless lessons from Mother and Miss Mable, I was almost 0.01 percent thankful today. Thanks to them, I knew I wouldn't make a complete fool of myself in front of so many people.

Inside the grand ballroom, ladies in elegant gowns and men in immaculate suits mingled, the air filled with a subtle blend of perfume and cologne, mingling with the faint scent of polished wood and fresh flowers. The soft hum of conversation created a comforting yet slightly overwhelming background noise.

I leaned closer to Eugene and whispered, "Now I understand why Mother put up such a fuss about this."

"What do you mean?" Eugene asked, his voice low but curious.

"Look around us," I replied, gesturing subtly with my gloved hand. "Almost everyone in the high society circle must be here. This is a gala to flaunt your family's titles and position. It's a statement to society of what each family stands for, and at the same time, it's also an occasion to get matched with a potential 'suitable' suitor."

Eugene nodded, a faint smile playing on his lips. "That's actually quite an accurate analysis of the situation."

Our conversation was interrupted when Nora spotted us. She executed a dignified curtsy and greeted us, "Hello, Sir Eugene. Lady Ariadne. I hope you had a pleasant journey."

Her demeanor had shifted, marked by frequent blinks and a touch of fidgetiness, a hint of shyness, and unmistakable nervousness. Eugene seemed equally out of sorts. Both of them stood there, staring at each other, leaving me sandwiched awkwardly in between. I nudged Eugene's elbow, silently urging him to break the silence.

"Hello, Lady Nora. Our journey was pleasant. How was yours?" Eugene finally managed to say, his voice steady but his eyes betrayed his unease.

"It was nice for me too," Nora replied softly, her eyes darting between Eugene and me. And then there was silence— a very unwelcoming awkward kind. Is this how it's going to be once they get married? I truly hope not. Both of them better get their act together.

In an attempt to ease the atmosphere, I faked a sense of excitement and said, "Hello, Nora. You look absolutely incredible today. I'm feeling a bit parched. Brother, why don't you fetch us something to drink?"

Nora immediately said, "No, it is fine. I would hate to impose."

Eugene chimed in, "It's no bother at all," and excused himself to go fetch the drinks. I was fairly certain he was relieved to have a reason to step away from the awkward encounter for a while.

As soon as Eugene walked away, Nora turned to me, her expression earnest. "How do you think that went? Do you have any suggestions as to how I can get along with your brother?"

Why would she ask me that? I'd only known him for a mere three months, after all. But I couldn't exactly say that, now could I? So, I inquired, "Nora, I must ask... why is there so much awkwardness between the two of you?"

She shyly admitted, "Well, I mean, this is only the third time we've had a chance to really talk to each other without our parents' presence. Once our engagement was finalized, I had to leave for France, and that didn't leave us with many opportunities to interact. You'll understand how it gets once you get engaged to someone."

I was silent for a moment, processing this new piece of information. "I see. That does make sense," I said slowly, trying to imagine myself in her position.

Soon, Eugene returned with our drinks, and we made a few attempts at small talk. Fortunately, we were saved from further awkwardness as a few other people joined our group. The conversation shifted towards how I was feeling, whether I truly didn't remember Miss Dane or Mister Gordeua, and everyone shared a good laugh over some embarrassing incident from the last formal gathering. In summary, it was a peculiar evening, but I was thankful to have Eugene by my side. Even Nora ended up being so helpful.

Most of the discussions revolved around suitors, dresses, and some cherished old paintings, and occasionally featured superficial flattery. Many ladies and gentlemen congratulated Nora and Eugene repeatedly on their engagement. It seemed they were viewed as an ideal match in society's eyes. Both hailed from well-respected families with long-standing connections. Eugene, in particular, had garnered significant accomplishments, while Nora carried herself with such grace and elegance. How could anyone not love them together? They were a perfect picture from the outside.

The compliments and flattery swirled around me, each one more grandiose than the last. The air felt thick with insincerity, and my forced smiles began to ache. I caught myself glancing longingly at the exit, my chest tightening with the need to escape this gilded cage. The chatter of voices and the constant, superficial laughter were like an incessant hum that grated on my nerves.

I watched Eugene and Nora closely. Eugene's posture relaxed, his laugh more genuine, while Nora's eyes sparkled as she gracefully engaged with those around her. They seemed to thrive in the crowd, their earlier awkwardness melting away as they found refuge in the social rituals. It was as if the presence of so many people allowed them to hide in plain sight, no longer needing to fill the silences or worry about forced conversation.

Meanwhile, I felt like an imposter, struggling to maintain the facade of effortless charm. My heart pounded as I fought the urge to flee, feeling more and more like a fish out of water with each passing second.

I was trapped amidst the mindless chatter when, out of the corner of my eye, I caught sight of those familiar ash-blond, curly locks. Xavier Henderson had made an appearance. I had a small hunch that he might attend, but now that he was here, I found myself at a loss for what to do.

Xavier looked different tonight.

He was even more handsome, dare I say, quite attractive. I could feel the hint of a smile tugging at the corners of my lips when I saw him. But I quickly quashed that impulse, laughing internally at the absurdity of it all. Why on earth would I smile upon seeing him?

He stood out in the crowd, impeccably dressed in a tailored black suit that hugged his frame perfectly. A dapper bow tie added a touch of sophistication, while his curly hair, though carefully combed, retained a hint of its natural wildness, giving him an effortlessly charming look. He was surrounded by a group of admirers, both men and women, who seemed captivated by his presence.

As the son of the president, his status and wealth undoubtedly contributed to his allure, but it was his striking features, sharp intelligence, and easy confidence that truly set him apart. His single status only added to his mystique, making him the focal point of many hopeful glances and whispered conversations. Despite having met him just twice, I felt a sense of relief at the sight of a familiar face, even if it was from a distance. It was more of a passing observation rather than a deep interest—something along the lines of, "Oh, he's here. Nice. Let's move on."

In the background, the faint strains of instrumental music serenaded the ballroom. Positioned in one corner of the expansive space was a group of eleven musicians, each wielding a unique instrument. Their harmonious melodies resonated beautifully throughout the grand ballroom, thanks in no small part to the towering ceiling, designed with acoustic perfection in mind.

Among the musicians, some skillfully played the violin and viola, while others drew deep, soulful sounds from the cello and bass. Amidst this symphony of sounds, one instrument stood out—the piano. Its elegant notes added a distinct layer to the music, enriching the atmosphere.

The formal dancing had commenced, and I watched as numerous couples gracefully glided across the polished floor. They moved in perfect harmony, almost like performers putting on a show for the spectators. But that was not the truth. These couples had been rehearsing these dance routines since childhood, practically from the time they were able to walk. Each song had its designated routine, and every child learned them, ensuring a seamless and synchronized display of elegance and tradition on the dance floor.

I still vividly recall the look of despair on my governess's face when I dared to ask her what a box step was. Despite numerous attempts at dance lessons, I was a hopeless student in this subject. Miss Mable often looked like someone who wanted to run away from me, for I was nothing short of a dancing nightmare.

But even after enduring those excruciating dance lessons, I had no real intention of actually dancing with someone at this gala. While the gala had its charms, it also had its flaws. And I was so exhausted by all those forceful interactions. So, when everyone around me found dance partners, I decided to quietly slip away to the balcony. It seemed like the perfect escape from the formalities of the evening.

Chapter 15

ARIADNE

December, 1899

The balcony doors, made entirely of glass, offered an unobstructed view of the sprawling grounds beyond. As I stepped out, the chilly air nipped at my skin, and I instantly regretted my choice of attire for such a cold night. In the carriage, I was wrapped in a thick fur coat, but one of the servants took it upon themselves to take care of it upon our arrival. Nevertheless, despite the cold, it was the sight before me why I decided to stay here a bit longer.

Above, a full moon adorned the inky black sky, surrounded by a multitude of twinkling stars that together created a picturesque nightscape. It was as though they were still, ultra-high-definition captures hanging on the walls of a magnificent gallery. Below, the vast expanse of green lawn stretched out, meticulously manicured plants adorned the landscape, a central fountain glistened in the moonlight, and, as the crowning glory, there was a breathtaking view of distant, snow-capped mountains. It was a scene of pristine tranquility.

Leaning my elbows on the railings, I gazed upward. Just above me, was a dome-shaped structure with intricate geometric designs. Ones that were almost mesmerizing—each pattern a testament to the craftsmanship, drawing my eyes over and over again to its elaborate beauty.

I was lost in the serenity of the moment when a familiar figure slipped onto the balcony—Xavier Henderson.

It was rather comical cause there he was, attempting to hide himself, just like me, although in a more literal sense. He was so engrossed in his own game of hide-and-seek that he didn't even notice my presence as he entered.

Moments later, a group of ladies wandered onto the balcony, and it took them a few seconds to realize I was there as well. They immediately curtsied in a show of respect, and one of them inquired, "Hello, Lady Ariadne. Have you seen Mr. Henderson by any chance? I believe he walked in this direction."

I looked toward the pillar, and our eyes locked once again. And in that brief exchange, I saw the echo of our shared history—the narrowed eyes of suspicion, the raised brows of curiosity, the softening gaze of admiration, and the subtle nod of gratitude.

I bit my lip to suppress a grin, feeling the spark of a playful idea. Should I help him, or should I get him into a bit of trouble for fun? He seemed ready to leave, probably assuming I would reveal his hiding spot due to my delayed response. But then, a sense of reality hit me. This was Xavier Henderson we were talking about. I saved his life, and he helped keep my secret. It was a fair trade. I couldn't play tricks on him like this. I shook myself back to reality and blurted out, "I think I saw him heading towards the east stairs."

Hearing this, they immediately bid their farewells and left. A few seconds later, he walked towards me, scratching his head in embarrassment.

"Hello once again." Xavier rubbed the back of his neck, his cheeks turning a faint pink. "Umm... this is embarrassing. You saw it all, didn't you?"

"If you mean hiding from a few ladies... umm... yes, I did." I couldn't help but smile, the amusement evident in my eyes.

Xavier's cheeks flushed a deeper shade of red, and he ran a hand through his hair, avoiding my gaze. He came to stand beside me, our elbows almost touching but maintaining a slight distance apart. After a few seconds of silence, he asked, "What are you doing here?"

"Enjoying the cool weather and escaping all of that pomp," I said with a wry smile.

"A bit cold for that, don't you think?" His eyes narrowed slightly, then widened, a curious tilt to his head as he studied me.

"That I agree." I nodded, wrapping my arms around myself to ward off the cold.

He leaned in slightly, his interest piqued. "Do you usually come to the AHA?"

"I recently started. It's a new hobby," I said, leaning in just a fraction closer. There was something about him that drew me in as well.

"So you like to hunt?"

"No, not hunt. Trap and skeet shotgun shooting," I corrected.

"Ahh... I see." His lips twitched into a small, amused smile. I wasn't sure what amused him more—my choice of hobby or me trying to correct him.

He gazed at the scenery before us. The landscape seemed to come alive within his deep and enigmatic eyes, as though they were intricately painted on the canvas of his irises. His gaze mirrored the breathtaking view that stretched out before us, capturing every intricate detail. I couldn't help but notice his long eyelashes, similar in length to mine. Both of us fell into a comfortable silence until he whispered,"Thank you. For this and Restersburg. I never got to say it." He leaned closer, his voice barely above a whisper.

I couldn't help but tease him, a sly grin playing on my lips. "Whoa, did Mr. Xavier Henderson just thank me for something? Interesting. Wonder what's wrong with him today?"

He chuckled softly. "I am a gentleman. I know when to thank someone."

"But you didn't the last time. Instead, if my memory serves right, you just continued to argue about breaking high windows, commenting on my weight, pestering me about my identity, and, I don't know, just bombarding me with more questions," I retorted with a playful glint in my eye.

"No-no, young lady. If I remember correctly, it was you who first started pestering me with questions," he countered, a hint of mischief in his voice.

"Whatever. Not that it matters anyway," I replied dismissively, though a small smile lingered on my lips.

Then we were silent, but the silence wasn't awkward; it was comfortable and soothing, like a moment of peaceful respite amidst the evening's bustling activities. It felt like we didn't need words at that moment, just enjoying each other's company in a calming and serene atmosphere. Both of us were barely a step away from each other. He was focusing on the scenery with a deep expression. His elbow now lightly touched mine. That point of contact, in all this coldness, felt warm.

I mentally noted the way he smiled. A smile like that on a face like his should be illegal.

After a long time, he whispered, "So, what now?"

"I heard that you worked with my brother in the past?" I whispered back, not exactly answering his question.

"Yes, I did. Did you know you are nothing like he described?" he commented.

"Oh. That makes sense," I said. "Although, what did that annoying human being describe me as?"

"That's an interesting choice of words, to call Eugene Bryant an annoying human being out of all. May I ask why?"

"That's a secret. But I do pity all your colleagues. Imagine their plight in having to deal with both of you at the same time."

"For someone who has met me just twice, you sure have a very harsh opinion of me. Why is that? What have I done to offend you?" he asked, sounding genuinely surprised.

I pretended to think really hard. "Ummm... let me think." Then, with a sly smile and my eyes slightly wider, I softly said, "Wait, now I remember. Because of you, I got involved in situations where I almost died."

He sighed. "Do you think I like being involved in life-threatening situations?"

"I hope not, because that might make you a masochist," I chuckled, nudging him lightly with my elbow.

"A masochist? Really? You are extremely strange for sure, Miss Ariadne."

"I can say the same about you, Mister Xavier," I replied with a playful grin.

"But seriously, that's not my fault, you do know that, right? About getting involved in life-threatening situations and all. Being that man's son comes with a lot of excess baggage. Had I been given a choice, even I wouldn't have chosen such a lifestyle," he explained, his tone carrying a hint of heaviness and sorrow.

His words tugged at something inside me. There was clearly more to him than the confident facade he showed. I found myself wondering what really made him who he was. What had he gone through to become this mix of serious and playful? How did he manage to handle the pressures of his life and still find moments to laugh? I wanted to uncover the stories and thoughts hidden behind those deep, ocean-blue eyes.

"By the way," he continued, his tone lightening, "How is it that we've never met before? Someone like you isn't easy to miss."

"I don't know," I shrugged.

He gave me a playful look and said, "Why wouldn't you remember? It's rare for a girl to forget someone like me."

I mocked him with a smirk, "Well, unfortunately for you, memory loss can make someone forget even the most unforgettable faces."

Then, suddenly, as if he had just processed my words, he said, "Wait, what? Memory loss-induced personality change?"

I couldn't help but laugh at his shock. I mean, seriously, what was he thinking, being so bold? "Oh, who do you think you are? Why should I be the one to remember you when you couldn't?" I challenged, thoroughly enjoying our playful banter. "Listen more, buddy."

He looked a bit confused but decided not to pry. I could see his soft lips stretching into a teasing smile as he said, "At least you get the joke, buddy," emphasizing the word.

We seemed to both realize at the same time that we were, in a way, buddies now. The word echoed in my head... buddy, buddy, buddy. We were buddies. That's a kind of relationship. But then my brain went into overdrive. Were we just buddies? This didn't feel like just buddies. It felt more. It felt personal. It felt intimate. Was this flirting? Was he flirting with me? Was I flirting back? What were we doing here, really?

I mean, sure, I was 26 in reality but turning 21 soon in this body. But I had never really dated... was this playful banter? Was I overthinking the situation? Ariadne, focus!

We continued our conversation, and it was as if an invisible current flowed between us, keeping our exchange alive and charged with electricity. My mind raced with thoughts and yet, I could carry on our discussion with effortless ease. Internally, however, my thoughts were a whirlwind, dissecting every comment, savoring every smile, memorizing the depth of his voice, and the way his lips moved as he spoke. It was like my mind was on high alert, all while I maintained a poker face on the outside.

A few minutes passed, and we continued to talk. That's when I spotted my mother and Nora's younger brother beyond the balcony's glass doors. It was only moments before they spotted me back.

"Shit... Not again!" I muttered in frustration.

Xavier immediately noticed the change in my expression. "What's wrong?"

"It's my mother... and Borris Fulton," I explained, my voice tinged with annoyance.

"So?" He still looked puzzled.

I sighed. "Well, my mother is obsessed with the idea of me getting married. And since Nora Fulton is marrying my brother, naturally, she wants to set me up with my soon-to-be brother-in-law."

He raised an eyebrow, clearly amused. "All mothers want their kids to get married. Just tell him no."

"Are you serious? It's not that simple. Last time they came over for dinner, I spent the whole evening dodging the topic. I avoided him like the plague, but he's persistent. And now he's dragging my mother into this."

"Wow. Sounds like you've got your hands full," he joked, feigning sympathy.

"It's a lot more difficult and strange than you can imagine. Navigating life as a woman in 1899 is no easy feat."

He locked eyes with me once again, and a warm, knowing smile played on his lips. He leaned in slightly, his warm breath caressing my ear, sending a delightful shiver down my spine as he whispered, "Since you just saved me, let me return the favor."

My heartbeat quickened as his fingers gently closed around mine. They were surprisingly soft, a stark contrast to the chill in the air that sent shivers down my spine. He guided my hand to rest on his elbow, and an unspoken, intimate connection seemed to spark between us. With our steps perfectly synchronized, he began to escort me towards my mother and Borris Fulton.

"What are you doing?" I whispered in protest.

"Saving you," he replied, his words making me feel all sorts of warm fuzziness inside me.

Xavier approached them with a polite smile, "Good evening, Mrs. Bryant, Mr. Fulton. I hope you're having a pleasant evening." It took them a few seconds to process what they were seeing, their eyes widening slightly.

My mother replied, "Hello, Mr. Henderson. How have you been? What brings you to the balcony instead of enjoying the gala inside?"

"I'm very well, ma'am. I was just escorting Lady Ariadne to the dance floor." I shot him a shocked look and nudged his elbow. What! Why? I am not dancing. Xavier Henderson, what the hell are you doing? But he completely ignored my actions.

My mother immediately chirped in excitement, "Oh really! Well then, we won't keep you. Please, go on."

He took my hand and led me inside. The song had just ended, and the heat inside the room, against my icy-cold skin, was extremely soothing until I sneezed.

"Excuse me." Which was followed by a few more.

He kept looking at me and started to laugh. His laugh had a boyish charm to it, a lightness that drew you in, making everything around us feel just a bit brighter.

"Don't laugh!" I scolded, which made him laugh even more.

Once my sneezing fit had subsided, I asked, "What was that? Why would you say that? I'm not dancing."

"Is that how you thank someone? Your mother would have forced you to dance with him anyway. Better me than him."

"How does that make it better? Now she's just got the same ridiculous idea, but with another person."

"Stop being so dramatic. It's just a dance. Look around you. Everyone's dancing with multiple partners. One dance doesn't mean you're getting married. How old-fashioned are you?"

Did someone born and raised in the 19th century actually tell me that I was old-fashioned? Me? Someone who was literally born in the 21st century? I couldn't help but note the irony of this situation. "I am not old-fashioned, you idiot. It's just... Xavier, I'm being really serious. I sincerely cannot dance. I'm horrible at it!"

"That's the problem? Relax. Don't worry and follow my lead. I'm a great dancer."

"No. You don't understand. I'm seriously horrible. Ask Miss Mable. She'll tell you. So please, let's just leave the dance floor. Maybe enjoy a drink or some dessert."

The soft tune of the piano had just started playing in the background. All the partners surrounding us had taken their dance positions. Xavier grabbed my right hand in his and held my waist with his left, pulling me slightly closer. He leaned in, his voice a soothing whisper as he softly said, "Relax. It's rude to leave the dance floor once the music starts. Now come on. Follow my lead."

My face flushed, and my stomach churned with nervous energy. I could feel the heat rise to my cheeks, and my fingers trembled slightly against his as I imagined every eye in the room following our every move. Or maybe it was just my overactive imagination. Either way, the next seven minutes were excruciatingly awkward.

Xavier held my hand and led me onto the dance floor with a grace that made it look effortless. His poise was undeniable, and he gently encouraged me to follow his lead. Mentally, I tried to count the beats and recall the dance lessons I had taken. We moved through a series of intricate steps: forward, backward, a twirl, and a bow. We shifted to the right, joined a line of dancers, curtsied, and offered a polite clap.

Our hands remained intertwined as we navigated the dance, but despite my best efforts, I was always a few beats behind. I stepped on his toes three times and even managed to bump into the couple next to us. Each mistake made me cringe inwardly. But despite my clumsiness, he didn't let go of my hand. Instead, he held it even more firmly and whispered, "Calm down, and don't look so panicked. The key to dancing is maintaining control of your facial expressions. So smile and stop being so rigid. Loosen up."

"I seriously hate you for dragging me into this," I whispered back.

"Shush. Take a deep breath, smile, and follow my lead."

Xavier continued to lead with a composed demeanor, and I gradually started to find my rhythm. I focused intensely on his footsteps, occasionally looking up to smile. Despite his encouragement, I knew I had stumbled my way through. Seven mortifying minutes later, the song ended, and I curtsied as gracefully as I could before quickly guiding him off the dance floor just as the next song began.

"See, that wasn't so bad now, was it?" he said, a touch of amusement in his voice.

I gave him an exaggerated, sarcastic smile. "You're so lucky we're in a ballroom full of people because if we were alone, I'd punch you for that."

"Ouch, so mean," he replied with a playful note. "I was just trying to help. Violence is never the answer."

"They were all laughing at us. Didn't you see?" I sighed, exasperated.

"No, they weren't. Stop being so self-conscious. There are so many people in here, it's hard to get all their attention, even if you are this beautiful. Trust me, I know from experience."

Did he just say I looked beautiful? Immediately, he realized what he had just said, and I could see the corners of his ears turn red, but his expression remained straight. Either he was a complete flirt who was great with flattery, or he was too simple-minded and straightforward. But that didn't matter. Because just like how I noticed the slight change in his expression, he noticed mine. And yes, we gazed into each other eyes a little longer then necessary but both of us were unsure.

The silence at that moment was painstakingly loud. Both of us were unsure what to say next. Luckily at that moment, I spotted a familiar blond wearing a stunning dress who was walking towards us.

I exclaimed, "Petra, du siehst toll aus! Was machst du hier?" (Petra, you look amazing! What are you doing here?)

"Ich kann dasselbe über dich sagen. Das Kleid sieht toll aus. Ich habe dich fast nicht erkannt." (I can say the same about you. That dress looks amazing. I almost didn't recognize you.)

"Hello, Mrs. Maybane. How do you do today?" Xavier interrupted, regaining his composure, just like me. We needed that jolt of reality—desperately.

"Hello, Mr. Henderson. I am good. Nice to see you once again. I must say, you both look great together. What an adorable couple. And both of you pretended you didn't know each other the last time, huh? Don't worry, I am not that dumb. I will pretend I didn't notice." She teased.

He slowly pulled his hand away from mine, leaving traces of warmth behind on my skin. "Mrs. Maybane, thank you for the compliment, but we are not together," he said a bit abruptly.

I joined in, my voice a mix of relief and embarrassment. "Yes, Petra. We aren't."

"Oh, I'm sorry for the misunderstanding. It's just that you two looked so adorable together. Your dance was really cute," Petra said genuinely, though I could sense she wasn't entirely convinced.

I knew it. I had made a fool of myself. Frustrated, I blurted out, "See! I told you everyone would notice my dancing. Why did you drag me onto the dance floor?"

"It wasn't that bad. A little awkward and stiff at times, but seriously... it was fine. Right, Mrs. Maybane?" Xavier tried to reassure me.

Petra smiled warmly. "Of course, dear. It was fine. Why worry so much? Half the people here are either drunk or too preoccupied with the atmosphere."

Eugene joined us then, greeting Xavier and Petra before turning to me with a playful smirk. "Excellent dance, sister. I'm proud you didn't fall, even if you were completely out of rhythm."

"It wasn't that bad for someone who had to memorize all those ridiculous dance routines in just two months. I think I was pretty decent," I defended myself, trying to sound confident.

"Yes, yes. That's why I said I was proud of you," Eugene teased, though his tone softened when he noticed how bothered I was. "You did great."

And just like that, the rest of the evening passed with occasional jokes, champagne, and, as Petra had said, an overall intoxicating atmosphere.

Chapter 16

XAVIER
April, 1900

It's fascinating how often you run into someone when you wish for it most. That was the case for us. Our meetings weren't frequent—maybe once a week, sometimes every two—but they were always meaningful. Her ash-blond hair always stood out, capturing my attention even from a distance. Her silhouette was unmistakable in a crowd. And then there were those days when she knew exactly how to catch me off-guard.

Be it accidental encounters on the bustling streets of the shopping districts or intentional meetings at formal gatherings which she openly expressed her dislike towards—we bumped into each other often. And then there was the Agnor Hunting Association (AHA), where we bumped into each other the most, partly by intention on my part and purely by accident on hers. At least that is what I think.

She did love her visits there.

When I first got to know her, I used to think that she was someone who preferred her own company. It didn't take long to realize I was wrong. In just one winter, she'd built a circle of friends—four, to be precise. There was Petra Maybane for starters. A friendship that she somehow managed to make it work. Then there was Emmeline Ashford, wife of Henry Ashford, whose family runs the Ashford Publishing House. They are new money but a powerful family who got hands on a printing press early on. So now, most publishers publish stuff via them.

Then came Aurelia Montagues, only daughter of Nathaniel Montagues. They were simply a very rich-old money family who had investments throughout industries. A lot of their investments were in British companies. However, they were one of those families who had managed to make investments in the Americas as well on something called the Xerox which no one truly understood. And lastly was Chrisa Emmerson, daughter of Morris Emmerson who was also a prominent member in the political circles more so in the transportation industry. He was the one importing all the new automobiles in the country at exorbitant rates—which somehow people were willing to buy.

Somehow all of them were similar to each other. People who shared the same interests. From shooting competitions to intense book club meetings that often delved into intense debates about politics, cultural norms, or frequently passionate discussions regarding the latest romance stories and theater performances—they covered it all. They were quite the topic amongst the guests and employees. A boisterous bunch who loved to talk and challenge. Few found their meetings absolutely fascinating to come across. Opinions and ideologies clashing in the confines of a library, tucked in the corner with good food, humor, and drinks—it was unique in a way. But for some, they were quite the cultural shock. Not that it bothered her or any of them for that matter.

Who would dare talk back to the only daughter of the Bryant's household or wives and daughters of esteemed influential families?

Yes, it was indeed that kind of circle of friends—One that symbolized power. One that could sway certain political opinions, if they so desired. Yet they didn't. They preferred independence and peace. Freedom to be. The further away from conflicts, the better. Such was their belief. They enjoyed their time in the company of each other, inside the cozy confines of library walls, where no one was welcome, unless invited. And no, it was not some exclusive private group of friends, which other ladies dreamed to be a part of. In fact, on the contrary, many wished to not be associated with them due to the fear of being too vocal and stand out. In a time where blending in and enjoying mundanities was the norm, very few dared to stand out. However, I can't exactly say that their private group of friends was that inclusive either. They were picky too.

But then there was me and her. Buddies of sorts. Two individuals who loved to talk.

Our conversations wove a diverse tapestry of topics, spanning from the weighty matters of gender diversity in politics to the most trivial debates, on why some random dish that she loves is so much better than our traditional Agnorian pie. In reality, she was really fun to talk to. She always had this curious blend of intellect and weirdness going on around her.

Once, when the two of us were caught in a sudden rain, she looked at me with this childish glint in her eye, and with delight, suddenly said, "Did you know this fresh scent after the rain is called Petrichor? It's caused by this tiny bacteria called actinomycete. Isn't it fascinating how these tiny microorganisms have such a significant impact on our everyday lives?"

Firstly, why did she know this? And how did it matter. Yes, she was weird. Truly strange. But fun to be around.

She loved to share the weirdest lyrics and the quirkiest tunes that once again, I'd never heard before. She preferred upbeat music over classics. She was a true explorer at heart. One born with the gift of painting vivid verbal pictures of far-off destinations as if she'd walked those streets herself. She'd recount tales of charming eateries hidden in the heart of East Asia, describing them with such detail as if she had truly tasted them.

But how could she have? A trip like that would have taken months if not years and she would never have had the opportunity so far—to travel alone, so young and so far. She spoke of her desire to witness the vibrant shades of the northern lights, describing their ethereal dance of colors across the Arctic sky. She was a dreamer who had this beautiful spark for life.

Despite my best efforts, I had embarked on countless quests to track down these elusive authors or musicians she often mentioned, scouring libraries and rare stores far and wide. Yet, somehow, these artistic treasures remained just out of reach.

But she was not the only one, who was strange. I think, I was a bit too.

For some reason, I always wanted to tell her how fascinating I found the space to be. And sometimes I even spoke to her about the intricacies of faith. I was a nonbeliever. Surprisingly, so was she. Which was blasphemous if anyone found out. But we knew we could share secrets. I'd love to pester her and tease her. She was so much fun to annoy. But often, when I questioned her about the mysteries of the universe and delve into the depths of my existential dilemmas—she didn't give me a reaction. Instead, all she would say was how one day, I was going to find the answers. And until then, I should focus on the present; for the future is boundless.

It was frustrating at times. Cause it felt as if she knew the answers, but for some reason desired to keep it to herself. For someone who embraced adventure and the thrill of the unknown, it was confusing how she could remain indifferent to the wonders of modern innovation. I mean, how can someone not be captivated by the marvel of the radio or the promise of the submarine? Once, I had come across this young woman named Marie Curie—a scientist hailing from France. She had delved into something called radioactivity, sparking newfound enthusiasm for the future among certain scientific circles. Yet when I told her all this, with an almost ominous undertone, she cautioned that not all discoveries bode well for the future.

However, each time we met, I was swayed by her charm.

It wasn't your typical polished elegance, but her very own style. She carried herself with a touch of untraditional grace, something that might seem a bit unruly at times. However, be it her dreams, her desires, or the way she said my name, those eyes always managed to hold me still and make me pause. She could render me thoughtless at times.

Something had shifted since that conversation on that winter night. I felt it. And I was certain she did too. No matter how much she tried to conceal it, she enjoyed my company, just as I relished hers. It was the simple truth. But what I truly felt unsure of was, was I just another one of her buddies like the rest or would she be willing for something more?

I didn't want to go there. To bring this discussion up. Honestly, I was just scared. What if she chooses to leave or never talk? She was one of my only friends after Chris left. And I would have hated to lose that. So silence was what I chose. And it was not bad of a space to be in. To just be friends, and talk—once in a while or sometimes a lot!

Before I knew it, the middle of April had begun. The cold days were starting to loosen their grip, giving way to a bit of warmth. The world had a different smell now—more floral and earthy. Today marked yet another one of my father's strategic campaign maneuvers, masterfully designed to pluck at the heartstrings of the general public.

He walked onto the podium with his slight limp, a visible souvenir from a war injury he bore—one that he took immense pride in. He never missed a chance to remind everyone of the sacrifices he made for Agnor's freedom, using his limp as a symbol of his dedication and strength.

With an air of authority, he turned his gaze toward the onlookers surrounding the podium, and a hushed anticipation filled the air. The crowd leaned in, their collective attention captured by the hoarse, deep, and resonant timbre of his voice in the microphone, which carried his words to every corner of the assembly as he began.

"Good morning, everyone. I extend my heartfelt gratitude for gracing us with your presence on this significant occasion as we pay tribute to one of the most monumental victories in our history—the Great Revolution. This revolution was no small feat. The liberties we presently relish are a testament to the monumental efforts, unwavering sacrifice, and tireless dedication of our forebears."

With pride and unwavering confidence, he addressed the audience, the room falling into utter silence. The speech unfolded, extolling the victory that led to Agnor's emancipation from a tyrannical rule, transforming it into a constitutional republic. His voice grew stronger with each sentence, filled with the fervor of a man who believed himself the rightful shepherd of a nation.

He proceeded to laud the current administration's accomplishments, emphasizing their readiness to advance into the future and embrace the possibilities of the twentieth century. This event, it seemed, marked the initiation of the government's endeavors toward Agnor's envisioned growth and prosperity. He stressed that this symbolized a shift in the government's approach in light of the new century's arrival.

As he continued, I found myself drifting away, my attention waning. It's not like I didn't know where this was going. To others, his voice sounded majestic. One that brought forward the promise of a great future. To me, it was the same voice that held the power to bring back my deepest fears. Every scolding, each punishment, the constant reminders of how I was one of his living disappointments. He might be a good politician, but he was a terrible father.

Memories of harsh words and cold stares flooded back. The time he berated me in front of his cabinet for a minor mistake, the countless times he compared me unfavorably to my brother. Yet, as the President of a prominent nation, how could he reveal to the world that his family life was a failure?

After what he had driven my eldest brother to do, my mother couldn't even bear to look at him, let alone offer support in his campaigns. I could myself, hardly stand to be in his presence. The burden he had placed on my brother had been insurmountable, to the point that it almost led to his death. My brother survived physically, but the person he once was had been irrevocably changed, lost in the abyss of our father's expectations.

And yet amidst all this, what my father cared for the most was his desperate need to maintain the facade of a flawless president with unwavering family support. He was a man obsessed with control, both politically and personally.

Eventually, he concluded his speech, and applause rippled through the crowd. The time had come to unveil the massive statue, and the excitement was tangible. Cameras flashed as the red cloth fell, revealing the Grey rock sphere, held by a trio embodying unity: one soldier, one citizen, and one common man. A symbol of struggle and responsibility. Sculptor

Rudyard Griffiths and architect Thorpe Yates beamed with satisfaction, toasting to their achievement with a second glass of champagne.

  I exchanged handshakes and smiles with many, while journalists diligently noted every detail of the event. The primary goal of this gathering was to alter public opinion, but the outcome rested in the hands of these journalists. Regardless of the actions taken, the press had the power to scrutinize and criticize. Freedom of the press was a cornerstone of our society, and the government never interfered or censored, recognizing their immense influence. So I truly hoped that their articles would reflect this administration positively. At least positive enough to justify the substantial amount of funds allocated for this event.

  As the afternoon carried on, I found a way to slip away from the bustling crowd. The day had been quite exhausting, especially when you have to maintain this specific image that everyone expects to see.

  I wandered the surroundings, soaking in the architectural marvels and natural beauty of Agnor University. It was incredible. I had once considered studying here, but my father considered it unnecessary. Instead, he insisted on private tutors and British universities. Isn't it ironic, that despite being a leader, he found our educational institutions inferior? He wished to focus more on issues like trade and the military over education.

  The thought made me sigh heavily.

As I was wandering through the hallways, I overheard a group of students playfully teasing each other about the crowd outside.

"Look at that guy," one of them pointed out with a grin. "Trying to impress Miss Thornton in the brown hat, huh? Damn, she's gorgeous as always."

Another student laughed, shaking his head. "No way! She's way out of his league. Plus, there are rumors she's getting engaged soon. Look at the lady behind her; she's the real stunner."

Then, I heard a voice that sounded oddly familiar. "If you want to win someone's heart," she said with a hint of amusement, "don't talk like that in front of the one you wish to impress." Her comment was met with another round of laughter.

A third student, grinning mischievously, added, "And what about that guy over there? He looks like he's had one too many snacks and now needs a bathroom break!"

The familiar voice responded playfully, "Nah, he's probably had too much to drink. Look at the way he's walking. He's got no clue where he is."

Her eyes sparkled with amusement, and I couldn't help but wonder what she was doing here, blending in effortlessly with the students. She wore a simple flowy bottle-green dress, paired perfectly with an elegant off-white hat. Her hair was meticulously woven into a single braid cascading down her back. She sat gracefully on the windowsill, legs crossed, exuding ease and confidence as she commented on the scene outside.

Curious, I entered the room quietly, but the wooden floor creaked beneath my weight. All heads turned, their smiles quickly fading to more serious expressions.

One of the students greeted me hesitantly, "Mr. Henderson... umm... good afternoon." The others quickly followed suit, except for one.

Seizing the moment, I remarked with a hint of sarcasm, "Looks like you all enjoy making fun of our esteemed guests."

"How dare we, Sir. Umm... we were just admiring the... setup," one of them stammered.

Another, more nervous, added, "It's a beautiful sculpture, Sir. Very modern. Very meaningful."

Finally, she spoke up, looking at me with a twinkle in her eye. "Oh, come on, Mister Xavier, you're ruining our fun."

I raised an eyebrow and asked, "Well, Miss Ariadne, is this your idea of fun?"

Stepping away from the windowsill and taking a few strides toward me, she crossed her hands behind her back and responded casually, "Yes, it is. There's no harm in a few jokes to lighten the mood. Plus, no one is getting hurt, right?"

Suppressing a smile, I replied softly, "I see."

Turning to the other students, Miss Ariadne clapped her hands and said, "Come on, boys. Relax. He's not going to eat us. You're scaring them... Xavier." She was always informal with everyone, always addressing people by their first names unless absolutely necessary.

I chuckled softly, shaking my head. "Oh, I'm sorry. That wasn't my intention. I was just curious about what you all were up to. Anyway, why didn't I see you at the ceremony?"

Miss Ariadne pinched the bridge of her nose and let out a sheepish smile. "Caught, wasn't I? Well, boys, it's been nice meeting you all. I hope my suggestions were helpful, and I trust you'll submit your assignments on time. As you can see, I've been summoned downstairs, so I must take my leave."

One of the boys interrupted, his voice pleading, "Wait, Miss Bryant. Are you leaving already? Can't you help us with just one more question?"

She sighed, taking the piece of paper and pencil from his hand with a resigned expression. Perching on the edge of a desk, she quickly scribbled equations, explaining how they needed to substitute one of the variables from the first part and then derive it similarly to question number three. As a few boys peppered her with questions, she provided concise responses, and they nodded in understanding.

Once they seemed satisfied, she stood up, looking at them one last time. "Well, I really need to take my leave now. If you still don't understand what you need to do or how to solve it..." She raised a finger for emphasis, "Go bother your professors, not me."

With a warm smile, she turned to me. "Well, Xavier, shall we head back downstairs?"

I nodded, and we began to walk. As we crossed the hallway and descended a flight of stairs, I asked, "What was all that about?"

She shrugged casually. "Not much, really. I was just wandering around the campus when I saw them gathered in that classroom."

"How do you know them?" I asked, glancing at her curiously.

"I don't," she replied, shaking her head with a slight smile.

I arched an eyebrow. "I assume there's more to that sentence."

She sighed and continued, "Alright, I'll admit it. Out of curiosity, I asked them what they were discussing because they all looked so serious. They were having a tough time with some questions in their assignment, so I offered some suggestions. After helping them solve a few questions, we just chatted for a bit. Which later turned into coming up with theories and scenarios about what the guests were up to. We were just having some light-hearted fun, you know? Anyway, I was also about to head downstairs when you walked in."

I couldn't help but tease her. "So, you just 'casually' helped some university students with their math assignments?"

"Yeah, it was just some high-school-level math. It was pretty easy, honestly." She shrugged again, looking away.

"That wasn't high-school-level math; it was university-level. It's really difficult. Who taught you all of this?" I asked, genuinely curious.

Miss Ariadne hesitated briefly, then answered, "No one. I like to self-study from time to time since I have a lot of free time on my hands. And haven't you realized by now, I am smart." She gave a small, deflective smile—using humor to steer the conversation away. It was a habit that most would fail to notice, but somehow, I always picked up on it.

Then she smiled again, but it wasn't one of her bright, radiant smiles. Instead, there was a hint of sorrow behind it.

This kind of smile often graced her face, as if she carried the weight of a heavy past. It was a stark contradiction to, as she liked to say, her memory loss-induced personality change. Yet, despite the occasional glimpses of her burdened spirit, she never uttered a word about it.

"Hmm... I see," was all I could manage. Her ability to learn such complex subjects on her own was incredibly impressive and yet extremely suspicious. But after all this time, why was I even surprised? Yes, she was smart. To a great extent even.

As we headed back towards the ceremony, she asked, "Do you also aspire to become a politician like your father?"

"No, absolutely not. I despise all of this," I said, the words spilling out before I could even think. I glanced at her to gauge her reaction.

She laughed at my strong refusal, her eyes sparkling with amusement. "Same here. I absolutely despise all of this too. It's so political, biased, agenda-focused, and pointless. Tell me, what do you want to do in the future?"

"I'm not sure," I replied. "You know, I'm already doing well for myself. Helping my father out is sort of my job now. I don't really have a say in all this." I shrugged, feeling a bit resigned.

She looked at me and sighed, a mix of empathy and frustration in her eyes. "That's not what I'm asking, Xavier. I want to know what you want to do. Something you want to study or pursue? Astronomy, researching technology, sports... it can be anything. What's your dream?"

Her question hung in the air, making me pause and think. I pondered for a few moments, but nothing came to mind. "I don't know. What about you?"

She smiled and gazed in the direction of the press. "That. I want to be a journalist." Her eyes sparkled with enthusiasm. But then her expression darkened. She looked at me and continued, "But I can never do that here."

I asked why, though I already knew the answer. As her expression turned somber, she whispered, "You know why. Who would hire a female journalist in this time period?"

It was a grim reality, and I empathized. "I'm sorry. I wish I could do something."

"It's fine," she replied with understanding. "It's not your fault. But thank you for the thought. It's kind of you." She gave me a kind smile, though there was a trace of sadness behind it.

"You know, there's someone I'd love for you to meet," I said, attempting to change the topic.

She looked at me with suspicion. "Who?"

"Remember the man you praised so highly at Restersburg?" I hinted.

"Chris? Is he back from the border?" she asked, her curiosity piqued.

I shook my head. "No, not him. The other one. Demion Marshall, your famous university researcher, and lawyer. Remember him?"

Her eyes widened with surprise and excitement. "Wait, he's here? Really? No way!"

I pointed to the other side of the garden where a few people were casually enjoying some snacks. "Right there."

Her eyes came alive with delight as she noticed his tall figure in the crowd. Demion, as always, was subtly blending in with the surroundings. His brown hair neatly combed, with his dark grey suit.

While Demion wasn't a widely known figure, the way she spoke about him had sparked my curiosity. So, I had to pull numerous strings to access those so-called banned university papers she had praised so highly. Upon carefully reading those papers, I could see why she found them remarkable, just as she had described. The ideology represented inside them was truly incredible, with minute findings and brazen views on the current economic policies that set them apart. With such detailed, evidence-based scrutiny of the current ruling government's economic policies, it's no wonder they were banned. But what he wrote was the truth. His work, despite being banned, contained thought-provoking ideas and a critical eye that had potential to look for the future.

"But what's he doing here?" she asked, her eyes glinting with curiosity.

"He's been hired as an entry-level advisor for the government, focusing on the legal aspects of the Slovain community," I explained.

A knowing smile spread across her face. "Figures," she said, as if it were the most obvious thing in the world.

I raised an eyebrow, puzzled. "Why does that not surprise you?"

"Sometimes, you just have a hunch. And my hunch is he is going to thrive in this role. But how did he get in? Wasn't he working in a private law firm literally a few months back?" she asked, her brow furrowing.

"How do you think? I saw his work. It was really good. Extremely controversial. He has guts—that man. To write something that provocative about the ruling government's policies. But it was good. So I made a recommendation," I said with a wink.

"Oh my god, you didn't! That's awesome," she exclaimed, her face lighting up with excitement.

She was about to head straight to talk to him, but I stopped her with a hand on her arm. "Miss Ariadne, are you truly planning to approach him just like that?"

"Yes, of course. Why?"

"And what are you planning to say? 'Hi there, remember me in Restersburg? I helped you not shoot the son of the president and save an old dying man from excessive bleeding?'" I mocked, raising an eyebrow.

She paused, realization dawning. "Oh, right. Maybe that's not the best introduction."

I shook my head, grinning. "Seriously, despite being so intelligent, you can be quite clueless sometimes. How did you even manage to fool Eugene all this while?"

"Ugh, fine," she replied with a hint of frustration. Then, linking her arm with mine and looking at me earnestly, she added with a mix of politeness and sarcasm, "Could you please provide me with an introduction, Mr. Xavier?"

"And why must I do that, young lady?" I teased, raising an eyebrow.

"Because I asked you," she said, her tone daring me to refuse.

Her brazenness was always funny and endearing. She knew full well that I would help her out. How could I not? We were buddies now.

Chapter 17

XAVIER
August, 1900

Arguing with Demion was like trying to outshine the sun. He spoke only when he was certain, and when he did, his knowledge and conviction left no room for doubt. What surprised me most, though, was his willingness to listen. When he didn't know something, he leaned in, eyes intent and focused, his questions precise and thoughtful. It was as if he was assembling a mental puzzle, each piece fitting perfectly into place as he absorbed every detail. In a world where most people were either talkative or silent, he was a rare blend of both, mastering the art of conversation in a way that made every interaction with him intellectually invigorating.

It was this duality—his ability to speak with authority and listen with genuine curiosity—that drew people to him. It certainly drew me. In a circle of friends where everyone was eager to be heard, Demion stood out by making everyone else feel heard. He didn't just wait for his turn to speak; he engaged, probed, and reflected, making each discussion richer and more meaningful. That's why becoming friends with him was so easy—it felt like he valued your thoughts as much as his own.

Just like me, Ariadne also enjoyed his company. But she had a knack for asking him really tricky questions. One day, while we were drinking tea in the sitting room at the AHA, she asked him out of the blue, "Demion, if given a choice, would you save five people by killing one or save one person by letting five die?"

Demion leaned back in his chair, the leather creaking under his weight. He rubbed his chin thoughtfully. "That's a tough one, Miss Ariadne." He stared at his tea, his fingers tracing the rim of the cup as the steam rose, swirling like his thoughts."Morally, it's a question of doing the greatest good for the greatest number versus sticking to strict principles of right and wrong."

Ariadne tilted her head, intrigued. "Explain."

Demion sighed, setting his cup down gently. "You can approach this problem in two ways. One way would be to act to maximize overall happiness or minimize overall suffering. So, saving five people by sacrificing one would be the choice that benefits the most people. But another way is to focus on the morality of actions themselves rather than the consequences. Is it right to kill one person, even to save five? Morally, that could be considered absolutely wrong."

Ariadne's lips curled into a knowing smile, her eyes narrowing with a playful glint as she leaned slightly forward. "All valid points, but which one would you choose?" She was clearly enjoying pushing his buttons.

Demion ran a hand through his hair, his frustration was evident. "You're putting me on the spot again. If I really had to choose, I'd probably lean towards the greater good by sacrificing one, but it's not a decision I'd ever want to make lightly. Every life has equal value."

Ariadne's playful demeanor shifted; her smile faded and her brows knitted together as she leaned in, her voice lowering. "Interesting. But what if that one person was someone you loved?"

Demion's eyes darkened, his voice lowering. "Oh, come on. That makes things so difficult!" he exclaimed. "Personal attachment can cloud judgment. It's easy to say we'd make the logical choice, but emotions often drive our actions more than we'd like to admit. Honestly, if I could, I'd sacrifice myself to save the loved one and the remaining five people. I'd choose that."

Ariadne shook her head, her tone turning earnest. "Demion, sacrificing oneself is noble but also a coward's way out. You can't always choose to sacrifice yourself to protect others. What if you could protect more people in the future if you stayed alive? Then morally, you'd be choosing to sacrifice yourself today only to let many more people die tomorrow."

The room grew tense, the debate was heating up. I decided it was time to step in. "Oh my god, give the poor man a break, Miss Ariadne. There's no right answer. Also, remember this is all hypothetical. Why are we talking about killing people or killing yourself? Let's just all choose to not die or kill, okay?" I laughed, shaking my head, trying to lighten the mood.

Ariadne just smiled, her eyes sparkling with amusement. Most of their discussions often got heated like this. Neither ever had a proper conclusion, and instead of finding answers, it often left you with more questions. But Demion found something uniquely refreshing about her company. She challenged him and provoked his thoughts, and their conversations often left him contemplating new perspectives long after they ended. It didn't take him long to realize that she was the same person we met in Restersburg, which only made him more eager to learn more about her.

However, aside from being great company, Demion was actually an excellent advisor. After my recommendation, he was initially assigned to provide basic recommendations on minor legal aspects concerning the Slovain community, such as improving sanitation in their neighborhoods. However, it soon became evident to everyone how remarkably capable he was. His keen insights and strategic thinking saw him being consulted on more significant issues like equal wages and job prospects. Even my overbearing father, a man not easily impressed, had subtly mentioned Demion's name one day—a rare nod of respect from someone so notoriously reserved.

Demion's influence grew, and he started attending many official meetings, often accompanying me to various events. It became routine for us to work together daily, navigating the complex political landscape of Agnor.

One afternoon, as we were working through some policy drafts, the soft rustle of papers and the steady ticking of the grandfather clock were the only sounds in the room.

"You know, Demion," I said, breaking the silence. "Just making policies isn't enough. We need to talk to these people, understand their needs and struggles."

He nodded slowly, his brow furrowed with concern. "But it's not that easy. They won't welcome us there. They don't trust us. It's too dangerous."

I leaned back in my chair, meeting his steady gaze. "Didn't you once tell me that change doesn't come from a distance? To truly make a difference, we need to understand their struggles firsthand. That's the only way we can create policies that truly help them."

Demion sighed, running a hand through his hair. "I know I said that. But there's always a right time to act. And you and I both know, these days—it's just not it. Our focus needs to be on improving Agnor's relations with the British. Things are getting really bad."

I sighed deeply, feeling the suffocation of the situation. "All I've been hearing these past few months are heated discussions about this topic. Things are escalating. Agnor has heightened security across all its borders and is even considering imposing curfews to curb tensions. But more curfews mean worse conditions for the Slovain community. They take on all the odd jobs—cleaning streets, sanitation, waste management, working in factories, and what not. If curfews are implemented, they'll be the first to lose their jobs. And if their livelihood is affected, there will be more conflict. As a nation, we can't risk internal conflict when we're already facing external tensions."

Demion nodded thoughtfully, his eyes reflecting the gravity of the circumstance. "You're right. It's a delicate balance. We need to find a way to address their needs without compromising national security. But even I don't know how to approach this."

Weeks later, the inevitable happened: curfews were implemented.

Just as Demion and I had feared, the living conditions for the Slovain community deteriorated rapidly. Our relief measures were falling drastically short, and Agnor teetered on the edge of internal conflict. With all funding redirected to external security, the situation had become truly dire.

Since childhood, I had wrestled with my feelings about the Slovain community. I had seen them break laws and lash out, but I had also seen their pain and the relentless injustices they faced every day. Growing up, they were always painted as the villains—illiterate, filthy, unruly troublemakers. The press thrived on sensationalism, casting them as either dangerous agitators or pitiable victims, depending on what sold best. Meanwhile, my father's colleagues boasted of their righteousness, speaking of justice while turning a blind eye to the systemic inequality they helped maintain.

I felt torn—truly torn. For the first time, I yearned to form my own opinion, to find my own path, unswayed by external influences. I remembered the disapproving looks from my father's colleagues when I had questioned their views, the silent dinners where my thoughts clashed with their words. For once, I needed to break free from their shadow and see the truth for myself. Demion and Ariadne always had this vision to make a difference, questioning everything and seeking answers. But I never had the courage to do any of that. So that day, I made a decision... I had to see all of this myself. I had to meet these people and truly understand what was going on.

On the day of the first meeting, I slipped into their neighborhood around half-past seven, blending into the evening shadows. I had studied the area meticulously, noting the patrol schedules and identifying potential hideouts. A lot of discreet planning had gone into making this work.

To ensure I wouldn't be recognized, I disguised myself meticulously. Ragged clothes hung loosely on my frame, dirt smeared across my face and hands. I tousled my hair and smudged it with grime, creating a haggard appearance. My reflection in a broken window showed a figure no one would associate with the real me. It felt insane how easy it was to discard my real identity simply by changing how I looked.

The first meeting took place in an abandoned church. For almost fifty years, no one had used this space. The church's once-grand facade was now crumbling, with ivy crawling its way up the stone walls, giving it an eerie, yet oddly serene, appearance. Broken stained glass windows cast fragmented, colored light across the dusty structures, creating a mosaic of forgotten stories. Inside, the air was thick with the musty scent of damp wood and decay, and the floor creaked underfoot, littered with fallen plaster and debris that crunched with every step. A worn altar stood at the front, its surface covered in a thin layer of dust that puffed into the air if touched. The flickering candlelight from scattered lanterns cast long, dancing shadows, making the space feel both sacred and desolate. The distant sound of dripping water echoed in the stillness, and the cold, damp air clung to my skin.

That day, as I looked around, I saw people of all ages gathered, their faces illuminated by the soft, wavering light, sharing their struggles in hushed tones and offering solace to one another. The murmurs of conversation and occasional sniffles filled the hollow space, creating a hauntingly intimate atmosphere. As I observed, I saw a few extremists, but most were ordinary people seeking a voice, a platform to air their grievances.

Watching the community huddle together in the cold church, sharing what little they had, I felt the stories of 'unruly troublemakers' unravel. They weren't villains; they were survivors. These were not the criminals or rebels I had been led to believe they were. They were human beings, trapped in a cycle of poverty and prejudice.

But that wasn't enough. I wanted to learn more. Understand more. So I decided to attend another meeting.

At the second meeting, the experience deepened. Planning and preparing for it was exhausting; the anxiety gnawed at me every step of the way. The worst part was the lying. I couldn't tell anyone—not even Demion or Ariadne—because I knew they would try to stop me. And that's why I hated doing this even more. I knew how important it was, but I also knew I was making some rash decisions. Every moment was a tightrope walk between doing what I believed was right and risking everything.

The second meeting was similar—peaceful and heartfelt. I spoke with many members, listened to their stories, and even played with a few children. Their living conditions were appalling: filthy, overcrowded, and suffused with a perpetual stench that clung to my clothes and hair long after I had left. Their reality was far worse than I had ever imagined. They lived in abject poverty, their water polluted, their opportunities scarce. The walls of their homes were damp and crumbling, the air thick with the smell of mold and despair. As I sat there, a profound sadness washed over me. The police were unyielding, even towards the youngest and most vulnerable. How could my father allow this to happen? He had the power to change things, yet he remained passive. For once, I wanted to do something meaningful, but I felt utterly powerless.

One of the biggest risks of attending these meetings was that I couldn't leave the neighborhood until dawn. Hiding in narrow alleys to evade the strict police patrols was both exhausting and dangerous. Each night, I held my breath, praying I wouldn't be caught. Complacency breeds danger. Just because I had evaded capture the last two times didn't mean I was safe or knew how to handle things.

But today, everything changed. During the third meeting, the police raided the gathering.

The room erupted into chaos as officers stormed in, their heavy boots pounding like a death knell. People screamed. Chairs clattered to the ground. The air was thick with fear and sweat. I pressed myself against the cold stone wall, my heart racing. I needed to escape—quickly. I couldn't get caught. But then I saw an officer raise his baton to strike a six-year-old child. Without thinking, I lunged forward, shielding the child with my body. The baton came down hard. Blinding, searing pain shot through me.

"Stop!" I shouted, my voice trembling with desperation. The officer's eyes narrowed. He struck me again, kicking me as I huddled over the child. "You worthless filth, why can't you people ever just stay in your lane," he spat, his words dripping with contempt.

Pain exploded in my side, a white-hot fire that left me gasping for breath. But I refused to back down. I fought, desperate to protect the child, but I was outnumbered. The blows came relentlessly—punches, kicks. The metallic taste of blood filled my mouth. My ears rang with the sounds of chaos—screams, heavy boots stomping, and the sickening thuds of batons hitting flesh. I lost count of the hits as my vision blurred.

As I lay on the ground, beaten and bruised, the cold, hard floor pressing against my battered body, I saw the terrified faces of the Slovain people around me. Their wide eyes glistened with fear and helplessness, the flickering candlelight casting eerie shadows on the walls. I had failed them. The officers dragged me away, my limbs limp and unresponsive, my vision fading in and out. My last thought before darkness claimed me was, I had really screwed up this time.

When I regained consciousness, I was in a cell. The cold stone floor pressed against my bruised skin, sending chills through my aching body. The air was damp and musty, carrying the stench of mold and decay. The dim light barely illuminated the bleak room, casting long, haunting shadows. Pain shot through me as I tried to move, every muscle protesting with sharp, relentless agony. I could hear the distant drip of water echoing through the silence, each drop—a reminder of my confinement. I was in jail, and now, everything was at risk.

Chapter 18

A RIADNE

August, 1900

I was deep in a dream, drifting through hazy images, when a soft touch on my shoulder pulled me back to reality. Violet's voice—usually calm and composed, was edged with an urgency that sliced through the remnants of sleep.

"Please, my lady, wake up," she whispered, her breath warm against my ear.

I squinted, trying to fend off the faint hint of dawn filtering through the heavy curtains. The room was cloaked in the soft blue shadows of early morning, and my body ached to return to the comforting embrace of sleep. Groggily, I brushed her hand away. "The sun's barely up, Violet. Can't it wait a little longer?"

Violet leaned in closer, her face pale and eyes wide with worry. Strands of her usually neat hair had escaped their pins, framing her face in disarray. "I'm terribly sorry, my lady, but it cannot wait. There's a phone call for you in the servant's quarters. Please wake up."

I let out an irritated groan, struggling to sit up. "What now?" I muttered, frustration thick in my voice. I blinked against the dim light, my gaze settling on Violet. Strands of hair escaped her usually neat pins and her crumpled nightgown clung awkwardly to her frame. She never looked like this.

I sighed deeply, trying to make sense of the situation. "Who would call me so early in the morning, especially in the servant's quarters?"

"It's Mr. Henderson—Xavier Henderson. He wishes to speak with you urgently. He called the servant's quarters to ensure that no one would find out," she whispered, her voice trembling slightly.

"What? Are you sure?" I groaned, the early morning grogginess making it even harder to process what she was saying.

"Yes, I am. Please, get up and come with me. I don't want us to get caught. If anyone finds out, you know what problems it could cause." She glanced around nervously, her fingers twisting together.

With a soft groan, I rose from my bed and fumbled for a scarf to fend off the morning chill. "Okay, okay, fine. Let's go."

We walked softly downstairs, moving through the kitchen and the narrow, winding hallways. During the day, this part of Clairborough Manor was chaotic—filled with the clatter of dishes, the hum of conversation, and the bustling footsteps of servants. But now, it was eerily quiet, the silence almost palpable. The faint aroma of last night's supper lingered in the air, mingling with the scent of polish from the well-trodden wooden floors.

We reached the small common area where the servants relaxed when off duty. The room had a cozy yet worn feel to it, with a large, scarred wooden table dominating the center. Surrounding it were mismatched chairs and cushions, threadbare from years of use. In one corner, an imposing black telephone with a rotary dial sat incongruously, its sleek, modern lines stark against the humble, timeworn furnishings. The dim light from a single hanging bulb cast long shadows, making the room feel even more intimate and secretive.

I walked up to the telephone, the floorboards creaking softly under my feet. The cold receiver felt heavy in my hand.

"Hello?" I said, my voice tinged with mild irritation.

As I held the receiver to my ear, a burst of static preceded Xavier's voice. His words tumbled out quickly, breathless and strained. "Ariadne, thank goodness you picked up."

I let out a sigh and replied, "Do you know what time it is, Xavier? Why on earth are you calling me right now?"

"I sincerely apologize. But um... I need your help. I've gotten myself into a bit of trouble. It's a delicate situation, and I'd rather it didn't end up in the newspapers. You know how that can be. I really need your help. Could you please bail me out?"

"Did you get arrested?" I gripped the receiver tighter, my knuckles whitening. "What's going on? Are you hurt? What have you done?" My voice sliced through the quiet, sharp, and unyielding. But underneath the edge, worry crept in.

"Relax. I'm fine. It's not much, I promise. Please just help me out." he pleaded. I could hear the panic rising inside him, along with the occasional crackle of the telephone lines.

I hesitated for a moment before responding, "Xavier, don't you have anyone else who can help you out? What exactly am I supposed to do?"

"I know you're resourceful. Please, figure it out! Get Demion to help," he implored.

I groaned, realizing I was about to be dragged into this mess. "Damn it! Ugh... fine. Where are you?"

He provided me with the address, which I mentally noted. "Thank you so much. I really owe you one."

"Yes, you do. Big time," I muttered before hanging up. I took a deep breath, bracing myself for the day ahead. "I won't be able to leave until a little past ten. Stay put and try not to stir up more trouble!"

"Thank you so much. I won't, I mean, what more trouble can I cause?"

"You better!" I retorted, my voice carrying a mix of annoyance and genuine concern.

Violet kept giving me an anxious yet skeptical look.

I raised an eyebrow. "What's the matter?"

"It's nothing, my lady," Violet replied tentatively.

"What is it?" I insisted.

She hesitated, then spoke carefully. "It's just that... I'm aware of your close friendship with Mr. Henderson, and you were quite firm back there. I understand it's a serious issue, but the way you laid into him was quite a sight. I wish Lady Nora could muster up even half of your courage to stand up to Sir Eugene. Then this household would truly brim with liveliness."

I rolled my eyes, a smile tugging at my lips. "Oh, please, don't make it sound so dramatic. With Nora and Eugene's child around the corner, this house is going to have plenty of liveliness. Although, I can't wait to meet my future nephew or niece." Truly, for a couple who barely knew each other, they sure decided to have a child really fast. Barely one month after their marriage, Nora was already pregnant.

"Oh yes, that is indeed true, my lady." We both laughed at that thought. But nothing helped calm the nerves inside.

The morning light had barely seeped through the curtains as I paced the room, my thoughts racing. The faint chirping of early birds outside did little to calm my nerves. Getting Xavier out without attracting media attention was going to be tricky. I needed backup, and Demion was the obvious choice. Over the past months, our friendship had deepened, and I knew his bond with Xavier was even stronger. If Xavier needed help, Demion would do anything to assist him.

I paused, gripping the edge of the table, the cool wood grounding me. But I also knew why Xavier had called me first instead of Demion. While Demion was brilliant and resourceful, getting Xavier out quietly required money and connections—things Demion didn't possess yet, but I did. Honestly, for someone who knew the future, it was nothing short of captivating to witness him as a legend in the making.

Demion's role in the impending struggle against the British was set to be pivotal. Signs of an approaching war were everywhere, like distant thunderheads slowly rolling in, dark and foreboding. This war was destined to be a turning point in Agnor's history, and now it loomed closer than ever. While many remained unaware of its true magnitude, I knew how horrifying it was going to be. The tension was heavy and inevitable, like the facade of calm air before a storm. The anticipation of the pain and loss to come made every moment feel like a slow march toward disaster. The war was no longer a distant historical event buried in textbooks; it was becoming an unavoidable reality—my reality—creeping into my life with each passing day.

I clenched my fists, my nails digging into my palms. January 3, 1901, loomed so close. Each moment was filled with a growing sense of dread. This conflict would not just shape the fate of our nation but also tear through the lives of those I held dear. Even after ten months here, I felt powerless, drifting through life with no real purpose.

But those thoughts shouldn't occupy my mind today—is what I told myself again and again. Today was about figuring out a way to get Xavier out of jail without anyone finding out. I grabbed the phone, the cold metal sending a shiver down my spine, and made a quick call to Demion. Our conversation was brief but urgent, the tension in his voice mirroring my own.

It took time, but we managed to piece together the grim reality. Xavier had been caught in an abandoned church where he was rounded up during a police raid on the Order of Slovain Extremists (OSE). The authorities still had no idea they had apprehended the president's son, but to make matters worse, Xavier was injured—bruised and beaten.

A shiver ran through me, as if icy fingers were tightening around my heart, spreading chill through my veins. We were dealing with something far beyond our capacity to resolve alone. Charging into the police station was out of the question.

I sat down, my mind racing. Both Demion and I knew this situation was beyond our control. We needed more help—someone with more power and influence. Someone who couldn't be ignored or taken for granted. I wasn't that person. But I knew who was. When I first arrived, I would never have trusted someone like him with any secret. But now, I had no choice. I needed my brother. I needed Eugene.

It wasn't easy.

In fact, it took two whole days to get Xavier out. And that involved a lot of lying. Demion and Eugene skillfully executed a meticulous but effective plan. The forged documents that they created were a marvel of deceptive craftsmanship: employment contracts that looked aged and weathered, as if they had been filed away for years; time-stamped records with carefully smudged ink to suggest hurried, authentic signatures; and identity certificates featuring grainy, indistinct photographs stamped with the family crest.

Luckily, there were no biometrics to verify people's identities in this time period.

All we needed were these documents with the family stamp to vouch for him. The story they concocted was that Xavier—now Luca—had been running errands when the curfew began, leaving him stranded. Seeking refuge in an abandoned church, he encountered a few old men and children. Mistaking the gathering for harmless loitering, he decided to stay. Realizing too late the true nature of the meeting, he found himself arrested before he could report it.

This narrative was rehearsed extensively. One of our contacts within the police station prepped Xavier on the details, ensuring both sides told the same story. With the backing of the Bryant family's first son and Demion's legal expertise, the plan had a solid foundation. Yet, it wasn't just the story that secured Xavier's release; a substantial bribe, which Eugene surprisingly provided without hesitation, greased the wheels.

Eugene's calm demeanor throughout the ordeal was unexpected. He only asked me one thing: "Do you really want to help Xavier?"

His tone was serious, his eyes searching mine. "If you don't, he'll still be okay. The difference is, that everyone will know the truth."

I felt a pang of empathy for Xavier. I knew the consequences he would face if his father found out. Their relationship was already strained, filled with distant memories of a cold, calculative man and a childhood marred by harsh expectations. I couldn't let him face that. "Yes," I said firmly, my voice steady despite the turmoil inside. "Because I'm the only one he can trust to help him."

While Demion and Eugene handled the legal and logistical aspects, I focused on providing Xavier with an alibi. For that, I turned to Emmeline Ashford, one of my new friends whom I had grown close to over the winter. Her family owned the Ashford Publishing House, essentially the gatekeepers of all news. Emmeline didn't ask too many questions—which I was truly thankful for.

Our friendship had blossomed quickly. Emmeline was as fierce as she was intelligent, with a competitive spirit that matched mine. We bonded over our shared love for shooting; afternoons spent at the range often turned into spirited contests that neither of us wanted to lose. Her temper, however, was even worse than mine. She despised the notion of settling down, much like I did, and her fiery independence drew me to her. We reveled in our mutual disdain for societal expectations.

Emmeline was a force to be reckoned with—sharp-witted and unafraid to speak her mind. I admired her resolve, and despite our new friendship, I felt I could trust her implicitly. Unlike Petra, who was a lot older, Emmeline was around my age. So it was also easier to get along with her. She could relate to my day-to-day problems a lot more. Which made spending time with her so much easier.

When I told her I needed rumors circulated about Xavier being out of town, attending events, participating in charity work, or traveling on the outskirts to gather support for his father, she simply nodded. "Consider it done," she had said. No questions asked.

Over the course of the ordeal, we faced numerous close calls. At one point, a journalist got wind of a "mysterious arrest" at the church, but Emmeline swiftly quashed the story, replacing it with a scandal involving a minor politician. Her deft manipulation of the press was masterful, and I couldn't help but marvel at her skill.

The rumors were our most potent weapon. We meticulously crafted a web of deceit, knowing that the best way to conceal a lie was to bury it under a mountain of others. If people discovered that many of the stories were false, they would begin to doubt everything, including the truth. The public's tendency to question the validity of each piece of information worked to our advantage.

We spread layers of misleading tales, each more wild than the last. Stories of secret meetings, false identities, and outrageous scandals flooded the newspapers, creating a smokescreen that hid the real events. Emmeline's network of informants and her keen understanding of public psychology were instrumental. People love a scandal, but they tire of uncertainty. Once they discovered some stories were fabrications, they dismissed all of them.

All those months of working on sports gossip—thanks to Olivia and Mateo—had trained me well to tackle such issues. The skills I honed in crafting salacious tales of athletes and team scandals were now invaluable.

In an era of no internet, our task was both simpler and more challenging. Information traveled more slowly, giving us time to react and redirect the narrative. However, it also meant that once a story took hold, it was harder to counteract. In the stillness that followed our orchestrated plan, I felt a mix of relief and trepidation. Success was fleeting, and the shadow of impending danger loomed ever larger, pressing down on my every thought.

Chapter 19

ARIADNE

August, 1900

It took two agonizing days to deal with the situation, but Xavier was finally free.

Demion helped him get bail, and I volunteered to pick him up. I needed to see his face, to talk, to shout, to understand what in the world had possessed him to do something like this. But the moment I saw him, my heart ached. The anger that had fueled me dissipated, replaced by a deep sorrow.

His face showed it all—the struggles, the fear, the exhaustion. I could see the bruises on his hands and legs, stark against his pale skin. Luckily, his face wasn't marred, but the haunted look in his eyes spoke volumes. He had been through hell. He looked at both of us and sighed, "Thank you, truly."

My throat tightened, and any words I had prepared to say vanished. The weight of his ordeal rendered me speechless. Demion, sensing my inability to speak, stepped forward and broke the silence, his voice gentle but firm, "What were you thinking, Xavier? What happened?"

Xavier's eyes flickered with a mixture of shame and defiance. In a soft, almost hesitant whisper, he admitted, "I attended the Slovain community's meetings."

We already knew what had happened, but Xavier's side of the story filled in all the gaps and loopholes. The implications of what he had just admitted to were tremendous.

The president's son, arrested at a Slovain community meeting on that side of town? The potential public backlash and damage to his father's reputation would have been immeasurable if anyone had found out. What in the world had he been thinking? I had nothing against the community, but Xavier, of all people, should never be associated with them. However, I couldn't say a word.

Xavier looked slightly uneasy as he glanced between us but told us everything. He went on, "It was supposed to be fine. None of this was supposed to happen. I took every possible precaution, believe me! I understand how grave this could have been."

But these excuses were just that—excuses. He sounded like a child who had to confess because he'd been caught. Just because things didn't turn out horribly didn't make it right. In his case, he was fortunate that only something bad had happened. The worst-case scenario was too terrible to even contemplate. I refused to let my mind go there.

Xavier shot back out of nowhere, his eyes narrowing with irritation. He had noticed my silence so far but he knew I was disappointed. "Don't give me that look."

"Look at you in what way? Do you even comprehend the gravity of what you're confessing right now?" I retorted, my voice soft but biting—enough to make him flinch.

Then Demion stepped in as a voice of reason. "I understand what you're saying, Xavier. But you must realize that the government is closely monitoring this situation—your father's government. If anyone had discovered your identity, do you have any idea of the immense trouble you could have plunged yourself into? The chaos and complications you might have unleashed on your family? If you felt so strongly, you could have consulted us about this."

Xavier hung his head, a heavy sigh escaping his lips. "I know. But, I just wanted to form my own opinion for a change without it being dictated to me. Plus, nothing had happened the last two times I went there. So, I really didn't expect things to get so heated this time. It was such chaos when the police arrived. It all happened so suddenly and before I knew it, I was caught."

'Nothing had happened the last two times I went there.' Those words loomed over my head as if someone had just pricked my soul. This was not the first time he went. He had intentionally, repeatedly decided to put his life at risk.

And for what?

An internal conflict—a cleaner consciousness. I know that forming an opinion on your own is important. I have myself had so many dilemmas like this. But this was not the time. Xavier, out of all people, knew how tense the political climate is these days. How could he be so foolish? We are going to go to war with the British barely a few months later.

The blasts, the riots, the poverty, the deaths, the loss that was going to follow in the upcoming months is going to be unprecedented. And Xavier's family was going to be in the center of it all. Every single move he made today was directly going to have an impact on him in the future. But just like everyone—he was oblivious with no idea of what was coming.

As he spoke, I could see how heavily his voice was laden with regret and sorrow, and the shock of what he had witnessed was unmistakable. He was in denial, having just been exposed to one of the harshest living conditions out there. For someone who had been brought up in luxury, where everyone admired him because of his family, the experience had left him truly shaken to the core.

That's when Demion spoke. His voice truly carried the wisdom of the man he would one day become. "I understand the feeling of powerlessness; it can be truly disheartening. It makes us realize our vulnerabilities. But in these moments of vulnerability, we find our true strength. We should also remember that we're not truly powerless. Yes, your father's government has its flaws, some significant ones at that. But it is in acknowledging these flaws that we lay the foundation for meaningful change. However, meaningful change doesn't happen overnight, as Miss Bryant often reminds us. It's a gradual process, marked by subtle shifts in public opinion and the cultivation of gradual ideological transformations. These small ripples in the fabric of society can create waves of lasting change. We must raise our voices, but we must do so judiciously. It's all about timing. You've had quite a shock today, Xavier. But for now, let's get you home."

Demion decided to walk home on his own. I think it was his way of subtly giving Xavier and me some time to talk alone, something I really appreciated today. "I will drop him," I said, then simply got up and left.

As I drove, we both sat in a suffocating silence, each second stretching into eternity. Seven long minutes passed before Xavier finally spoke, his voice a tentative whisper. "Can you say something? Why are you so quiet?"

"What do you expect me to say?" I replied softly, my frustration simmering beneath the surface.

"Anything. Your silence is unsettling."

"Then stay unsettled," I retorted, my voice harsh yet soft, barely masking my anger.

I suddenly pulled the car off the main road, onto a narrow, isolated lane where there wasn't a soul in sight. What I needed to convey, the sheer depth of my emotions, couldn't be confined to mere words while driving. Since he had been so persistently pushing me to speak, I was determined to let it all out in this remote location. I was seething, truly exasperated.

"Do you want me to tell you that you were wrong? We both know you weren't. But you acted foolishly. If you intended to make a stand, you should have been more cautious. Do you comprehend the danger you placed yourself in? If your identity had been exposed at that gathering, you could have faced dire consequences, even death. Remember Restersburg? You've been chased your entire life, targeted for your position, especially by members of that community. I know you're driven to bring about change, but this was not the way.

You were risking your life. Do you understand the gravity of that? How could you be so foolish?"

Words felt inadequate to express the turmoil inside me. Xavier wasn't just a presence in my life; he was one of the most important souls I'd known since I came here. He was woven into the very fabric of my existence, embodying warmth, kindness, and an unyielding spirit despite his scars. I knew too well the pain etched into his heart: the neglect from his mother, the crushing disappointment of his father, and the painful absence of his brother. He had borne an enormous burden. And when his closest friend, Chris, was sent away, he was truly alone.

But now he had Demion—he had me. We were there for him. So why wouldn't he seek us out? Why wouldn't he confide in us? His loss mirrored my own. It was exactly how I felt when Olivia, the person who made me feel the safest, was gone the moment I arrived here. Yet, Xavier's presence had truly helped me.

Since when did I care so much? I hated this feeling of helplessness, the vulnerability of caring deeply for someone. I didn't even realize when my eyes became moist. Seeing how he took his own life for granted pained me. My affection for him ran deeper than words could express. I was consumed by a profound desire to shield him from life's hardships, to protect him from suffering. He just kept looking at me as I laid it all out. His gaze revealed how deeply I was affected by everything.

Tenderly, he reached for my face, his fingertips warm and gentle as they brushed away the tears welling up in my eyes.

"I am sorry," he whispered, his voice soft and heavy with regret.

"Don't look at me," I muttered, turning away. I didn't want him to see me this way. My emotions overwhelmed me. But instead of letting me pull away, he drew me closer. His arms wrapped around me, strong and reassuring. I could feel the steady rhythm of his heartbeat against my cheek.

I had never cried since I started living here in this time period. Even when I woke up an entire century in the past, I didn't shatter. Yet here I was, on the side of a road, letting all my pent-up emotions pour out. His hand gently stroked my hair as I finally allowed myself to break down. The scent of him, a mix of familiar cologne and something uniquely Xavier, filled my senses, grounding me in the moment. The warmth of his body, the firmness of his hold, all combined to make me feel protected and understood. His embrace allowed me to unleash this wave of emotions.

It took a long while to regain my composure, but he didn't let go. He held me close, gently patting the back of my head as if soothing a child.

After a long time, once I finally started collecting myself, I just realized what I was doing. The mental panic arose; I was in the middle of the road, hugging a man, hugging him... with tears in my eyes. In a sudden burst of self-awareness, I gently but hurriedly pushed him away.

Seeing I was doing fine, he suddenly said, "You know there are rumors everywhere that I'm courting you?" His eyes had once again found that playful glint, despite the exhaustion.

"What?" I wiped my face and looked at him. I was sure, I looked like a mess. But so did he.

"If anyone saw us right now, don't you think this would confirm it?" He grinned.

"Shut up. No one believes them anyway."

"Oh really? Even now, when I call your house at dawn? When your brother helps you bail me out? Your family is quite open-minded. How did they end up with such an old-fashioned daughter?" he teased, a playful smile tugging at his lips.

"You could have gotten me in real trouble, you know? You're lucky that Violet was the one who picked up the call. If anyone else had picked up the phone and decided to call my mother, you would have been stuck in jail, and I would have lost all my freedom to go out."

"Or maybe your mother would have pestered you more about us courting." He chuckled. There was something in the way he said it, a hint of playfulness and something more that I couldn't quite place.

"She's already pestering me enough. Let's not add fuel to the fire," I sighed.

He laughed and then leaned in, his face mere inches from mine. His eyes, with that oceanic depth, seemed to peer into my very soul, drawing me in with an irresistible force. It was as if he could see every hidden part of me, every secret I tried to keep. My chest fluttered with an almost painful intensity, a mix of longing and vulnerability. The intensity of the moment mirrored my own racing heartbeat, pounding so hard I thought he might hear it. I felt utterly captivated, unable to look away, every fiber of my being drawn to him.

"Then let me," he whispered, his warm breath grazing my lips.

"What?" I managed to utter, barely above a breathless murmur. Did he just ask me out? The thought raced through my mind. Each word hung in the air like a promise.

"Then let me court you," he repeated softly, his eyes locked on mine, leaving no doubt about his intentions.

I wasn't sure what happened next or how it happened, but I found myself leaning in, and our lips touched. It was the softest kiss, a moment when time seemed to stand still, and our world narrowed to just us. His lips were warm and soft. The brief contact was electrifying, sending shivers racing down my spine and igniting a tingling sensation that coursed through every fiber of my being.

We both pulled back at the same time, slightly shocked by what had just happened. Our eyes met again. His deep ocean-blue eyes were utterly still and focused, like mirrors reflecting my own face back at me. That gaze, unrelenting and magnetic, made it impossible to look away. It always had this effect on me, drawing me in like a tide I couldn't resist.

Then we were kissing again, but this time it was different—charged with newfound intensity. The tenderness was gone, replaced by a heady mix of anticipation and excitement. His hands moved to my waist, pulling me closer, and I felt a shiver run down my spine. The overwhelming wave of emotions surged through me, making my knees weak and my heart pound even faster. Every touch, every movement, ignited a fire within me that I couldn't quite pinpoint but was powerless to resist.

My hands found their way to his hair, fingers entwining in the dark strands curling over his ears as he pulled me closer. For the first time, I kissed him—truly. His nose brushed the side of mine, and I lifted my mouth under his—trying to close the gap between us. Our slow breaths pressed us into each other, and his hands squeezed my sides. The passion that had been simmering beneath the surface was suddenly unleashed. I had no idea what I was doing anymore. Our lips moved together, creating this symphony. Every fiber of me desired this man—longed for him. So we kissed. For a long—long time.

The past two days had been incredibly exhausting, a whirlwind of emotions that took me on a roller coaster ride. I cycled through annoyance, concern, anxiety, dread, shock, anger, and eventually a surprising tenderness and compassion. But in all my wildest imaginations, I could never have expected it to end the way it did—me kissing Xavier Henderson—me kissing him as if there was no tomorrow.

From the night we first met, I knew there was something between us, an undeniable connection that drew me in. At first, it was intrigue and mild attraction. How could I not be attracted? He was beautiful. But as I got to know him, that initial spark deepened into something far more profound. It stirred my soul—a love still in the making, a feeling that left me in awe of its existence.

Yes, I guess—or rather, I knew—I didn't just care for him; I loved him. Deeply. Truly. Utterly.

Chapter 20

A RIADNE
August, 1900

Three days. It had been three days since we kissed, and then he had disappeared.

I stared at the book in my lap, its words swimming into meaningless shapes. The room's silence pressed in on me, making every creak and whisper seem like his footsteps. The book lay open on my lap, its pages a haze.

Why did he disappear like this? What had he been thinking? The questions spun in my mind, refusing to let me move past those few minutes. I couldn't stop replaying our last encounter, dissecting every word and gesture. Had I misread the situation?

I went everywhere, hoping to run into him, but he was nowhere to be found. I thought of calling but I just couldn't bring myself to do it. Did I just get ghosted in a time when ghosting wasn't even a thing? Why hadn't he reached out? He was the one who asked me out—not the other way around.

Deep down, I always felt there was something more about him, something beyond friendship. He wasn't perfect, but he was perfectly imperfect, and that's what drew me in.

He made me feel at ease as if I'd known him forever. His quirks, his ability to be foolish and reckless one moment, then tender and caring the next, made him stand out. With him, I could be myself, and that felt so rare.

But it was the way he spoke to me, always with a quiet respect, that made my heart stutter. His kindness didn't waver, even when I was at my most difficult. We had a balance, a mutual understanding, but did it go deeper than that?

I needed to process this—process him. We needed to talk. Him and me. But he was nowhere to be found.

The ticking clock echoed through the room, a reminder of time passing, and the silence felt deafening. The room, with its high ceiling adorned with intricate moldings and chandeliers casting a warm, golden glow, seemed to mock my turmoil. The ornate, gilded mirror above the marble fireplace added an air of grandeur, reflecting the lush surroundings. Through the tall, draped windows, the afternoon sun streamed in, casting long shadows and illuminating the room's deep, rich colors. Despite the opulence, it felt like a gilded cage.

I sighed for what felt like the hundredth time, the weight of the unsaid pressing heavily on me.

Nora suddenly stood up, her voice loud and agitated, breaking the heavy silence. "My God, Ariadne. What's going on with you? Why are you in such a daze? I'm the one dealing with swollen feet, crazy food cravings, and nausea, and yet I feel more put together than you. What's the matter? Talk!"

Her agitation was somewhat new—a side effect of her pregnancy, I reminded myself. But if she was reacting like this, how badly was I really behaving? I glanced around—no servants, just me and Nora in our enormous living room. I looked at her seriously. I needed to talk to someone; otherwise, I would go crazy. Despite her usually calm demeanor, Nora knew how to keep a secret.

"I don't know what to do," I whispered, closing my book with a thud.

"Is this about Xavier? Did you guys have another argument? Don't take it too seriously. Even I'm used to it at this point."

"No, it's not an argument!" I exclaimed.

"Alright, alright. If it's not an argument, what happened?"

What was I supposed to tell her? That we kissed and everything was perfect and beautiful but then he disappeared? Just thinking about it made me feel so agitated. Everything was perfect. More than perfect. We were lost in each other. Our lips intertwined. Just the thought of that moment made me feel breathless—like my chest felt tighter. It was as if I was on autopilot, doing things, reacting to things in ways that I never ever could have consciously done. And then there he was—reacting the same way, yet making it better.

I now knew one thing—he was skilled. Xavier Henderson knew how to kiss a girl. Truly. Deeply. Passionately. His lips moved with such tantalizing precision, making every touch, every breath, feel electric—irresistible even.

I was kissed once, after high school. It was a fond memory. And I have heard Olivia give me the tiniest minuscule details about her passionate encounters. But this was something different. It was raw. It was instinct. It felt natural. We had acted purely on instinct!

And then when we both had finally managed to stop, there was so much joy in both our eyes. Well, there was also minor panic. This wasn't 2025; it was 1900. Had anyone seen us, the aftermath would have been disastrous. My reputation would have been ruined. I mean, it was still just a kiss. But it was one in public. Out in the open, inside a car. Not that I genuinely cared about societal judgments, but I was aware that such a scandal could have serious repercussions, the kind that no one would willingly subject themselves to.

But even then, we both were so glad it had happened. But now, where was he? He told me he would call—the next day precisely. But he hadn't. He had simply just disappeared. Xavier Henderson, what have you done to me?

I leaned in a little closer as Nora sat down beside me. I tried to phrase all that I was thinking about but all I could come up with was, "We sort of engaged in a moment of attraction, and since then, he has simply disappeared. I need to talk to him, but I don't know what to do. Please help me. What should I do?"

"Wait, is it finally happening?" she exclaimed in excitement, too loudly.

"Shush, Nora. Softly, my dear sister-in-law. Let's not broadcast this to the world."

Nora gave me a perplexed look but realizing her reaction had been loud, tried to calm herself and asked, "What do you mean you engaged in a moment of attraction? He is not even courting you."

My fingers fidgeted with my dress as I avoided her eyes. "That's true, but also not entirely true."

"Explain," she demanded authoritatively. Eugene's personality had been rubbing onto her.

"Well, he kinda asked me if I'd let him court me," I mumbled softly. Even I couldn't control my expression. The sheer excitement that I felt at the prospect of us together now.

"Me goodness, what?" she exclaimed in shock.

But even the excitement couldn't help calm the turmoil within. I found myself on my feet, unable to sit still, pacing the room as I tried to unravel the mess I'd created. The words spilled out of me uncontrollably. "That day, he was sitting so close, saying all those things. I can't explain it; it was the atmosphere, the emotions. I was overwhelmed by what had occurred earlier. And a lot had happened that day. All he was helped me do was regain my composure. But then he started saying all these things—all these perfect things and we just... reacted on pure instinct. I leaned in, and we kissed. And then it just happened. But... he hasn't called since then."

Nora leaned back, her calm facade momentarily slipping as she processed my words. In a serious tone, she asked, "You both kissed. Before marriage. And you didn't even stop him. Heavens, Ariadne Bryant."

At that moment, I felt like Nora's whole world just came crumbling down. Intimacy before marriage, was that even a thing? I am pretty sure she was the kind of person who had no idea what physical intimacy even meant until the night of her marriage. If I was her, this world would have been truly such a frightening one to live in. Especially the world one would live in post-marriage where as a woman, one got so much more freedom to be.

I nodded guiltily. "Ariadne, what were you even thinking? I'm glad things are progressing in this direction. Finally, you both are realizing your feelings for each other. But when a guy asks you for permission to court, the rational thing to do is act shy and ask him to get permission from your parents. Maybe even say yes to affirm the affections, not kiss him."

Just as Nora was about to respond, Violet entered the living room with an urgent announcement. "Lady Ariadne, Lady Nora, Mister Xavier Henderson is here. He urgently wishes to speak with you."

"He's here? Right now?" I asked, baffled. Just like that? So easily?

Nora, acting uncharacteristically direct, replied, "Yes, send him in. They need to talk. I would like to talk too."

Nora suddenly looked at me slightly sternly, "You wanted to talk, and now he is here. So talk to him. Get on the same page. But, Lady Ariadne Bryant, I am serious; in absolutely no circumstances is anything like your last encounter permitted. Five feet apart at all times. I will be waiting outside the room. I am going to give you some privacy. But respect it."

As Xavier entered, Nora looked at him and in a polite manner, said, "Mr. Henderson, it's a pleasure to see you here. Unfortunately, my husband is currently at work. And with the state I am in, I need some rest. Until my husband comes back, I will ask Lady Ariadne to accompany you. I think you both need to discuss many things."

Then she left, and we were alone. The sight of him had once again unleashed so many emotions. He looked better now, his bruises almost non-existent. He was also dressed better. Even from a distance, I could smell his unique scent, a mix of cedarwood and something distinctly him. It was the same scent that had now been imprinted on my memory, triggering a flood of feelings.

He was looking at me—the same way as last time, with that intense gaze. As he slowly took a step towards me once the door closed, I abruptly yelled, "Stop!"

He was taken aback by my reaction, his eyes widening slightly. "Did I offend you by any chance?" he asked gently, but I could see the mental panic rising in his eyes. He was nervous.

I wanted to scream, "Yes! Where had you disappeared? Why have you ignored me? What were you thinking? Do you know how I felt these last three days?" but instead, I remained silent, avoiding eye contact. He took a hesitant step closer.

His worry and anxiety were evident. His hands twitched, his expression a mixture of regret and desperation. In the most caring manner possible, he gently asked, "Ariadne, please say something."

I finally whispered, "You disappeared."

"Ahh... that."

"'Ahh... that'?" I mentally rolled my eyes in frustration. How could someone be this dense?

"I had something important to take care of, and I wanted to look a little better before I came to see you. I didn't want to freak your family out with my bruises. But they took forever to fade," he explained, his words trailing off.

"So you just disappeared? You couldn't have called?" I asked. Frustration boiling under my skin.

"Yes, I could have, but I really wanted to talk in person. I am so sorry. I truly didn't think you were this anxious. Plus, I didn't want your mother to start pestering you again—like you mentioned last time." He chuckled softly.

How could he actually have the audacity to chuckle right now? This man—the nerve of him, to laugh as if everything were just fine. At that moment, I truly wanted to throttle him. To make him suffer. "Oh, I am so glad you find this funny. Now that you are doing just fine and seem to have finally found some time, Mr. Henderson, what do you want?" I snapped, my voice dripping with sarcasm.

"Ariadne, come on. No need to be so harsh. What do you mean by what I want? What do you want? I'm willing to do whatever you wish. Tell me, and I'll follow your command."

I remained silent, letting the tension hang in the air. I knew what I wanted, but how could I make it easy for him? I wanted him to squirm, to feel just a fraction of the agony I had endured these past three days. I waited and waited. Watching his anxiety grow. Now he was finally getting how pissed I was.

"I am truly sorry, Ariadne. Please, don't be mad. I really was getting something extremely important done. I promise I will tell you all about it. Please." He begged me. Pleaded. I could sense the desperation. So I gave in.

This was supposed to be a beautiful moment. A moment of reunion and accepting our feelings for each other. So I let it be. I had the rest of my life to slowly torture and agonize him. So finally, I said, "Fine."

"What?" he asked, his voice tinged with uncertainty. He knew what I meant but still waited for me to say it properly. So I did. "Stop being dramatic. 'Fine' is your answer."

He suddenly stood up. The joy radiated out of him as he processed that I was no longer angry. And then he asked cheekily, "Fine—I forgive you for disappearing away, fine—I was absolutely breathless by the way you kissed me, fine—I have missed you every second of these last three days, Fine—I still hate your guts, or is it 'the fine'—that says yes to the question I asked you that day. There are various ways a 'fine' can be interpreted, Miss Bryant." He slowly walked towards me, saying all these things, and all I could do was roll my eyes.

"'Fine' is your answer, Mr. Henderson. Take it or leave it," I said, trying to keep my tone stern. But as the words left my lips, his arms wrapped around me, pulling me into a tight embrace. The silence in the room seemed to grow a hundred times louder, filled with the unspoken emotions between us.

His sudden joy was evident, his eyes sparkling with happiness. I felt it too—the tinge of suppressed butterflies trying to surge out of me, like an electric current. He pressed his forehead to mine, and we stood there, grinning like a couple of fools. The world outside ceased to exist, and in that moment, all that mattered was the goofy, heartwarming anticipation of what our tomorrow could look like together.

We stayed like that for a good few minutes until he leaned in further, his lips just inches from mine, his warm breath grazing my skin. How could one smell so good—I thought to myself. "Thank you for not running away, especially after how I reacted. I haven't been able to stop thinking about it. About you. About me. About that..." His eyes flickered to my lips.

"Me too." A sly smile tugged at the corners of my mouth.

"You don't hold back, do you?" he teased, a mischievous sparkle in his eyes, as if daring me to reveal more.

"I thought that's what you liked about me?"

"I never said I liked you," he said with a smug grin, his tone dripping with amusement.

"Oh, so you don't like me. You just casually took advantage of an innocent lady, and did things that could potentially ruin her reputation?" I challenged, my voice low and provocative.

"No—no. Let me clarify; the lady took advantage of me in that situation. Who else could possibly take a young man all the way out to an isolated road and do such unmentionable things..." he began, his voice dropping to a husky whisper, trying to defend himself.

"Excuse me? I didn't take advantage of you?"

He looked at me with mock defeat, his eyes smoldering. "Let me complete my sentence. And now I am going to be a gentleman and take responsibility to make you the happiest person I have ever known." His voice was filled with a mixture of excitement and sincerity.

"Firstly, I am not a responsibility. I am perfectly capable of taking care of myself, Mr. Henderson."

"Noted, Miss Bryant."

"Secondly, healthy communication is the core crux of a relationship. So you better not disappear again!"

He nodded, his gaze never leaving mine.

"And lastly, that's quite a claim to live up to, you know, Mr. Henderson?" I smirked, leaning in just enough to feel the heat radiating from his body.

"I know, Miss Bryant, and I promise to do everything to live up to it." He leaned in again, our breaths mingling, the air between us charged with anticipation. His hands tightened around my waist, pulling me closer. My heart raced, the tension between us almost unbearable.

I was in his arms, hugging him back, feeling the magnetic pull between us, when suddenly the door swung open. Nora's abrupt entrance shattered the moment, leaving us breathless and longing.

We both immediately let go and jerked away.

Her eyes narrowed on both of us. "What are the two of you doing?"

"Miss Ariadne Bryant, five feet apart at all times. Do those words mean nothing to you?" Nora sighed with frustration.

Her gaze then fixed on Xavier, and the intensity of it could hardly be described as merely piercing. Xavier wasted no time in offering his apology. But he had completely lost his ability to speak coherently. He was such a nervous mess. I internally laughed at that sight. Oh my god—I loved it. "I am sincerely sorry. I didn't mean to offend you—her—I mean anyone. What I mean to say is..."

Before he could complete what he was trying to say, Nora shifted her attention between the two of us and commanded, "Sit."

Which we obeyed, taking our respective seats on the sofa—intentionally a little far apart. As Nora sat down, I noticed the relief that washed over her face. Her hand resting on her pregnant belly. She often suffered from severe back strain during these late stages of pregnancy. "I'm assuming the talk went well?" Her question was directed at me.

"It was fine," I said, emphasizing the word "fine" in a delightful manner. One that made both Xavier and I smile instantly. But the moment Nora's eyes narrowed on me further as if to reprimand me, I immediately stated, "We are officially courting if that's what you wanted to know."

I could see Xavier's gaze on me. His eyes once again mirrored the depth of what we both were feeling inside. Those suppressed nerves were once again trying to break free inside me. Both of us blushed as our eyes made eye contact.

Nora sighed and remarked, "Heavens, is this what I'm supposed to deal with from now on?"

"What do you mean?" I asked.

Ignoring my question, Nora turned her attention to Xavier and asked, "Mister Xavier Henderson, I must ask you, are you serious about this?"

He replied sincerely, "I am, indeed. And I truly apologize. I had no intention of being disrespectful to Lady Ariadne."

She looked at the both of us as the tension inside the room grew. "Ugh, fine. Who am I to keep two souls, who so obviously can't stay mere inches apart from each other?"

And we both could feel the excitement of what this meant. I stood up and hugged Nora as I kissed her cheek, "Thank you so much, dearest sister-in-law. I promise I will make it up to you."

"Just behave well, the two of you. And Mr. Henderson, I think you should speak to the rest of the family. Make sure to seek their permission. That is how things are traditionally done and I really hope the both of you follow them. Traditions are what make things more structured. Beautiful. Ordered. Respect that. Okay?"

Xavier reassured her, "Of course, I shall. I was planning on speaking to them today if Ariadne had consented."

"Today itself?" she exclaimed.

"I think so. I am sure Mother will be overjoyed. Which means Father and Eugene won't have much of an option," I chimed in, a playful tone in my voice.

"Wait, wait... don't you think you both should wait and maybe ask some other time? Ariadne can give them a bit of a warning too. No need to rush so much." she suggested.

We exchanged glances, but neither of us wanted to wait. Nora sensed our impatience. "Fine, do what you think is fine. Mr. Henderson, please stay back for dinner. I think this is going to be a long and eventful evening." I could see her mentally rolling her eyes.

Xavier nodded, and as if sensing the atmosphere, Nora suddenly instructed both of us, "Go for a walk, you two. Violet will be your chaperone. Now, please leave."

To which we just laughed.

Third-wheeling between the both of us was not something Nora was ever willingly going to sign up for. She didn't even utter a word of warning this time. As if it was her silent permission to be alone—just a little bit. Sort of like a blurred boundary that we could slightly cross but respect. And that is exactly what we did.

Chapter 21

A RIADNE

August, 1900

My fondness for Nora had grown since our first meeting, and she had become a dear friend. But now, my attention was solely on the curly-haired, ocean-eyed man beside me. His slightly disheveled hair and semi-formal attire made it impossible to look away. Every detail captivated me, from the faint freckles on his cheeks to the way his eyelashes bent over his eyes. Today, every nuance stood out, and I wanted to memorize him, to engrave every aspect of him into my being.

He noticed my gaze, and though our eyes locked, neither of us looked away. We continued walking, our steps synchronized yet deliberately apart, along the path around Clairborough Manor. The manicured lawns stretched out in every direction, a pristine image of nature's beauty. I might have admired it more if my mind weren't so preoccupied. The mere two steps between us felt like an insurmountable chasm. I wanted to close the gap, hold his hand, declare to the world that he was mine. Instead, I held back, my fingers curling into fists at my sides.

This feeling was new to me—unsettling yet oddly pleasing. I couldn't fathom how I could feel so possessive about someone. But with Violet chaperoning us, closing that distance was impossible, leaving me mentally exasperated once again.

The gravel path crunched under our footsteps, bordered by carefully trimmed hedges and dotted with elegant stone benches. As we ventured further, towering trees surrounded us, their canopy creating a mosaic of light and shadow on the ground. The sun filtered through the leaves in golden rays, and the air was filled with the earthy scent of moss and the faint fragrance of blooming flowers.

After walking a considerable distance from the main house, Violet suddenly spoke up. "My lady, I apologize, but might I take a short break? I appear to have hurt my ankle and would appreciate a moment to sit."

"Miss Violet, are you all right? Shall we fetch a doctor from the manor?" Xavier asked sincerely. It was another thing I found charming about him—his lack of pretense. He treated everyone with respect, and while he occasionally exhibited a 'rich-kid' attitude, it was never with bad intentions. He always meant what he said and carried himself with a courteous yet sometimes childlike demeanor.

Violet looked at me and smiled knowingly, and I couldn't help but smile back. Her perceptiveness was one of the reasons I was so fond of her, even if she could sometimes be overly dramatic. Today, however, I had no complaints. In fact, I felt like giving her a hug and a bonus if I could. I turned to Xavier and said, "It appears all she needs is some rest. Let us continue our walk. After a few minutes, I'm sure Violet will feel better. Right, Violet?"

Violet glanced at us, her eyes twinkling with a mischievous glint. "Don't take too long on your walk," she said.

I rolled my eyes and started walking away. Finally, Xavier seemed to catch on to what was really happening. He glanced back at Violet, then at me, a slow smile spreading across his face.

Once we were out of sight, Xavier gently took my hand and pulled me closer. The warmth of his touch sent a shiver down my spine. We stood under a beautiful oak tree as he softly whispered, his voice a mix of relief and urgency, "I thought she'd never leave us alone."

I nodded with a coy grin. "Me too."

The breeze swirled around us, but neither of us wanted to let go. His gaze pulled me in deeper with every second. "So when are you going to marry me?" he asked, his tone playful yet earnest.

I laughed softly, the sound mingling with the rustling leaves. "Marry you? You haven't even properly courted me yet, Mr. Henderson."

He slowly kissed my left cheek, then my right. I wanted to spend every single second with this man, get to know him, and learn more about him. But jumping to marriage felt too soon, too rushed. "Wow. Marriage, huh."

"Knowing you, you're going to insist on a longer courtship than usual, right?" he teased.

"How did you know that?" I asked.

His index finger tucked a strand of my hair behind my ear as he said earnestly, "Miss Ariadne Bryant, I've heard you talk about how unfair marriage as an institution is to women numerous times. I know you well enough to understand that you have no intention of getting married to me tomorrow. You want time to make up your mind."

I didn't want him to misunderstand, so I continued, barely thinking about what I was saying. "It's not that I am unsure, you know. I truly care for you and cherish you, Xavier. I don't think words are enough to convey how grateful I am to have met you once I came here. You were the only person with whom I truly felt the most comfortable, the only one I could show my most honest self to. I want to hear you say my name first thing in the morning and late at night. I want to share our laughter and sorrows. I want to hold your hand every time we go for a walk or share a dance. Yes, I do have problems with marriage as an institution," I continued, my tone growing firmer.

"The patriarchal structure of marriage, with its ingrained gender roles and unequal power dynamics, has historically placed women at a disadvantage. It's designed to restrict my freedom, stifle my ambitions, and perpetuate inequalities because I'm a woman. While I believe in love and partnership, I hesitate to enter a union that reinforces these norms. But I also know that the world is not ready for what I want with you in the year 1900," I added.

"The societal pressures and expectations placed upon women to conform to traditional roles are too deeply ingrained. As much as I wish it were different, defying these conventions would invite scorn and condemnation. To be frank, what I want with you is not marriage but partnership. To feel peace when we're together, find comfort in your voice even when we disagree, and feel a sense of belonging when our eyes meet. So yes, I will marry you because that's the only way to experience that partnership. But it would make me feel better if we could have a longer courtship. I want to explore our relationship on our terms, without the weight of everyone's expectations. I want to ensure that when we do get married, it's because we truly want to, not because we feel compelled to conform. My love for you has no correlation to any of these thoughts."

He waited until I finished, his eyes never leaving mine, absorbing every word. After my long rant, he smiled gently, his eyes softening with emotion. "I understand," he said, his voice thick with sincerity. "But please, don't work too hard on your wedding vows. If that's what you say off the top of your head, I don't know if I could ever keep up with you."

A warm smile spread across my face as I felt his sincerity. I reached out and gently touched his cheek, feeling the warmth of his skin under my fingertips. My eyes locked with his, conveying everything words couldn't. "How about we get married on the 17th of February next year?"

His eyes lingered on mine for a long moment until he softly said, "I would love to."

"That's it? Just like that, you're fine? No questions, nothing?"

His eyes crinkled as he started laughing. "Yes, of course. You just agreed to marry me in six months. Nothing you say is going to make it not fine. Although I do know my new favorite word."

I rolled my eyes and whispered into his breath, "Fine, is it not?"

"It is fine indeed." He whispered back.

"Do you know the first thing I ever noticed about you was how your hair curls up over your ear? For some reason, I could never look away."

"Oh really now?" he said, gently holding my hand and intertwining his fingers with mine.

"Uh-huh. But the first thing you told me was far from romantic," I teased.

"Why, what did I say?" he asked.

"Something along the lines of 'shush... they are close' or 'holy shit, you're a girl.'"

"It's not my fault that you were dressed as a boy the first time we met. I was in awe when I saw you berate those journalists with such passion. But you were definitely a bit crazy."

"So were you, Mister. But crazy or not, it's a take-it-or-leave-it situation."

"I shall take every single bit of it. Forever," he said as he gently kissed my index finger.

"Forever, huh?"

He once again kissed the tip of my index finger gently. "Forever."

And then suddenly, I saw the look in his eyes change—a change that mirrored mine. Neither of us could resist the urge any longer. He gently grabbed me by the neck, his warm fingertips contrasting with the cool surface of my skin as his lips met mine.

My breathing was shaky and shallow; his seemed nonexistent. We hovered there for a minute, too close but yet a fraction of a centimeter apart. He stared into my eyes, and I saw the last strand of his sanity break. Once again, we were kissing.

His teeth skated across my bottom lip as I sighed into his mouth, igniting a fire. He kissed me again, this time slower, deeper, rougher. He tipped my mouth up for more, and I grabbed his hair, pulling him closer. He leaned into me, pushing my back against the rough bark of the tree. A soft gasp escaped my lips as the texture scratched against my back.

He braced one hand on the bark behind me and held me close, unable to resist the magnetic pull. His teeth caught my bottom lip again, this time a little harder. The pleasure I felt from that sensation ran deep, sending shivers down my spine. This man was mine, and I was his.

Despite knowing we had to stop, the impropriety of our actions, neither of us wanted to. In that moment, propriety felt like a distant memory, and all that mattered was the intensity of our connection. Our breaths came fast and shaky as our tongues intertwined, exploring each other with an intensity that bordered on desperation. His hands scraped my waist, a touch I adored, and I responded by pressing myself closer against him.

Deep down, I was aware of the risk, the societal constraints that bound us. The fear of discovery, the potential for scandal, lingered in the back of my mind. But in his arms, those fears seemed to melt away, replaced by a fervent need to be closer, to feel more.

And then, suddenly, he sneezed, breaking the spell that had enveloped us. The wind was getting colder, and reality crashed back in, but all we could do was laugh.

"Let's go back. You still need to get permission from my family," I stated cockily as I stood up.

He chuckled, his eyes still bright with emotion. "Of course, Miss Bryant. But I promise you, this isn't over. Not by a long shot. But before all that—remember that really important task that I had to get done? Well, the real reason why I was three days late was because she took forever to make them." He turned around and pulled out a beautiful silver box from his jacket pocket. It was shining silver with intricate engravings, adorned with delicate floral patterns and scrolling vines, each line meticulously etched by hand.

I froze, recognizing it immediately. I let go of his hand and stepped back. "How do you have this? Who gave this to you?" I asked, my voice trembling.

Xavier's smile faded as he saw my expression. "I had it made for us. Isn't it beautiful? The lady who crafted it even told me a story to go along with it."

"Was she an older woman, with curly grey hair and a lot of wrinkles?" I asked urgently, my heart pounding.

"Yes, how did you know?" His expression grew serious, concern clouding his features. He looked at me for a moment longer, then gently touched my cheek. "Ariadne, what happened? Why are you crying?"

Memories of her cryptic words and the unsettling feeling she left behind surged through me. Her presence, her knowing eyes, everything about her felt like a puzzle I couldn't solve. She was more than just an old woman; she was a catalyst, a keeper of secrets that had altered the course of my entire life. And now, seeing those rings again, I felt a wave of fear and awe wash over me.

My cheeks were wet, and I was breathing heavily. In a shaky voice, I said, "This box has our engagement rings, right? Platinum bands. One with diamonds in the center."

His eyes widened. "How do you know all this? These rings didn't exist until this morning. I just saw them a few hours ago myself." His voice was laced with confusion and concern.

I continued to sob, the weight of realization crashing over me. The old woman's story echoed ominously in my mind: "The contents of this box hold the power to defy time and help its owners fulfill their destiny. But no one has been able to open it since that young couple's tragic death."

I had managed to open it in the future. I had worn the ring. I was able to do all those things and then got stuck in this time period. Bloody 1899—no, 1900. There was a war coming that would shake the whole country to its core. And Xavier and I were destined to die. Young tragic couple's death. That was us.

Xavier's face was a mix of fear and confusion. "Ariadne, please. Tell me what's going on. You are scaring me."

"Xavier, I know this is going to seem absolutely insane, but can we please go and see her now? I really want to explain everything, but I am so confused right now. I don't know what's happening. All I know is that we need to find her, or things are going to go terribly wrong." My voice trembled with urgency, my eyes pleading with him.

"Now?" he asked, eyebrows furrowed in concern.

"Yes, now," I insisted, my eyes wide and desperate.

"But we need to ask your parents' permission at dinner today," he replied, glancing toward the manor.

"There's still some time until dinner. We'll make it back in time. This is really urgent," I said, my voice rising with anxiety.

"What's more urgent than me asking permission from your parents for your hand in marriage?" he asked, exasperation creeping into his tone.

"Our lives and so much more! I don't even know. All I know is something really bad is going to happen, and I need to talk to that woman right now!" I exclaimed, my voice cracking.

"Ariadne, I have no idea what you are talking about," he said, his confusion turning into frustration.

"Xavier, I truly want to explain things, but you won't understand," I said, my voice cracking with desperation.

"Try me!" he shot back, his eyes blazing with determination.

"Xavier, for the love of God, can you please just listen? Please, I beg you. Take me to her now!" I shouted, my voice breaking as tears welled up in my eyes, my hands clenched into fists at my sides.

He stepped closer, his expression softening as he gently wiped the tears from my cheeks. "Fine," he said softly, his voice steadying me. "But please, stop crying. Will you tell me what all this is about later?"

I nodded, my voice shaky but earnest. "I promise."

"Let's go," he said, taking my hand firmly in his, a determined glint in his eyes.

Chapter 22

XAVIER
August, 1900

We left immediately. Violet informed Nora, who looked ready to protest until she saw the grave look in Ariadne's eyes—a look everyone in the house recognized. It was the same look she had the day she lost her memories and returned home from the hospital. They knew better than to stop her, especially when she looked like that.

Ariadne never seemed to realize just how much she affected those around her. She was lucky in a way because her family was always supportive and encouraging, even when they didn't fully understand her. I learned this as I spent time with Eugene—sometimes for work, sometimes for fun, and occasionally just to run into her.

Eugene once told me about the emptiness in her eyes, the rebellion in her behavior, and the completely different person she had become overnight.

"It wasn't just her personality that had changed; her knowledge and demeanor shifted too. She was smarter, wittier, bolder, but also more impulsive—a force to be reckoned with," Eugene said, his voice tinged with awe. "She used to be quiet, but now... now she's a whirlwind."

I could see what he meant. I saw it every time she walked into a room.

One day, Eugene and I were in the study, the scents of parchment and leather filling the air as we pored over some documents. The steady ticking of the grandfather clock was the only sound until Ariadne burst in, her presence commanding attention as always.

"We need to talk about the business," she declared, skipping any pleasantries.

Eugene looked up, raising an eyebrow. "What's wrong now?"

"The reliance on British suppliers—it's absurd," she said, pacing the room with restless energy. "We need to diversify. The Germans have better materials and terms."

Her father entered the room, sighing deeply. "Ariadne, it's not that simple. Politics—"

"Politics be damned!" she snapped, her voice sharp and clear. "We're shackled by tradition, and it's costing us. Why are we importing from the British when it's so expensive, Father? I've been talking to Petra. She has connections with reputable German firms. I've gone over the fine print. It can actually work. We can also send some people from our side to verify the possibilities. If we get the government to give us a permit, this could really make a difference."

I kept quiet, knowing how futile it would be to rely on my father's administration for support. Ariadne knew my limitations too well to expect my help in this regard.

Eugene glanced at her, then back at the documents, shaking his head slightly. "It's risky."

"It's necessary," she insisted, her eyes gleaming with determination. "If we don't adapt, we'll fall behind. Why can't you see that?"

Her father rubbed his temples, a gesture of mounting frustration. Eugene and I were sure he would dismiss her ideas. Instead, he surprised us.

"And what if this backfires?" he asked, his voice weary but genuinely curious.

Ariadne leaned forward, a smile of excitement spreading across her face. "Then we'll deal with it. But doing nothing is worse."

Her determination was infectious. Within weeks, the Bryant steel industry was abuzz with discussions about German imports. Eugene and her father were reluctant at first, but they started to see the logic in her arguments. They ran the numbers and scrutinized the facts and figures. What she said made sense, but they knew getting permits would be the real challenge.

That's when Demion entered the picture. His influence in the government was growing, and with his intellect and persuasive skills, a few ministers began to pivot. Without the Bryants' backing or Demion's persuasive skills, this whole plan would have failed. But together, they had the ability to make it work.

This shift was profound. The Bryant household, once rigid and predictable, began to embrace innovation and risk. Modernization as people would call it. Yet what no one knew was that the catalyst for all this change was Ariadne. She was the common link between all the stakeholders who made things possible.

No one outside the family truly knew of her pivotal role. To the world, it appeared as if Richard and Eugene Bryant were the masterminds behind this unconventional strategy. Yet, at the heart of this transformative decision was Miss Ariadne Bryant, influencing change from the shadows.

The entire household had started to see the world differently, influenced by Ariadne's fearless questioning and relentless pursuit of better solutions. Her presence was a catalyst, not just for business decisions but for personal growth and adaptability within the family. She had transformed not only their steel industry but the very fabric of their daily lives.

This was why it was so shocking to see her this way today.

Ariadne was a force of nature, a brilliant light that drew everyone in. She was funny, witty, bold, and breathtakingly beautiful—someone who made me feel like I could break free from the confines of my upbringing. Her laughter was infectious, her intelligence sharp, and her spirit unyielding. But behind her captivating eyes, there was a shadow, a loneliness and sorrow that only a few could see.

I had seen her in so many moments—arguing passionately and joking playfully. I had watched the way she looked at me evolve over time, from cautious curiosity to something deeper and more intense. Around me, she had started to laugh more freely, argue more fiercely, and eventually let her guard down. She felt free to show me her true self, unburdened by societal expectations.

She was the same radiant woman who had kissed me an hour ago, who had chosen to marry me. Yet now, seeing the hope drain from her eyes was terrifying.

During the ride to the shop, Ariadne stared out the window, lost in thought. Her silence was a stark contrast to her usual vibrant self. I glanced at her, my heart aching to comfort her, but I no longer knew what to say. She seemed so far away, trapped in her own world. The distance between us felt impossible to bridge, and it hurt more than I could put into words. I felt useless, afraid that anything I said might push her further away. Watching her like this, so isolated, made me feel helpless and alone, as if everything we felt for each other mere minutes ago was now lost in a void.

As we reached our destination, the sky had transformed into an ominous canvas of dark clouds, swirling with menace. The wind picked up, carrying the sharp, earthy scent of impending rain. The clouds rolled in with a foreboding intensity, casting long, eerie shadows over the river. The air grew cooler, its bite more pronounced, and the leaves rustled violently, whipped into a frenzy by the gusts.

The shop was right by the river, a tiny, rustic-looking store run by an old woman whose family had managed the establishment for over 200 years. It was quaint, with heavy stone walls and a sign that creaked gently in the wind. Inside, the atmosphere was a blend of opulence and mystery, illuminated by the warm, golden glow of gas lamps that cast flickering shadows on the walls.

Trinkets and jewelry adorned one side of the shop, glinting in the lamplight. Each piece seemed to tell a story, with intricate designs and aged patinas hinting at their long histories. On the other side, unique books filled dark wooden shelves, their leather bindings cracked with age. Some books were bound with strange letters, while others had delicate clasps. The air was filled with the cool, metallic scent of silver and gold mingling with the rich aroma of worn leather. There was also a faint hint of incense that smelled of sandalwood and spices—all blending together to create a unique and enchanting fragrance.

I had stumbled upon this place while hunting for books Ariadne had mentioned during our conversations. Somehow, this shop was the only one where I could find a few of them. As we entered the shop, Ariadne rushed in, her eyes scanning the room. The shop was devoid of customers. Neither of us could find the old woman. Instead, we found a young boy organizing things at the back. He was about around eleven years old, with well-combed hair, khaki shorts, a white shirt, and suspenders.

I approached him casually. "Hey kid, where's the old woman who works here?"

The boy looked up, his eyes widening slightly. "Oh, I'm not too sure, Sir. She left a few hours ago for some work," he replied, his voice polite but uncertain.

"Did she tell you where she was going?" Ariadne asked.

The boy shook his head. "No, ma'am. She just said she had some errands to run and would be back later."

Ariadne's expression tightened with frustration. "I don't need your apology, kid. Can you tell me where I can find her? It's urgent."

"I really don't know, my lady. Why don't you come back tomorrow morning? I'm sure she'll be back by then," he said politely, trying to be helpful.

"No, it's important I meet her today!" she insisted, her voice rising slightly, betraying her agitation.

I glanced at her, noting the impatience in her behavior, which was so out of the ordinary. "Why don't we come back tomorrow?"

"No! It has to be today. She's going to run away again, just like the last two times. It's a pattern," she retorted, her voice trembling with barely contained anger.

"How do you even know her?"

"I don't know her, Xavier! She just pops into my life whenever she wants and turns everything upside down. She's a bane in my existence," she exclaimed, frustration evident in her voice.

"Okay, calm down. No need to get angry. She's not here, and there's nothing we can do about it. Let's go and come back another time," I said, trying to soothe her.

"No!" She stomped outside the store, heading towards the backyard, possibly into the old woman's house.

I grabbed her hand. "Ariadne, stop! We can't just barge into her house, no matter how urgent it is. It's rude."

"Let go, Xavier! Can't you just leave me alone? Please," she pleaded, her eyes filled with a mix of desperation and anger.

"Just a few hours ago, you told me we would spend the rest of our lives together. Forever, remember? And now you want me to leave you? What happened to finding peace in each other's presence, to finding comfort in each other's voice when we disagree? Were all those just false words?"

Ariadne's expression softened for a moment, but the storm of emotions in her eyes didn't subside. She pulled her hand away, and that's when we saw the old woman walking in the backyard towards us.

"Well, well, it appears you have found me again, young lady," the old woman said, her voice calm—almost amused.

Everything in Ariadne's demeanor changed the moment she saw her. "You!"

Chapter 23

XAVIER

August, 1900

It was all so sudden.

I had never seen her this way. The rage that burned in Ariadne's eyes was like a deadly black fire ready to consume everything in its path. "Why would you do this to me?"

But the old woman somehow still managed to stay calm. Her gaze was steady, her tone calm and measured. "Calm down, dear. All I did was sell you one of my trinkets. I told you quite clearly that its contents held the power to defy time, to help its owner fulfill their destiny. Remember, the box chooses its owner, not the other way around. The box chose you for a reason. Isn't that a good thing? I never told you to open it. That choice was yours alone. But perhaps, it's a choice that will reveal more than you ever anticipated."

"How is anything good in this situation? Because of you, my entire life was turned upside down. You sent me here with no way back home. Why? And these bloody rings..." Ariadne harshly placed the box back into the old woman's hands. "You can bloody keep them!"

"Such anger is not good for a young girl like you, my dear," the old woman sighed.

"Don't—just don't. Why would you do this to me?" Ariadne demanded, her voice trembling with a mix of fury and desperation. "You sent me here, where I know no one, where I had to start my life from scratch. And now you mock me with this cruel joke? You told me this box was made by a young man in the late nineteenth century for his lover, that it held the power to defy time and help its owner fulfill their destiny. You said no one had opened it since that couple's tragic death. You tricked me into buying it!"

Her anger was a storm, but suddenly, the rage melted and turned into deep sorrow. Pain that could be seen. She was crying now—profusely, her eyes red and swollen, tears streaming down her face. Her voice cracked with every word, each syllable laced with heartache. It was as if it hurt to form words, but she did.

"If what you said is true—and I know it is because you're the reason I'm living almost a century in the past—then the young man who asked you to make these rings was Xavier. The one I want to spend my life with, the one I love. And if that wasn't enough, now you're telling me he is going to die a tragic death. What the hell is wrong with you?" Her voice wavered, the raw emotion palpable. "Why would you do this to me? And what destiny was I supposed to fulfill in this year?"

The old woman's expression softened. "My dear, I was always honest with you. And all that you just said just recounts our past encounters. So what is it that you really want to ask? Why don't you ask that? The real questions that keep bothering you."

I could see how broken Ariadne looked at that moment. She turned to me, her gaze full of love but so full of pain. Then she looked back at the old woman and said, "Is he really going to die?"

The old woman laughed, a sound that sent chills down my spine. "Look at the irony. You want to know if he is going to die and not whether you are going back? Interesting. Why is that? All I have heard you do is complain about how you wanted to go back. How you missed your life there. Is that no longer the case? Do you actually want to live here now?"

"Please just tell me, is he going to die? Can I prevent it?" Ariadne asked, her voice breaking.

"Discussing a man's future in front of him is never a good thing, my dear," the old woman replied cryptically.

I could no longer contain my confusion. What in the world were they even talking about? I grabbed her shoulders, my grip firm but not harsh, trying to pull her back to reality. "Ariadne, look at me," I urged, searching her eyes for a sign of reason. "I am not going to die. I am twenty-three and fit, with no health issues. Everyone in my family is healthy. So trust me—I am not going to die." My voice softened, a desperate plea for understanding. "And what does she mean by 'go back'? Go back where?"

"Xavier, I am so sorry," she said, her eyes filled with a heartbroken expression.

"Can someone please tell me what's going on?" I demanded, my voice rising with frustration.

The old woman sighed deeply, her gaze steady and calm. "Dear girl, you are going to go back to your time period very soon. In fact, on the very date you came here. You were just a guest who was meant to live here for a year in that body. You are a divine intervention. A facilitator. A catalyst for things to flow and move in the right direction. I just needed you here to simply exist, and start the ripple effect."

"What does that even mean?" Ariadne's voice trembled with desperation and confusion. "I am no one. Why me?" Her eyes darted around the room as if searching for answers. "What did I even do here? Chase some nonsensical hobbies, travel, fight with this girl's mother, and argue with this girl's brother. If I was truly here to bring change and fulfill some destiny by traveling to the past, I would have prevented the blood war that's going to start next year. Saved Agnor from British rule. Saved the Slovain community from the injustices they faced. Prevented Restersburg's destruction." She shook her head, tears welling up in her eyes. "But what did I ever change? I did nothing but simply live my life."

"It's always amusing how you humans think you are the main character of the story. Didn't you hear what I said? You were a divine intervention. A facilitator. A catalyst for things to flow and move in the right direction. I never said you were meant to save people or be the one to propel change. And as for what you changed, remember that even when a tiny butterfly flaps its wings across a continent, it can cause a storm on the other side of the planet. You were a living being who did more than just flap your wings—you talked, lived, educated, fought, and did your best to survive in an environment that wasn't in your favor. What I needed from you was your survival instinct. Imagine the chaos you created. Imagine how much you changed and influenced without even knowing it."

"What?" Ariadne's eyes were wide and unfocused, her voice barely a whisper as if she couldn't fully grasp the words.

The old woman stepped closer, her gaze piercing and unwavering. "If you truly want to know what you changed, let's start with the most obvious one," she said, her tone measured and deliberate. "You are the reason Demion Marshall joined the government. How do you think a nobody like him would have gained the power to change the fate of Agnor and ignite the freedom struggle? It's the same for all pivotal figures. We need facilitators to propel change. Someone to push the first domino for the domino effect to begin."

"Think about it," the old woman began, her voice steady and patient. "How did Gandhi become a freedom fighter? It all started when he was thrown off that train in South Africa because of his race. That single act of discrimination created a ripple that eventually led to a movement for India's independence. Or consider Alois Schicklgruber, Hitler's father. If he hadn't been born out of wedlock and later married Klara Pölzl, Hitler wouldn't have existed. Only two of Hitler's parents' children survived infancy—imagine if he hadn't been one of them. Would the horrors of the Holocaust have happened? Maybe, but they happened because of him. These seemingly small events set off ripples of destiny that changed the course of history. Do you think it's all just coincidence?"

My mind spun. Gandhi? Hitler? The Holocaust? These names blurred together, each one more alien than the last. I felt my heart race, each beat echoing in my ears. The old woman's words seemed to drop like stones into a vast, turbulent lake, sending ripples that reached deep into my core. I clenched my fists, trying to anchor myself, but the weight of her revelations pressed down on me, making it hard to breathe.

The old woman continued, "You want to know what you changed? Let's start with Chris Baxton. Remember the brown-haired fellow you met at Market Square? If you hadn't intervened, Mister Xavier here might have gotten severely injured. Chris would have had to resign for failing in his duty. Without your help, he wouldn't become the senior officer whose contributions are crucial in the great war next year."

"But we lost that war!" Ariadne shouted, her eyes wide with frustration. "That war plunged Agnor into ruin. Xavier's father's government fell because of it. My dad told me time and time again how much our nation suffered. Blasts, riots, poverty, countless deaths. So why does it matter if Chris gets promoted?"

"Such naivety, young girl," the old woman replied, shaking her head. "You need to lose something to gain something. Losing the first war was necessary for Agnor to be rebuilt. Do you think that foolish Benjamin is capable of leading this country to greatness? That man can't even confront his own fears and parades a fabricated war injury. Did you know he shot his own leg to get an early discharge because he was too afraid to participate? He used deception to gain political praise for a battle he ran away from. Chris needed to be posted at the front to become the commander-in-chief for the final war and lead this country to victory in 1947. You did what you had to do. So, good job. What more do you want?"

Ariadne's face contorted with anger and sorrow. "If I did such a good job, why sentence Xavier and me to a tragic fate? You sent me here without my consent, and now that I truly love someone, you condemn us to a fate where he dies and I go back to the future. Isn't that too cruel? If you're so grateful, reward me. Reward us. We are not mere puppets in your story."

"Fine, point taken," the old woman said, her tone softening slightly. "But I'm sorry. I have nothing against this man, but he is fated to die. It's a necessary inflection point in history for certain wheels of fate to turn. It's far too complex for me to explain, and honestly, I don't have the power to change that. Is there anything else you want to know? Since you think I've been so harsh and cruel."

All this time, I was too stunned to speak. In just a few minutes, I had learned that Agnor was on the brink of a devastating war, that Demion would become a crucial hero for our nation's freedom—my best friend Chris was destined to lead the fight as commander-in-chief, bringing about freedom forty-seven years later. I had discovered that Ariadne was from the future and would soon return there. And as if all this wasn't enough to shatter my reality, I had just learned that I was going to die. The dark irony of it all twisted inside me, making me want to laugh at the absurdity and cry at the inevitability.

A bitter laugh bubbled up inside me, the irony of my situation almost too much to bear. Mustering all my courage, I looked at the old woman and asked, "If you know the destruction and death that's coming, why don't you stop it? You clearly have the power to create interventions. Why not intervene to bring about positive change instead of negative? Why ruin something to build something new? Why cause so much death to bring forth a new era?"

The old woman's eyes softened, a hint of sadness in her gaze. "Wise questions, young man. But sometimes we need to lose something to gain something. Destroy something to build something new. Loss creates value for creation. This is how the universe has worked far beyond your mind's understanding. It's a cycle of destruction and rebirth, necessary for growth and evolution. Without the hardships, without the struggles, the triumphs would mean nothing. It's in the crucible of adversity that true strength is forged, and from the ashes of the old, the new arises, stronger and more resilient."

The old woman's words hung in the air, heavy with the weight of a truth that was difficult to accept. The philosophy she tried to explain was far too harsh, yet it carried a certain undeniable logic. Life, with all its complexities and seeming injustices, was a tapestry woven from countless threads of cause and effect, each strand a result of the others, each action leading inevitably to the next.

Ariadne's face was now a mask of anguish, her eyes searching mine for answers. But I knew she found none. Cause all she could see was despair. "So, what now?" she whispered, her voice breaking. "What do we do now?"

The old woman's gaze softened, just a fraction. "Just live the way you lived so far. Cherish the time you have. Very few get the gift of saying goodbye to their loved ones. I gave you that. You make the most of the moments you are given, and you trust that your actions, no matter how small they seem, will have a profound impact. You, Aria, were brought here for a reason. Your presence has already set the wheels of destiny in motion. Embrace it, and know that even in the face of loss, there is purpose. And remember, Xavier and you also had to meet for a reason."

We were caught in a current of fate far beyond our control, yet within that current, we still had the power to make choices, to love, and to live fully in the time that we had.

The old woman turned to leave, her figure blending into the shadows as she opened the door to head back inside her house. As she disappeared, her final words lingered in the air, a cryptic whisper that hinted at the unknown. "Remember, it's not the length of time that defines a life, but the depth of the moments you live. Sometimes, what seems like an end might merely be the beginning of a new and unexpected chapter."

Ariadne and I stood there, holding each other, trying to find comfort in the uncertainty of our future. The weight of what we had just learned pressed down on us like a physical burden, heavy and suffocating. And then she broke down, her body trembling as she cried, full of anguish. Her sobs were raw and heart-wrenching, the sound of someone grappling with overwhelming hopelessness. She clung to me as if letting go would mean losing everything.

"Xavier, I don't want you to die. I want you to live. I want to grow old together. I want to get married and live our lives. Why? Why do we have to go through this?" Her voice was thick with desperation and despair.

I held her tighter, my own heart breaking. "Shush... I don't know what's going to happen anymore. To be honest, I barely understand anything. But all I know is that all we have in control is this moment, today. She said you were supposed to be here for just a year. What does that mean? When did you first come here?"

"2nd of October," she whispered, her voice almost drowned by her sobs.

"But that's less than a month away," I said, realizing too late how those words would affect her. Ariadne's crying intensified, her grief palpable.

"Okay. It's fine," I lied, trying to sound reassuring. "We have a month. We make the most out of it. I have so many questions you need to answer. I want to know the time you come from. How many people are fortunate enough to know what the world would look like in the future? One month, Ariadne. One month to live fully with each other."

"Stop pretending. You know how horrible this is," she said, her voice hollow. The emptiness in her words mirrored the void that was opening up inside me. A tear rolled down my cheek, and I knew no amount of pretense could keep us together.

"No matter how strong I try to be, I've just learned I'm going to die, and you're going to leave me in less than a month. I am sorry but I am trying really hard to hold it together. But I can't... not anymore." My voice cracked, betraying the fear and sorrow I felt.

Ariadne looked up at me, her eyes red and swollen, filled with anguish that matched my own. "This isn't fair, Xavier. None of it is fair. I finally found you, and now I have to lose you. How am I supposed to go back and live my life knowing that?"

I brushed a tear from her cheek, my hand trembling. "I don't know, Ariadne. But we have to try. We have to make every moment count, even if it's just for a short while. We owe ourselves that much."

We stood there, wrapped in each other's arms, as the reality of our situation settled in. The future seemed unbearably bleak, a dark cloud hanging over our heads. But in that moment, all we had was each other, and the fragile hope that somehow, we could find a way to make these last days meaningful.

Chapter 24

ARIADNE
August, 1900

It had started to rain, a cold, unrelenting downpour that mirrored the turmoil within me. But it didn't matter. Just like everything else. The old woman had called me a catalyst, a facilitator—a meaningless gust of wind that propels war and elevates people to positions of power to then eventually stop it. In a way, it felt fitting. She had just reassured me that it was not my burden to carry. That my destiny wasn't something grand like saving people and stopping wars. It was simply to flap my wings like a meaningless butterfly and create chaos that might work in her divine favor.

Xavier and I walked back through the narrow gate that led us to the entrance of the shop. His hand held mine tightly, a silent promise that he was ready to brave any storm with me. And that's why it hurt more. I hadn't known until the moment she had said it, how much I wanted this man beside me.

As we made our way down the path, a familiar shadow emerged from the misty rain.

"Eugene, what are you doing here?" Xavier asked, his voice breaking the silence before I could even process Eugene's presence.

Eugene didn't reply immediately. He was dressed in a dark blue shirt and brown pants, both soaked through by the rain. His hair was plastered to his forehead, and his eyes were hollow, reflecting the same anguish we felt. His expression was one of deep concern and sorrow, his usually sharp features softened by the rain and the gravity of the moment.

"Brother, what are you doing here?" I asked, wiping the remnants of tears from my eyes. I looked like a mess. Drenched in rain, my clothes clung to my silhouette, my makeup smeared, my eyes swollen, and my voice raspier than I expected it to sound.

"Nora sent me. She was worried about both of you," he said softly.

Eugene stepped closer, his eyes scanning my face with a tenderness I had rarely seen from him. He hesitated for a moment, then gently wrapped his arms around me, pulling me into a warm, comforting embrace. Mister Eugene Bryant, the antithesis of affection and care, an embodiment of a cold exterior with a softer heart, who always argued and seemed to hate my guts, was now hugging me. It was funny how I actually thought of him as an elder brother now.

"I am so sorry," he whispered.

Hearing his voice broke me down further. "I don't know what to do," I sobbed. His arms tightened around me, and he gently patted my head, his touch tender and reassuring.

On our way back home, neither of us spoke a word. Eugene simply drove through the rain, the rhythmic pounding on the roof the only sound breaking the silence. We tried to make ourselves look slightly more presentable, and it worked, but nothing we did could wash away the grim, hollow feeling of horror that lingered in our hearts.

To my great surprise, no one at Clairborough Manor seemed to realize that something was wrong. As for our disheveled appearance, I think they all simply assumed we were caught in a bad storm.

Eugene insisted that Xavier stay the night and join us for dinner, citing the worsening weather. Xavier just nodded and smiled, too exhausted to argue. As the three of us moved through the motions of the evening like ghosts, the servants displayed a hidden sense of excitement in their behavior. They shared hidden glances and secret smiles as if they all had some internal secret to feel excited about.

In my room, the all-familiar routine began as Violet moved with her practiced grace. She drew me a warm bath, the scent of lavender filling the room as steam rose from the water. I undressed, my movements stiff and mechanical, and stepped into the tub. The touch of warm water amidst all that cold and shivering felt really welcoming.

After my bath, Violet helped me into a soft linen chemise. She then selected a simple, flowy dress made of light cotton, its loose fabric hugging my figure in the right corners and flowing in the right ones. She added a touch of powder to my face, a hint of rouge to my cheeks, and carefully applied a delicate fragrance to my wrists and neck. The motions were soothing in their familiarity, yet my heart felt heavy with the weight of everything that had transpired.

As she worked her way through my hair, I stared at my reflection in the mirror. The woman looking back at me seemed distant, almost unrecognizable, yet I had gotten used to seeing this face. The simple but necessary grooming, and the elegant attire—had all become part of my routine. Last October, this same routine had freaked me out, and yet the irony of it all was how accustomed to it I was now.

"Is there anything else you need, my lady?" Violet asked softly, her eyes meeting mine in the mirror.

"No, thank you, Violet," I replied, my voice barely above a whisper. "That will be all."

She nodded and left the room, leaving me alone with my thoughts.

I took a deep breath, trying to anchor myself amid the storm of emotions. I had to stay strong—not for myself, but everyone else.

There was no need to dampen everyone's mood. Plus, Xavier, Eugene, and I had already agreed to this before heading into the dining room. No one needed to know what had transpired. In fact, it was a relief in some ways. In less than a month, Mother and Father's real daughter would be coming back. To them, it would be as simple as her memories returning and me simply forgetting this past year when everything was chaotic. I wondered if they would miss this version of me.

Dinner flowed with the usual precision. The long dining table was set with an array of delectable dishes, each course arriving seamlessly. The first course consisted of a delicate soup, creamy and rich, served with freshly baked bread. We all took a small bite of the bread and a little sip of the soup. I felt the warmth spread through me, soothing some of the turmoil within.

The servants moved gracefully, refilling glasses and attending to every need without a word. They brought us food with practiced ease as Mother and Father made small talk, their voices a gentle murmur in the background. Nora tried to make light jokes, her laughter like a tinkling bell that cut through the tension. I caught Xavier's eye and we exchanged a fleeting smile. Although our minds were elsewhere, we tried our best to be present. Eugene, too, leaned in, nodding and adding a comment here and there.

The second course featured a succulent roast, surrounded by perfectly roasted vegetables and a savory gravy. The aroma filled the room, making everyone's mouths water. The room was filled with the clinking of silverware, the soft hum of conversation, and the occasional burst of laughter. Father recounted a humorous story from his youth, and we all laughed. Sitting at the table, I realized just how much I had grown accustomed to everyone and how deeply I would miss them.

As dessert was served—a light, refreshing sorbet followed by an assortment of fine cheeses and fruits—Nora turned to Mother with a playful glint in her eye. "Mother," she said lightly, "Ariadne and Mister Xavier wanted to say something today."

Xavier and I exchanged startled glances. We had never told Nora that we were skipping the announcement. I swallowed hard and said, "Um... so what we were going to say was..."

I looked at Xavier, hoping he would help, and he stuttered, "Um... I guess..."

There was a long, tense pause. What were we really supposed to do? Tell them the truth? That I was going to go back soon and Xavier was likely going to... I pushed the thought away, forcing a smile.

Unable to contain her excitement, Nora blurted out, "Oh my goodness, they want to get married, everyone. Will you give them your blessing?"

I stared at Nora in shock, my eyes widening. Internally, I rolled my eyes. Why must you do this to me, dear sister-in-law?

My mother's eyes lit up with pure joy. "Finally, there is going to be a wedding. With the way the both of you were proceeding, I was expecting this to happen when I nearly died."

Father gave a knowing smile. "I also knew this was going to happen for quite some time. I am glad the two of you finally came to a decision."

Xavier looked at me, and I met his gaze. We shared a mutual understanding—if one month was all we had, then let's make the most of it. And this was the best way to start. So we decided to take this moment to simply take a pause.

"What do you mean you expected this?" I exclaimed with a playful smile. "I just made this decision myself, a few days ago."

"Well, to be fair, you were quite taken by me," Xavier teased, his eyes twinkling. "I have that kind of effect on people."

"No, I wasn't!" I protested, laughing.

Eugene chimed in with a grin, "Well, with the number of times Xavier insisted on hanging out with me, he was definitely quite taken by you, sister. Even I expected this announcement at some point."

"What is everyone even talking about? We weren't that obvious," I said, still laughing.

Nora rolled her eyes playfully. "Oh yeah, you weren't obvious at all. Especially the last three days."

"My goodness, everyone stop," I laughed, holding up my hands in mock surrender. "First, you wanted me to get married, and now I am. Don't push my buttons unless you want me to change my mind."

Xavier leaned closer, his eyes wide with mock pleading. "Oh no, no, no—please don't change your mind. I am perfectly happy with how things are."

"Of course you are," Eugene said, rolling his eyes with a grin.

Mother's eyes twinkled with excitement. "When are the both of you planning to get married?"

Xavier sat up straight, taking my hand under the table and squeezing it gently. "The 17th of February next year, if that works for everyone," he replied, his eyes betraying a flicker of sorrow.

Mother looked at Father with a playful smile. "They came prepared with all the answers," she joked, patting Father's hand.

"My goodness, my youngest daughter is finally getting married. I truly thought it was never going to happen," my mother said, her voice catching as she wiped a tear from her eye.

And just like that, the mood shifted. We were joking, having fun, and toasting to the future. Eugene, Xavier, and I exchanged meaningful glances. We all knew that wasn't happening, but we enjoyed this fleeting moment of joy and excitement, pretending, if only for a while, that everything would be fine. I really needed this momentary respite—the warmth of family and laughter wrapping around me like a comforting blanket.

Chapter 25

A RIADNE
August, 1900

After dinner, Mother and Father decided to retire for the night. Nora, visibly exhausted from her pregnancy, also retired early to get some rest. The thought of not being able to see my future niece or nephew brought a bittersweet pang to my heart. Especially knowing that by the time I go back, they would be long gone from that time period as well, having lived their entire lives.

However, keeping that thought aside, just as everyone wrapped up their day, I turned to Eugene. "How much of it all did you hear today?"

He looked at me with a soft but sincere gaze. "Since that woman started talking about you being a divine intervention, facilitator, and catalyst," he replied. He noticed the servants moving around and added, "Why don't we continue the rest of the conversation in my study?"

Xavier and I agreed, and that's how the three of us headed upstairs.

Eugene's study was meticulously organized, reflecting his precise nature. The familiar scent of wood and books welcomed us as we entered. The chandelier cast a soft glow over the room, highlighting the dark wooden bookshelves filled with an array of books, their spines a mixture of well-worn classics and newer volumes. The central mahogany desk, meticulously neat with its closed ink bottle and arranged pens, reflected Eugene's precise nature.

I sat down on the plush leather couch beside Xavier while Eugene moved to the ornate cabinet by the wall. He opened the glass door and carefully selected a flask of whiskey. The light from the chandelier caught the amber liquid, making it glow warmly. He took three crystal glasses from the cabinet, placing an ice cube in each with a satisfying clink. Then, with practiced precision, he poured the whiskey, the liquid swirling around the ice before settling.

As he walked over to us, he held out one of the glasses to Xavier and then me. I gave him a questioning look. Was Eugene Bryant offering me a glass of whiskey?

"What? I know you drink, sister. I've seen you sneak my flasks plenty of times."

"Wait, you knew?" I exclaimed in horror.

"Of course, I knew," he replied, narrowing his eyes with a grin. "And don't think I haven't judged you for it every single time."

Then he sat down in front of us with his glass in hand as well. We clinked glasses, and both men took gentle sips whereas I, in one swift motion, chugged mine down and set the empty glass back on the table with a determined thud. The burn of the whiskey was sharp but welcome. I needed it today.

Both of them stared at me in shock, their eyes wide. I looked at them with a sly smile. "You said you knew I drank?"

"Well yes, but I wasn't sure you did so, that well," Eugene said, raising an eyebrow in surprise.

"Well, I am more of a wine person, but I could really use some liquid courage to process today."

Xavier chuckled but then finally asked the burning question on both of their minds. "Who are you really?"

The room fell silent. I felt the weight of their gazes, the anticipation hanging thick in the air. Taking a deep breath, I tried to organize my thoughts. It was time for me to tell them—tell them everything. This was the moment of truth.

"Let's start with the basics," I began, my voice steady but tinged with the gravity of the situation. I paused to gather my thoughts, aware that what I was about to reveal would change everything. "Remember when we met at the hospital, Eugene?"

Eugene nodded, his brow furrowed. "Yeah, you said your name was Aria Gibson. Aged 25. Living in apartment 24, Luxe Tower..."

"Martin-Cross Street, Portmaine City, in Agnor. Right. That's where I lived—live. I was born in the year 2000, and I was 25 years old when I first came here. So now you understand why I was so on edge and confused about who everyone was. I didn't know you guys. I had no idea why I was here. I literally thought it was a dream until I met that old woman again when I ran away—which had led to that breakdown. It was one of the weirdest experiences of my life."

"Heavens, 2025? That's one hundred and twenty-five years from the future," Eugene exclaimed, his voice full of disbelief.

I nodded. "Yes. My real parents were Ethan and Emily Gibson. They were amazing—everything I could hope for. But they passed away when I was fifteen in an accident, and then my aunt and uncle took care of me. Even though they were great, they were never really my parents. However, Olivia was the one person I truly cared for and thought of as my family. She was my older cousin and also my biggest support system."

"That's the person you were calling for that day at the hospital," Eugene remarked.

"Yes. That's pretty much the gist of my background. It's nothing grand."

"The couple you admired when you suggested the date for our wedding... were those your parents?" Xavier asked, curiosity evident in his voice.

"Yes, it was the date they got married. They were truly amazing and loved each other with such grace. Their love was genuine and honest, built on trust and open communication. They laughed together, shared dreams, and supported each other through every challenge. It was a partnership in the truest sense—equal, full of respect and joy. They made even the ordinary moments feel special, simply because they were together. That's the kind of relationship I wanted us to have," I said, a soft smile playing on my lips as Xavier gently held my hand. "My dad was a history professor, and my mom worked in R&D for IoT devices."

"Wait, I don't understand. What is all that stuff?" Eugene asked, his brow furrowing in confusion.

"R&D stands for research and development. It's where new products and technologies are created and tested. IoT stands for the Internet of Things, which refers to a network of physical objects—like household appliances, automobiles, and even clothing—that are connected to the internet and can communicate with each other. My mom's job was to test these ideas and see if executing them was feasible," I explained, noticing their confused expressions.

"Let me start from the basics. There is something called the internet," I began, seeing their lost expressions. "Think of the internet as a vast network that connects millions of devices around the world. It's like an enormous library, but instead of books, it holds information in a digital format. Imagine being able to access newspapers, books, and letters from all over the world instantly, without waiting for them to be delivered."

Eugene's eyes widened slightly. "How? That sounds impossible."

"The internet allows people to communicate instantly, no matter the distance. It's like having a conversation through a telegraph, but much faster—within a fraction of a second," I said, smiling at their expressions of awe.

"And this 'internet' is common in your time?" Xavier asked, leaning in with curiosity.

"Yes, it's an essential part of daily life. Almost everyone has access to it. It's a bit addictive. It's hard to imagine living without it once you're used to it," I explained.

"The Portmaine City I live in is incredible. It's nothing like you've seen before. It's a hub of economy and commerce, always bustling with life. There are these tall skyscrapers, some as high as a hundred floors, all made of glass and steel. At night, the city lights up with neon signs and streetlights—it's really something. But there's also a downside—unemployment is rising, inflation is through the roof, and living costs are really high."

"Wow," was all Eugene could say, his mind grappling with the image of such a future. But then his expression turned dark. "But what was all that about the upcoming war and British rule?"

I took a deep breath, feeling the weight of what I was about to share. "Well, to be honest, I don't remember everything perfectly. When I was a child, my dad used to tell me all these stories about our history, but that was a long time ago. Then I studied some of it in middle school as part of my history syllabus, so my memory is a bit vague. But what I do know is that next year, we are going to war with the United Kingdom. And we're going to lose. Badly."

I locked eyes with Eugene, my voice steady but urgent. "You have to be extremely careful. It's going to be a dangerous time to live in. But there is a silver lining—we eventually gain our independence in 1947, after a long and arduous freedom struggle."

Both Eugene and Xavier's faces contorted with anger. Eugene's jaw clenched tightly, his fists balled at his sides. Xavier's eyes narrowed, a storm of rage and frustration brewing within them. I could almost feel the heat of their fury radiating through the room.

"Can't we do something? Stop all this?" Eugene protested, his voice laced with desperation.

I shook my head, the weight of the truth pressing down on me. "I don't think so. Honestly, I don't even know how. All I know is that Demion Marshall is part of the solution, and as far as the old woman said, so is Chris Baxton. You have to support them. Use our power and resources wisely. And more importantly, keep Nora, Mother, and Father safe. You have a child coming soon. It's going to be a dangerous time, but always remember, we will win back our freedom. It might seem impossible, but it will happen."

Eugene's face tightened with resolve. "Are there any other hints you remember? People I could help keep safe? Things I could do to save more lives?"

I took a deep breath, racking my brain for any details. "Focus on hospitals. Invest more in medicinal research. Weapons only lead to more destruction, so safeguard our books and culture—knowledge is crucial. Support the Slovain community—they need it the most. And avoid Restersburg in 1933 at all costs—that's when the worst series of bombings happened."

"Bombings?" Xavier echoed, his voice filled with disbelief.

Eugene nodded, absorbing every word. "What if I send our family to Germany? Get them out before things get worse. I could stay back to help here."

"No! You can't." I exclaimed, my voice sharp with urgency. "Germany will be even more dangerous. Our war aside, the world is going to be in chaos. World War I and II are going to start in 1914 and 1939. Over 70 nations will be involved or impacted. I don't think anywhere will be truly safe. You need to protect our family's money. Invest in technology, the future, and medicine. And keep trading with those German industries we talked about, but pull out by 1913, before World War I begins."

Eugene's eyes widened with the enormity of the task, but they also hardened with resolve. "I'll do whatever it takes," he said firmly.

Xavier frowned, lost in thought. "But do you really think Eugene should get involved? What if his actions change the future you come from? We're talking about altering the past."

"Honestly, I'm not sure," I admitted. "But the old woman said I was a catalyst for change, someone to start the domino effect—the first ripple. Why else would she tell me all of this today? And don't you think she knew Eugene was listening? She told us everything, even when you were right there."

"But that's because I'm going to die," Xavier said, his voice tinged with sorrow. "Maybe she didn't care if I heard because what could I do? I'm going to be a dead man soon."

A heavy silence fell over the room. Fear gripped us all, a dark and unsettling feeling that seeped into our bones. The gravity of his words hung in the air, a stark reminder of the fragile thread on which our fates dangled.

After what felt like an eternity, Eugene broke the silence. "This is beyond our control," he began, his voice steady and calm. "What's done is done, and we must face what's coming with courage and resolve. Our primary concern now is to keep Xavier safe. That's our immediate goal."

He paused, his gaze meeting mine with a tenderness rarely there before. "And you, dear sister, it's a blessing to know you'll return to your own time. You don't deserve to witness the horrors of war. Your place is in the future, where you belong."

"But, Eugene..." my voice cracked with emotion.

Eugene gently held my hand to stop me. "No buts," he said softly but firmly. "You have the rare gift of knowing when you'll return. Use this time wisely. Reconnect with your friends, say your goodbyes, and cherish every moment with Xavier. It may not be fair, but it's the time you have. So make it count."

Eugene's voice softened, filled with genuine emotion. "And I would deeply regret not saying this today, so I'm just going to say it." He paused, looking directly into my eyes. "Dear sister, your name—whether Ariadne or Aria—has never truly mattered to me. Despite our rocky start, you have always been and will always be my sister. I don't care for you because we share the same parents; I care for you because of the beautiful soul you possess."

He took a deep breath, his eyes glistening with unshed tears. "You have this incredible resilience and a kindness that shines through even in the darkest times. I've watched you navigate through challenges with a grace and strength that is truly inspiring. You've faced every obstacle head-on, never letting fear or doubt overshadow your determination. And now that I know what you've been through, I feel this even more."

Eugene's voice wavered slightly as he continued, his expression serious but gentle. "The way you stood tall in front of Mother, the way you constantly argued with me to fight your case, the troubles and chaos you caused—you truly made this house lively. But more than that, you've shown me what it means to be truly courageous and to face adversity without losing sight of who you are." He smiled softly, a mix of pride and sorrow on his face. "I am going to cherish every single moment we've shared, and I can't begin to tell you how much I am going to miss you. I am truly thankful to have met you. My dear sister, you are a great spirit, and your absence will be felt more than you can ever imagine."

"I'm going to miss you too, Eugene. So very much," I said, my voice raspy with emotion.

Xavier looked at me then, his gaze deep and filled with a mixture of love and sorrow. His eyes held the weight of our shared moments, the pain of impending loss, and the determination to make the most of the time we had left. He reached out, gently brushing a tear from my cheek, his touch tender and comforting. His fingers lingered for a moment, tracing the path of the tear.

Xavier leaned in closer, his voice a soft whisper filled with unwavering resolve. "We'll get through this. Together." His hand found mine, squeezing it gently but firmly, a silent promise of support.

I could see the resolve in both of them, their silent vow to give me the farewell I deserved. To carry these burdens.

To face these moments of crisis. Their overwhelming love and support wrapped around me like a comforting blanket in the midst of the storm, warming the coldest corners of my heart. Their presence was a balm, soothing the raw ache of impending separation.

Chapter 26

XAVIER

October, 1900

These last few weeks were filled with painful joy. Every moment was precious yet fleeting. Each shared glance and touch was filled with love and the weight of impending farewell. She had said her goodbyes to all her friends, each parting a wistful reminder of her looming departure. The emotional toll was visible in her eyes, yet she faced it all with grace and resilience.

Her conversations with Demion were especially poignant, their roles often reversing in a unique exchange of wisdom and inspiration. Ariadne was determined to prepare him for the upcoming crisis, instilling in him the foresight he would need. She had unwavering faith in his abilities. Yet, the truth of her origins and the knowledge of the future remained a secret shared only by me, her, and her brother.

Her farewell with Violet was particularly heart-wrenching. Ariadne cherished Violet deeply, valuing her as a steadfast companion. Violet was more than just her maid; she was a true friend. I watched as Ariadne held her hands, speaking tenderly. Her words conveyed deep affection while masking the sorrow beneath, carefully choosing her words to hide the full truth.

I had seen her cry more times in these weeks than I could count. Each tear was a testament to her profound sadness. The thought of her returning broken, to a time where I no longer existed to comfort her, terrified me.

Despite the heartache, we tried to make the most of our remaining time. At her parents' insistence, we held an engagement party the previous night. Entering the grand ballroom, we were greeted by the hum of conversation, clinking glasses, and the gentle strains of a waltz. Guests turned towards us, some smiling, others behind polite masks. Ariadne's eyes sparkled as she squeezed my hand, masking the heaviness within. It was a joyous occasion, though tinged with the bittersweet knowledge that our wedding would never come to pass.

That night, she casually walked towards me and asked me to dance. This woman who hated the very idea of dancing made the first move. She was dressed in a stunning creation of soft teal and silver silk and lace, the fabric flowing gracefully with her every step. Her hair was styled in loose curls, cascading down her back, framing her face in such a beautiful light that she looked like she was glowing.

She held my hand, locking her fingers with mine. The warmth of her touch sent a comforting shiver through me. She rested her head on my chest as we moved in unison, her body pressed gently against mine. I felt her peace as she listened to my heartbeat, a steady rhythm that seemed to calm her. We moved together, our steps synchronized, lost in the music and each other. Her breath was warm against my neck, and I felt her heartbeat echoing mine.

The music enveloped us, a hauntingly beautiful symphony played by a pianist and a cellist, their melodies weaving together in a seamless dance of their own. The soft, lilting notes of the piano intertwined with the deep, resonant tones of the cello, creating an atmosphere of intimate romance. The room around us blurred into the background, leaving just the two of us in our private world.

She looked up at me, her eyes filled with unshed tears, glistening like the midnight sky. "Thank you," she whispered, her voice barely audible over the music. "For everything."

I pressed a gentle kiss to her forehead, my heart aching with love and sorrow. "No, thank you," I replied softly. "For giving me these moments."

Just as she was about to tear up, her parents gently pulled us apart, breaking the intimate bubble we had created. The crowd's attention had shifted towards us. Petra's light-hearted remark, "An earlier wedding might be better since neither of you seems capable of staying apart," drew laughter from the guests, momentarily lifting the heavy mood.

The room was full of love and support from most, but not everyone's intentions were pure. My father had praised me for this match, though his reasons were as cold and calculated as he was.

"Political benefits," he had said with a steely glint in his eye. He loved the prospect of having a stake in the Bryant Steel industry, envisioning how their support could bolster his upcoming campaigns. To him, our union was a strategic alliance, a way to consolidate power and influence. The way he spoke of it, as if Ariadne were merely a pawn in his grand chess game, sickened me. His voice had a clinical detachment that stripped the warmth from his words, leaving only the icy core of ambition.

I glanced at my father across the room. His stern face softened momentarily as he exchanged pleasantries with the Bryants, his charm a well-practiced façade. His entire life was a performance, meticulously orchestrated for power and influence. Even now, amidst the celebration, he was calculating his next move, his mind always a few steps ahead in the endless game of politics.

As I watched him, memories surfaced of the many times he had belittled my brother and me, his eyes always cold and calculating. I knew I was going to die. But at least this man—my so-called father, who had spent his life manipulating for power, was destined to be ruined. I wanted to see him crumble in the face of what was to come, to witness his pride and ego breaking down. As I stood there, surrounded by his façade of celebration, I felt a cold satisfaction knowing my father's carefully constructed world was about to burn.

On the other hand, my mother's indifference cut deeper than my father's cold calculations. She attended my engagement party out of politeness, her presence a mere formality. The empty gaze with which she looked at me hurt more than I cared to admit. She stood at the edge of the room, detached and disinterested, her eyes glazed over as if witnessing a distant, unremarkable event.

She had long since retreated into a world of her own, a silent protest against my father's domineering force. Her once vibrant spirit had been eroded by years of emotional neglect, leaving behind a hollow shell. Maybe she did love me. She just didn't know how to show it. For a moment, my eyes met my mother's across the room. I thought I saw a flicker in her gaze—a glimmer of the woman she used to be, buried beneath layers of apathy. But it vanished as quickly as it appeared, replaced by familiar emptiness. She turned away, lost once again in her private world.

As the evening drew to a close, I found a moment to steal Ariadne away from the crowd. We slipped out onto the balcony, the cool night air a welcome contrast to the warmth inside.

"Moments like these... they feel like stolen treasures. Do you think we'll ever have another chance to steal time again?" she asked softly, her voice barely above a whisper. Her words hung in the air.

I moved to stand beside her, taking her hand in mine. Her skin was cool, the slight tremble of her fingers betraying her calm exterior. "I don't know," I replied honestly, my voice as gentle as the breeze. "But I do know that whatever happens, these moments will always be with us. They're ours, and no one can take them away."

She turned to face me, her eyes shining with unshed tears. In the dim light, they glistened like precious gems, filled with a mixture of love and despair. "You're right," she said, her voice steadier now, as if finding strength in our shared resolve. "And I'm grateful for every single one of them."

I reached into my pocket and retrieved the small silver box, placing it gently in her hand. "Here," I said softly. "Take it."

Her eyes widened in surprise. "I thought I left it with the old woman. You got it back?" she asked disbelief in her tone.

"Yes. These rings might be ill-fated, but they brought us together. I don't want to give that old woman the satisfaction of taking something that belongs to us. This is our token of love, friendship, and union. Let's not give it away just because some divine being used it to manipulate us."

She looked down at the box, her fingers tracing its edges. "Xavier, I..." She hesitated, her voice catching in her throat. Then she nodded, her resolve firm. "You're right. Give me your hand."

"Wait, you're putting the ring on my finger first?"

She gave me a sly smile. "I like doing things a little unconventionally."

I laughed at her playful spirit and let her. Then I took the other ring and slipped it onto her finger. The simple gesture held the weight of eternity, a promise that transcended time and fate.

She placed her palm beside mine, comparing our hands. Hers was tinier, more delicate. She looked at our rings closely, her eyes reflecting the moonlight. With a glint in her eye, she said, "You got these engraved? Mine says 'Fine &' and yours says..."

"Forever," I finished, my voice choked with emotion. I pulled her into my arms, holding her as if letting go would mean losing her forever. We looked out into the night, the cool breeze whispering around us. Her head rested against my chest, and I could feel the steady rhythm of her heartbeat, a soothing counterpoint to the turmoil within me.

For a moment, the world seemed to stand still. It was just the two of us, wrapped in each other's embrace, holding onto the fleeting seconds that were ours. The scent of her hair, the warmth of her body against mine, the sound of her soft breaths—all these sensations etched themselves into my memory.

The stars above bore silent witness to our vow, their light reminding us that even in the darkest times, there is always hope. As we stood there, bound by love and the promise of what might have been, I knew this moment would remain etched in our hearts forever.

Ariadne believed she would return when the clock struck twelve. But as the hours passed, nothing happened. We joked, lazed around, and counted down multiple times, trying to make light of the situation so that we didn't break down. But nothing happened—not that night, nor the next morning, not even at lunch.

As we lounged in the living room, her laughter filling the air, for a moment, everything felt perfect. I began to hope that maybe this was just a cruel joke—that she was not going back. She earnestly shared names of stocks and companies for my future generations to invest in to become millionaires. She spoke of stories that famous authors would pen, which would end up becoming sensations.

Right in the middle of a sentence, her eyes sparkling with amusement as she recounted an incident in school when she won her first award for writing an essay, she suddenly paused, her brow furrowing in thought. I waited for her to continue, a smile playing on my lips, expecting her to tell me what the essay was about and why it mattered so much to her. But the reply never came.

One second she was there, and just like that, she was gone.

The room seemed to have frozen around me, the warmth evaporating into a hollow void. The woman I love was gone, lost to the past, or perhaps the future, leaving me with the gaze of a stranger—the real Ariadne Bryant. I reached out, my hand trembling, to touch her cheek, hoping it was a joke—hoping to feel a trace of the warmth that had been there mere moments ago. But she pulled back abruptly, her movements stiff and unfamiliar, as if I were an intruder in her world.

At that moment, I was left with a single, lingering thought.

Our time together had been brief, yet profoundly deep and meaningful. It wasn't clear whether this was a stroke of fortune or misfortune because we couldn't even claim that our love lacked strength. Maybe with time, it could have faded. But we simply weren't given the time to test it.

So in another lifetime, I hoped that perhaps the divine might take a bow and grant us the days we were denied. Let her story become mine, and mine become hers.

I imagined us gazing at each other as we grew old and frail. I longed for us to weather every storm side by side.

However, I knew, in this life, we were simply not meant to be. But in the next, I hoped we would be given the chance to last forever, to have it all, and to take life step by step until we turned to dust and returned to the beginning of it all.

But all of that was merely a thought—for in this lifetime, we were fated to be apart.

Chapter 27

A RIA

October, 2025

The first thing I noticed was the softness of my blanket, cradling me in a cocoon of warmth. My bed felt more inviting than ever before, the pillow perfectly cradling my neck. Even the room's temperature was just right—neither too cold nor too warm, but the perfect in-between. As I opened my eyes, a blurred haze of light filtered through, casting a gentle glow and an oddly familiar off-white ceiling greeted me. The smooth surface faintly shimmered in the morning light.

Then I heard it—the beeping sound of an alarm that I hadn't heard in ages.

I sat up in bed, scanning my surroundings. Everything felt peaceful, like the start of the perfect day. My senses were dull—incapable of recognizing where I was or understanding what was happening, but I knew I felt at home.

For the briefest of moments, I lingered in that morning haziness, a state where thoughts were absent and only the feeling of being in the present existed. But just as the room came into focus, it took only one blink for all thoughts to come rushing back—the dreams, the memories, the people—Xavier.

It had been a week since I had returned.

The world around me was a blur of constant movement—things flowed, people moved, sounds buzzed, and electricity hummed. For the first time, I realized just how much of a struggle it was to keep up with the relentless pace of modern life.

Everything felt too rushed—too hushed. I had forgotten how fast my life used to move. For the past year, my days had followed a slow, steady rhythm, like the beat of a drum. With a gentle breeze, fresh scent of earth, and the simple routine of mundanity.

So yes, I was playing catch-up.

This last week, I had allowed myself to take a moment to pause. I watched as locations blurred, scents mingled, and shadows danced. Yet, despite the rush and buzz, no distraction was big enough to keep my thoughts from drifting back to the memories of the past.

I had spent time with Mateo and Olivia. Their presence was the one thing I truly welcomed, grounding me in this reality that felt both foreign and familiar at the same time. I had definitely startled them that first morning when I broke down in tears, hugging them tightly as if I could fuse my fragmented self back together through sheer force of will.

"How are you?" I had choked out, my voice trembling with the weight of a year's worth of unshed tears. For them, it had been just one night. For me, it had been a year—a year of isolation, of transformation, of living a life they couldn't even begin to comprehend. I had all these stories to tell, dreams to share, and experiences to unpack. Yet, every time I opened my mouth, the words failed me. Instead of coherent sentences, only tears flowed—raw, unfiltered, and relentless.

But, in their expressions, all I could see was confusion, concern, and anxiety as if they were trying to understand why I was having a breakdown.

However now that it had been a week—seven days—one hundred and sixty-eight hours—I was done taking that pause. Now, it was time to run. To keep busy. To do anything to keep my thoughts full. I figured out my bills, cooked and cleaned. It was astonishing how exhausting I found it all. But now I was ready to scratch my brain and re-learn the nature of my trade. And the first thing on my to-do list was to get Luca Everett's interview done and dusted.

Imagine the irony of life—I had lived a year's worth of life overnight, and yet this man's interview had plagued my existence. But it all made sense. I had no grand purpose. I was that meaningless butterfly, flapping its wings to create small ripples of change, favorable chaos for some divine being. Living this life—with mundane routines and the simplest of joys—a meaningless being against the monumental weight of time.

I had tasted the depth of love, the sharpness of loss, and the relentless march of time in a span so short it defied reason. Perhaps that was the true irony: in the grand tapestry of existence, it was the fleeting moments that held the most profound significance. While others sought grand destinies,

I found meaning in the delicate beauty of a single heartbeat, a whispered word, a final glance.

I took a cab to the outskirts of Portmaine city. Amidst the serene landscape, I found his house—a living example of a modern aesthetic. The exterior was a combination of sleek, dark panels and warm wooden slats, creating a striking contrast that was both sophisticated and inviting. Large, expansive windows dominated the facade, reflecting the dense foliage. No one would have known that a house existed here unless they knew exactly where to go. It was private and secluded—perfect for a sports star. As I walked along the stone pathway leading to the main entrance, I felt an overwhelming sense of calm. It was truly a location in harmony with nature.

Just as I was about to ring the doorbell, the door opened, and Luca's personal assistant, Jane, who I had spoken to numerous times, ages ago, greeted me with a warm professional smile. "Hi Aria, apologies for making you come all the way out here."

"Oh, don't worry about it. It was a beautiful drive," I replied, politely.

"It is indeed," Jane agreed. "We generally don't conduct interviews at Luca's private residence, but unfortunately, I have some urgent work to attend to. No one else could drive Luca on such short notice, and I would have hated to reschedule again."

Sensing my train of thought, Jane added, "Luca can't drive. He has a fear of driving."

"Oh, I see. But it was no hassle at all," I replied politely.

"Also, can you please keep this address confidential? The press and fans haven't found out about it yet and I would like to keep it that way," she pointed out.

"Of course, I understand," I nodded. We left it at that. All the basic small talk was done, and we had already discussed every detail of this interview beforehand.

Then she guided me into the living room and handed me a cup of coffee. "Luca will be another twenty minutes, please, have a seat till then," she said before excusing herself. I had mastered this art—a perfect facade—one where I could pretend to be normal and go about my life as usual.

It took me two minutes to set my stuff up. My laptop was powered, and the voice recorder was in place. There was not much to do but admire this harmonious blend of soft, light-colored walls, wooden panels, and ceilings that created a calm backdrop. I walked toward the right side where lay this stunning book wall. The shelves were white which contrasted beautifully with the colorful spines of the books. Each shelf varied in height, accommodating books of different sizes and adding a dynamic appeal to the minimalist interior.

The book collections featured a wide range of genres, from classics written by Jane Austen, J.R.R. Tolkien, and George Orwell to rare history books chronicling Agnor's independence struggle and memoirs of the war. Then I found a book that stood out: the autobiography of Demion Marshall.

The moment I saw Demion's name on the cover, a rush of emotions overwhelmed me. I took a deep breath. "No, not now," I reminded myself. I wasn't going to have a breakdown here. I opened the book. It was titled, "Demion Marshall: The Man Behind the Revolution." I couldn't help but smile. He had been successful in igniting the flames of freedom.

As I read the first few lines, a soft, husky voice cut through my thoughts. "Are you a fan of history?" His voice was gentle but carried an underlying intensity.

I turned to see Luca, dressed in casual track pants and a navy blue t-shirt. His hair was a mix of dark black soft curls, and his gaze was sharp.

"Not exactly. Although I do have some newfound admiration for it. It was my father who was the true fan. He was a history professor, you see," I stated softly.

"Interesting," he said, his eyes reflecting a knowing smile, though there was a hint of pain in them.

"Are you a fan of history?"

He gave a slight nod. "I wouldn't call myself a fan, but I do love reading about that era," he said casually, pointing to a seat for me. And that's how we began the interview.

The profile aimed to delve deeper into who Luca Everett was beyond his successful football career. The goal was to uncover the man behind the athlete, exploring his motivations, personal experiences, and what truly made him tick. This wasn't just about statistics, game highlights, workout routines, endorsements, or press conferences; it was about the human story beneath his public persona.

Once the interview began, I quickly realized he was much more complex than the preconceived image I had of him. He had a profound passion for the unknown—space and technology fascinated him. He was a self-proclaimed geek of submarines and spaceships, often losing himself in the intricacies of their designs. His love for history was equally compelling; he frequently visited museums and donated considerable amounts to the restoration of relics and wartime research.

In his free time, he traveled extensively. He had explored the vibrant cultures of Japan, South Korea, and Thailand, each visit deepening his appreciation for Asian cuisine—a passion that surprised me. His adventurous spirit didn't stop there; he loved trekking and marveling at the natural beauty of Banff and Jasper. When asked about his dream travel destination, his eyes lit up as he described his longing to witness the northern lights. There was something about the magnificent dance of colors across the sky that captivated his imagination.

Luca was a dreamer with a beautiful spark for life, his curiosity and zest making him a truly intriguing individual. Contrary to what I had imagined, he was surprisingly introspective and understated. Despite his multifaceted personality, when I asked him why he chose a career in football, his response was unexpected. He explained that he had accidentally fallen into it, and because he excelled, he decided to continue. His journey was one of going with the flow, allowing life to take him where it may.

In truth, his answers related to his passion for football felt a bit bland, but he was tenacious and never skipped a day of practice. He liked the mechanical routine and eventually found his own unique way of loving the sport. Football wasn't his dream; it was his job—one he enjoyed and sacrificed a lot for. This revelation was funny to me; I had always assumed that professionals like actors, musicians, artists, and sportsmen pursued offbeat careers because it was their lifelong dream. But in reality, it could have also simply been just their job.

I had gathered enough for the compelling profile that Olivia and Mateo needed. So, to wrap up, I decided to ask him one last thing, "Well Luca, I think that was all. But if I could ask you one more question—what makes you want to wake up every day? If you had one wish, what would it be?"

His eyes widened, clearly caught off guard. "Umm... I'm not sure," he fumbled, his gaze locking onto mine. There was an intensity in his eyes, a vulnerability that made it difficult to decipher his emotions.

"Why the sudden question? This wasn't on the list, I believe," he said, a hint of depth in his voice.

"It's okay if you don't want to answer," I replied gently. "I just wanted to end on a more personal note. To be honest, the world already knows everything you want them to know. I was hoping you might share something more intimate."

He stayed silent for a moment, contemplating. Then he said, "Maybe there are some things I don't wish to share with the world because I want them to be intimate."

"I understand." I was ready to respect his privacy and move on, but then he interrupted, his voice softer, more vulnerable. "If I were to answer your question, I'd say this: my one wish would be to see the eyes of the person I love just once more, reflecting the depth of emotions they once did."

"Wait—Are you telling me on record that you once had someone you loved?"

He looked at me, his gaze unrelenting—almost as if I had touched a raw nerve. Something deeply personal and painful. He didn't answer for a long time, and then, with a sad smile, he looked away as he whispered, "Please forget it. That is not going on the record."

"Yes, of course! I am really sorry if that was something personal. I promise I won't include this in the article."

He silently nodded, and I began packing my things. Once I was done, just as I was about to head out, we shook hands. His grip was gentle yet firm, his hands much larger than mine. As I turned, my voice recorder slipped from my hand and fell to the floor with a thud.

"Shit, I am so sorry. I can be such a scatterbrain sometimes."

"It's all fine," he said, bending down on his knees to help me pick it up. As he did, a metallic silver chain around his neck slipped out from under his shirt, revealing a silver ring looped through it.

In that instant, I remembered his headshots. The ones from the photoshoot I had helped organize the week before I left. He had worn a deep V-neck to endorse a sports clothing brand that we advertised for. And there, right on his bare chest, was a silver chain with a platinum and diamond band. One that looked all too familiar. Acting on reflex, I grabbed his chain and examined the ring. My action jerked him closer to me—as I sat on my knees in front of him. He was mere inches apart.

There it was—a platinum band with "Forever" engraved inside. The same ring—the exact ring that I had put on Xavier's finger.

I looked up. He was staring at me, his eyes filled with a pain so deep, I could physically feel it.

"How?" I whispered, my voice barely audible.

"How do you think, Ariadne?" he whispered back.

And then there was silence—for all I could do was stare in shock as he said my all too familiar, borrowed name.

Epilogue

ARIA
October, 2025

The first emotion that washed over me when he called my borrowed name was relief. He was here—Xavier, now Luca. He looked different; his hair was shorter, and his once carefree demeanor seemed more subdued. His scent had changed too, a subtle mix of bergamot and fresh linen replacing the familiar cedarwood I remembered. Even his voice had a new timbre, softer yet still commanding. But despite these changes, the essence of him felt the same, and that unleashed a new wave of emotions. Questions—lots and lots of questions. But I had to be patient. I couldn't rush. Not now—not when he looked like a person who was ready to fall apart any second.

He brewed a pot of tea before we could talk. The fragrant aroma of chamomile filled the room, a soothing contrast to the tension hanging in the air. As he poured the tea into delicate porcelain cups, the steam curled upwards, carrying the subtle scent of honey and flowers.

Taking a deep breath, he said, "Before we begin, please tell me you are real. Tell me that you finally remember. Don't play with my emotions. Not now. Not after so long."

I placed my hand on his cheek. His skin felt foreign, but he had the same warmth. "I am. I remember everything. Or more like I finally lived the year you think I did. But how? How are you here?"

"It's a long story. I don't even know where to start. But the gist is, I died shortly after you left," he whispered softly but with a straight voice.

"How?" was all I could ask, my voice barely above a whisper.

"Ironically, I was assassinated right before the war began. Being the president's son made me a target. It was quick, at least. Immense pain as the bullet hit, but it was over in a second. Your friend Emmeline did extensive investigations, ensuring every detail of my assassination was publicized, hoping for justice one day. The details are all in the museum archives."

I tried to process the pieces of information he had just shared. So much had happened after I left. But he continued, "After I died, mere moments later, I woke up here, in this foreign land. Everything looked strange—felt strange. I had tried to imagine the future, but no matter how you explained it to me then, it was far different from what I envisioned," he said, his eyes distant, lost in memory.

Despite the pain and confusion in his eyes, a part of me was overwhelmingly happy to see him again. This was Xavier—my Xavier—standing right in front of me. My mind raced with questions, but I forced myself to be patient. He had been through so much.

"What happened? Why are you looking at me like that?" he suddenly asked.

"I don't know." My voice cracked. "I'm just so glad you're here. You have no idea how horrifying the last seven days were. I wish I could explain, but I can't find the words." At that moment, all I knew was I had to hug him. He embraced me back tightly, but I sensed a deep-rooted sorrow in his eyes.

"Actually, I do. How I wish it had been just a mere seven days of torment for me too," he said with a sad smile.

"What do you mean?" I asked, pulling back to look into his eyes.

"Remember our last conversation in your living room? When we laughed about the future and talked about your essay competition?" he said casually.

"Yeah, of course, I do. What about it?" I replied, confused.

"That conversation was ten years ago for me."

Ten years. The weight of his words hit me like a tidal wave. While I had only experienced a brief period of seven days—one that felt like agony—he had lived an entire decade without me. A decade filled with memories, experiences, and pain. I whispered, "That's impossible. When did you come here?"

"I came here on the 2nd of October, 2015. The day your parents died in that accident."

My breath caught in my throat, and my heart pounded in my chest. I stared at him, my mind racing to make sense of his words. "Why that day?" The question escaped my lips, barely a whisper, as my eyes widened in disbelief.

"You never told me that you were in the car as well," he continued.

"I mean, I was. But I don't really remember that time too well. I just knew that we were driving one second, and then there was glass shattering and darkness. And when I woke up, I was in the hospital."

"I need you to sit down," he said softly, holding my hand. His touch was gentle, a stark contrast to the intensity of his words. "I woke up on the morning before your parents' accident. Of course, my first instinct was to find you. I knew your address, but it was one from the future—the place you lived ten years from then. The place you live at today. So it took me some time to find out where you lived. It took lots of hunting through phone books and misguided lost walks until someone taught me how to search for it on the internet. Eventually, I pieced the information together, and I found out where you lived. I went there that evening and ran there frantically. But you were already in the car, heading somewhere. So I followed you. And then your family had that accident."

He slowly continued, "My first instinct was to help your family—all of you. To get each one of you out. Your dad noticed me and urged me to pull you out first. He was really worried. There was broken glass everywhere and I was so scared but I did. And barely seconds later after I pulled you out, the car was blazing in fire. That day has haunted me ever since."

"You are the one who saved me?" I whispered, my voice trembling.

"Yes, but I am also the one who failed to save your parents." He looked crushed, guilt written on his face. "I don't know if you are going to feel the same, especially after learning this, but I need you to know that I really wished I could save them. I simply couldn't."

A sharp ache spread through my chest. The weight of his guilt, the years he had spent tormented by that day, were palpable. Tears welled up in my eyes, each one a testament to the pain and gratitude I felt. He had saved my life, but at what cost?

I took a deep breath, struggling to find my voice. My mind was failing to form words, but I forced myself to speak. "You saved me. You gave me a second chance at life." I paused, hastily wiping my nose with the back of my hand. "I can't imagine how hard it must have been for you. But in no way are you responsible for my parents' death. Why would you even think that?"

I looked down, gathering my thoughts, then met his eyes again. "If you take things that way, then I could be held responsible for everyone's death during the freedom struggle. I could have changed the future. I was given every power and knowledge to do so. But I couldn't, could I? So do you think it was my fault?"

"Of course not, that's not your burden to bear. How could you have saved everyone? There were so many factors. So many people. So much happening behind the scenes," he insisted.

I ran my fingers through my hair, frustration evident in my movements. "Exactly. It's the same here. There were so many factors involved in my parents' accident as well. Just like how you could have saved them, so could I." I paused, taking a deep breath before continuing. "All I had to do was maybe not spend an extra minute looking for my jacket or take a last look in the mirror before leaving." I clenched my fists, trying to steady my trembling hands. "All I had to do was delay our departure by mere minutes, and they wouldn't have died. But things happen, and we have no control over them. Do you really think we have the power to change fate? Make an actual difference?"

I looked away, biting my lip, then turned back to him. "Do you remember the old woman's words? My role was that of a meaningless butterfly. Someone who had to cause chaos and create ripples. That was all. Maybe you were the same. Maybe all you had to do was cause ripples and start the wheels of change. Maybe all you were meant to do that day was save me. That's it."

He looked at me, his eyes reflecting a decade of pain and sorrow. "But I could have saved them, Ariadne," his voice broke as he sobbed, covering his face with his hands. "I was merely minutes late. I could have stopped you from getting in the car. Delayed your travel by mere seconds, and none of it would have happened. But I couldn't do anything."

He wiped his eyes and continued, "When you were in the hospital, the old woman came to visit me. And similar to how you felt, I was angry and furious. She had put me in the worst position ever. And after all of that, what was it even worth?"

"It was worth us!" I exclaimed, reaching out to grasp his hand. "That bane of the existence of a cursed woman's last words to us was to remember that it's not the length of time that defines a life, but the depth of the moments you live. We lived each and every moment given to us to the fullest. And you know better than anyone, they were very few." I squeezed his hand, trying to convey my conviction. "But the last thing she told us was that sometimes, what seems like an end might merely be the beginning of a new and unexpected chapter."

I met his gaze. "When I first woke up in October 1899, you think it didn't feel like the end for me? But it wasn't. It was the beginning of a beautiful new chapter, one that I am going to cherish for the rest of my life. One where I got to meet a new family... all those new friends and people. And you." I smiled softly, my thumb gently brushing over his hand. "Maybe you coming here, surviving that accident, and living through the last ten years was all in preparation for the beginning of our unexpected chapter. Don't you think? I know you made friends. You have the whole nation cheering for you at your games. You are an icon that people idolize. How many people do you think you have impacted by simply living your life and playing bloody football that you don't even consider your passion?" I asked.

"I thought about you every day. Knowing you were alive kept me going. It was the only thing that made this new world bearable—but I'll be honest, the football, the fans, the relentless practice, and maybe even the fame did help a bit," he confessed, his voice breaking as tears streamed down his face. Despite his tears, a small, wistful smile tugged at the corners of his lips.

He suddenly held my hand tighter. "Do you still love me? Despite everything? Despite the fact that I couldn't save your parents?" he asked, his voice trembling.

"Of course I do. And it's not your fault!" I exclaimed, my voice cracking with emotion. "I should be the one asking if you still feel the same way. I won't hold it against you if you don't. Not anymore. Ten years is a long time—a decade where you lived your life. And you're not just anyone. You're literally the nation's heartthrob. You must have had so many people who wanted to be with you, to love you. We barely spent mere months together and only had a few moments of true happiness as a couple."

I laughed lightly, shaking my head, "How is this fair? You get to be reborn as a rich and handsome football star, while I ended up as an aristocratic woman in a conservative society in bloody 1899."

He chuckled, running a hand through his hair. "Well, I agree. The moments we had together were rather few. And to be honest, I did try to move on."

He paused, his eyes looking down as if searching for the right words. My heart sank with worry—what if he really had moved on? But then he looked up, his eyes meeting mine with the same intensity as that fleeting day in August 1900, when he asked me if he could court me for the very first time.

"But loving you was like carrying a grief inside of me that I didn't want to leave," he said, his voice softening. "I missed you every single day. There was this constant ache in my chest, making it difficult to breathe. I'd dream about you recognizing me, holding my hand, us talking, and spending time together as if we had all the time in the world. But every time I had that dream, I'd wake up, and the pain of losing you was fresh again, always there, eating me up from the inside. But I also knew that when I went to sleep again, you would visit me once more."

He took a deep breath, his eyes glistening with unshed tears. "So yes, even after all these years, my love for you has only grown deeper. I still love you, so deeply and endlessly. It's foolish, to be honest, because I knew I was madly in love with a memory of a person who hadn't even experienced the moments we shared. But I hoped that if I waited long enough, maybe you would look back at me the same way, having lived those moments too. And so I waited—waited for a decade."

His words brought fresh tears to my eyes. I reached out, squeezing his hand. He looked up, meeting my gaze. "Everyone in this new life who knew me thought I was waiting for a fantasy, someone who didn't exist. And maybe they were right, for the most part. But even then, it was always you, I was waiting for. So yes, I love you," he admitted, his voice trembling with a mix of sorrow and relief.

We were both crying now. Tears streamed down our faces, our vision a blur as our eyes locked. Our breaths were shallow and ragged. We moved toward each other instinctively, as if drawn by a force beyond our control. Our lips met, and the world around us disappeared. This kiss was different. It was deep, passionate, filled with years of longing and unspoken words. I could taste the salt of our mingled tears, the sorrow, the joy, the pain.

His hands trembled as they cupped my face, his thumbs gently brushing away my tears. I felt the warmth of his touch, the softness of his lips moving against mine, and the desperate need to take in every breath he took. My fingers tangled in his hair, pulling him closer, refusing to let go. The intensity of the moment consumed us, each soft touch and gesture a testament to the years we had lost.

We finally pulled away, gasping for breath, our foreheads resting against each other. I could feel his breath on my lips, hot and shaky, mingling with mine. Our eyes met, and in that moment, we knew we had forever. The days we were denied were now ours to claim.

"Now we can finally let your story be mine and mine become a part of yours," he whispered, his voice thick with emotion. "We are going to grow old and frail but choose to live our life together. We are going to be fine..."

"Forever," I added.

I could see his eyes filled with the same emotions that mirrored my own.

We held each other tightly, knowing that despite the pain and loss, we had finally found our way back to each other. And that was all that mattered.

www.ingramcontent.com/pod-product-compliance
Lightning Source LLC
Chambersburg PA
CBHW070047080526
44586CB00013B/940